MODERN AGITATORS:

OR

Pen Portraits

OF

LIVING AMERICAN REFORMERS.

BY DAVID W. BARTLETT.

AUTHOR OF "LIFE OF LADY JANE GREY," "JOAN OF ARC," ETC. ETC.

NEW YORK:
MILLER, ORTON & MULLIGAN,
25 PARK ROW, OPPOSITE ASTOR HOUSE.
AUBURN:
107 GENESEE STREET.
1855.

AUBURN:
MILLER, ORTON & MULLIGAN,
STEREOTYPERS AND PRINTERS.

INTRODUCTION.

TO THOMAS BOX,

OF ENGLAND.

My Dear Friend:—Though thousands of miles of angry ocean lie between us, I shall never forget you nor your "Palatine Cottage." Its quiet, unobtrusive beauty, nestled as it is among trees, and flowers, and singing birds, I have never seen surpassed. To me it is doubly dear from the fact, that when I was but a boy, (yet with a heart full of earnest aspirations for a reformed world,) it was a second home to me. That sad, beautiful summer you nor I shall ever forget, nor will the dear ones of the "cottage" who watched me so tenderly when my brow burned with fever. I can see the exquisite sight from your windows even now, as I saw it then, and the fragrance of the flowers has crossed the Atlantic with me, and lingers round my heart still. So do the evenings rise up before me when you gave me such graphic pictures of the English reformers. It was new and intensely interesting to me, especially as I was deeply sympathizing with several important reforms.

I am in my native land again; months, years have passed

away since I said farewell to you. While I write, my windows open out upon a landscape not so beautiful, but more grand than yours—upon more gorgeous though not sweeter flowers than those at Palatine! I am in a new world, where we have our own beauties and defects. Here—God knows how my heart aches to say it!—here we need reformers as well as you; here the sorrowful plaint of the bondman, and the wail of the drunkard's wife are heard. And so remembering your word-pictures of English agitators, I send you a few plain, honest portraitures of some of our American reformers of the present time. They do not by any means include *all* of our distinguished reformers. I am obliged to *select*, and have very likely sketched some persons not so distinguished as others I have not mentioned. With one exception, the subjects of these pen-portraits are living men. Rogers was so brilliant a man, was such an original, and was so intimately connected with our anti-slavery agitators, that I could not resist the temptation to speak of him in this volume. I have, in almost every instance, made extracts from the writings of the persons sketched, knowing that often wise quotation will give a better clue to character than pages of mere description.

Begging that you will excuse the errors into which I may have unintentionally fallen in this book, which was prepared for *the people* of this country,

I am, always affectionately, yours,

DAVID W. BARTLETT.

CONTENTS.

MODERN AGITATORS.

N. P. ROGERS.

New England has given birth to few men, who, in point of brilliancy, genius, and genuine philanthropy, are the superiors of N. P. Rogers. George Thompson, after a few hours spent in conversation with him, declared him to be "the most brilliant man in America." There was a fascination about the man, a charm in his conversation, in his presence, which was as superior to *acquired* politeness as nature is to art. Few discovered from his conversation, that he possessed great powers of sarcasm and indignant eloquence. For he was one of the gentlest men that ever drew breath. In many things he was like a woman. His heart was sensitive, his fancy delicate, his love without bounds, and when insult was aimed at him, or when attempts were made to wrong him, he was silent. But when insult was aimed at the cause he loved so well, when his brother was wronged, his spirit rose lion-like, and he could throw his shafts of sarcasm home to the heart of an adversary, or could shower down upon his head the terrors of a denunciatory eloquence. He was a man overflowing with wit and humor. It showed itself in his conversation, in his speeches, in his writings. His bitterest enemies could not deny themselves of his brilliant newspaper writings, and many of their names were upon the subscription book of the newspaper of which he was the editor.

Mr. Rogers was born in Plymouth, New Hampshire, June 3d, 1794. His father was a physician of fine abilities, and his mother was a woman of more than ordinary intellect and heart. His parentage was excellent, and as he was a lineal descendant of John Rogers, the martyr, he had no cause to be ashamed of the blood which coursed through his veins. In 1811, he entered Dartmouth College, but through ill health was obliged to leave, after remaining one year. He returned afterwards, and took his degree in 1816. He shortly afterward engaged in the study of the law, and practiced it in his native state.

By nature possessed of extraordinary talents, when to these was added the discipline of a collegiate course, he was fitted to adorn any station in the country. He became thoroughly acquainted with law, and yet its practice was always distasteful to him. He seldom appeared in the courts to plead, for his spirit was of too fine material not to shrink from the rough conflicts of such a life. He remained in his office—it was in his native town—and counseled his clients, or prepared cases for the courts. His keen intellect won for him a fine reputation, and his advice was sought in intricate cases, far and wide. For many years, Mr. Rogers continued in the profession for which he was educated, but was never content with it. His love of nature was fervent, and the poetic instincts of his nature led him to abhor the dry technicalities of the statute book. He was born and lived among grand scenery, and his soul seemed to assimilate itself to the magnificent mountains, among the shadows of which he so dearly loved to wander. He gave up book-reading and read nature. The awful peaks of the White Mountains were more welcome to him than anything in Shakspeare or Byron, and the tender song of some early spring-bird more sweet and beautiful to his ear than the measured cadences of more modern poets. He had room in his heart for everything good and gentle, sublime or beautiful.

At last the anti-slavery agitation arose, and being a true man, and in tune with nature, he at once received into his great heart God's truth, and became *an abolitionist.* He gave up profession, pecuniary independence, comfort; and heart and soul espoused the cause of the slave. He removed to Concord, and became the editor of the far-famed *Herald of Free dom*, in which he wrote for many years some of the most brilliant editorials which have ever emanated from the newspaper writers of America. He adopted a style well calculated to attract attention; a pointed, homely, and, if we may use the term, a *Yankee* style. He eschewed the old rules, and being sure of always penning great ideas, cared little for the manner in which they were clothed. As a matter of course, he had to meet the cry "*you are before the age!*" and he answered it as follows:

BEFORE THE AGE.

"You are too fast." Well, friends, *you* are too slow. "You are altogether ahead of the times." Well, *you* are altogether in the rear of the times—astern of the times—at the tail of the times, if I must say it. And which is the most honorable and useful position? It is ahead of the times to denounce slavery, and demand its abandonment. But that is no reason anti-slavery is wrong, or unreasonable, or imprudent, injudicious, or any of the epithets a laggard age casts upon it. Is slave-holding right? Are the institutions that support it right? Are they for the happiness, benefit, improvement, usefulness, innocency of the people? These are the questions. "You are before the age!" Well, if I were not, it's high time I were. *You* ought to be before the age. The age is wrong. Whoever improves must go before. He must quit the age, wherein it is wrong, and the charge that he is before it is an admission that he is right. When Robert Fulton told them steam was better than wind on the water, or than horse-flesh on the land, he was before the age, though not a great ways before. He was n't many years ahead of it. The age is up with him now. They will begin to build him monuments by and by, because he is dead and it wont do him any good. They trod him under foot when he was alive, he was so far "before the age," and called him crazy! *Mono*maniac I suppose they called him. One poor man got the notion, some *ages* ago, that the sun did n't whirl round the earth, but that it was more likely and reasonable that the appearances that looked as if it did, were brought about by the earth's turning round on its own axletree. They came nigh hanging or burning him for it. They let him off, I believe, on the ground of insanity. They made him give it up, though, publicly, to save his life. The *Solemns* got hold of him—the reverend divines—God's specially called, ordained and set apart ministers—chosen of God to *guide* the people to heaven. They must know all about the sun and stars, and things up the firmament, for they are guides to heaven. They said it was contrary to the inspired book to say the sun stood still and the earth whirled round. It was contrary to "Joshua." So they made the man take it back. They are a *knowing* people, these divines. They are specially gifted of God. They *can't* mistake. They were *with* the age. This crazy man was "before the age," *now* it is admitted by the very *Solemns* themselves, that the earth whirls over every twenty-four hours, and the sun is as still as a mouse. The *Solemns* always admit things after "the age" has adopted them. They are as careful about the age as the weather-cock is about the wind. They never mistake it. You might as well catch an old, experienced weather-cock on some ancient orthodox steeple, mistaking the way of the wind, standing all day with his tail east, in a strong west wind, as the divines at odds with "the age." They can smell "the age." They *taste* it, at any rate.

Some of Mr. Rogers' most popular articles were written for the *New York Tribune*, over the signature of "Old Man of the Mountain," but they did not, to our thinking, quite equal his contributions to his *Herald of Freedom*. Some of these were written under circumstances which would have silenced the tongue or pen of any ordinary man. He was poor in health, poor, God knows, in purse, and an increasing family was upon his hands. And there were troubles the world knows not of with associates not so pure, gentle, and truly noble as he. We have spoken of his indignatory eloquence, and will quote a few paragraphs from one of his articles upon the martyr Torrey. It stirs the heart, even at this day, like the blast of a trumpet:

TORREY.

A New England citizen has been imprisoned and put to death without pretense of criminality—for mistaken philanthropy, at worst—*for philanthropy, undeniably*. But what can be done? Nothing, because of the spell slavery has shed over the land. Slavery may perpetrate anything, and New England can't see it. It can *horsewhip* the old commonwealth of Massachusetts, and spit in her governmental face, and she will not recognize it as an offense. She sent her Hon. Samuel

Hoar to Charleston, on a state embassy. Slavery caught him, and sent him most ignominiously home. The solemn great man came back in a hurry. He returned on a most undignified trot. He ran. He scampered—the stately official. The Old Bay State actually pulled foot—cleared—*dug*, as they say, like any scamp, with a hue and cry after him. Her grave old senator, who no more thought of ever having to break his stately walk, than he had of being flogged at school for stealing apples, came back from Carolina upon the full run—out of breath, as well as out of dignity. Well, what's the result? Why, nothing. They no more think of showing any resentment about it, than they would if lightning had struck him. He *was* sent back, actually, "by the visitation of God." And if they had lynched him to death, and stained the streets of Charleston with his blood, a Boston jury, if they could have held inquest over him, would have found that he died by the visitation of God. And it would have been "Crowner's quest law." Slavery's "Crowner's."

They have murdered Torrey. But there can be no inquisition. They have brought his body home. They "gave it to his friends," as they would the body of a man hung on the gallows. They have brought it to Boston. And they talk of having a public funeral, and an oration. They thought of having it in Park-street meeting-house. They might as well have expected it, for celebrating the obsequies of Tirrell, had he been hanged for murder, as the obsequies of the murdered Torrey. "Park-street" don't open to such obsequies. And such obsequies ought not to go in there if it did open. "Park-street" is at the bottom of the murder. Boston is hand in glove with it. The Bay State is. The nation is. It is as insensible as a dead dog to the murder of Torrey, when it ought to stir the land like the massacre of the 5th of March, 1770, when they shot down Monk in the streets of Boston; and "Maverick and Gray, Caldwell, Attocks, and Carr," in the old days of Hancock and Warren.

I will make no ado about it. It would be like clamoring to a burying yard. Torrey, to be sure, is murdered—but what of that? Who cares? He has been killed by slavery.

The love of nature, which was a striking characteristic of Mr. Rogers, exhibited itself constantly in his writings. What can be more beautiful than the following easy, careless paragraph upon

THE RAIN.

While I am writing, it is raining most magnificently and gloriously, out doors. It absolutely roars, it comes down in such multitude and big drops. And how refreshing! It waters the earth. There has been but little rain, and our sandy region has got to looking dry and distressed. Everything looks encouraged now, as the great strainer, overhead, is letting down the shower bath. The grass darkens, as it drinks it in, with a kind of delicate satisfaction. And the trees stand and take it, as a cow does a carding. They hold as still as a mouse, while they "abide its peltings," not moving a twig or stirring a leaf. The dust of the wide, naked street is transmuted into mud. And the stages sound over the road, as if they rattled on naked pavement. Puddles stand in all the hollows. You can hardly see the people for umbrellas—and the clouds look as though they had not done with us. The prospect for the Canterbury meeting looks *lowery*. Let it rain. All for the best. It is ext*rain*eous, but I could hardly help noticing the great rain and saying a word about it. I think the more mankind regard these beautiful doings in nature, the more they will regard each other, and love each other, and the less inclined to—enslave each other. The readier abolitionists they will become. And the better. The rain is a great anti-slavery discourse. And I like to have it pour. Nor eloquence is richer to my spirit, or music. That rush from heaven of the big drops—in what multitude and succession, and how they sound as they strike! How they play on the old home roof, and on the thick tree tops! What music to go to sleep by, to a tired boy as he lies under the naked roof! And the great low bass thunder, as it rolls off over the hills, and settles down behind them—to the very center, and you can feel the old earth jar under your feet—that is music, and poetry, and life. And if the lightning strikes you—what of that! It won't *hurt* you. "Favored man," truly, as Uncle Pope says, "by touch ethereal slain." A light touch, compared to disease's, the doctor's, or poverty's.

And here is a scene among the White Mountains, brought vividly to view by a few touches of his graphic pen:

THE NOTCH.

You roll along a mile or two, the road gently undulating through the majestic woods, and fringed with bushes of delightful green—when a vast and overwhelming opening breaks upon you, a boundless *room* among the mountains, walled on the left by the great Elephant mountain, the rock covered by stunted evergreens *precipicing* up two thousand feet—the blue sky itself scarcely visible over its eternal ridge. Before you, at the farther extremity, opens the Notch, *curtained* by the sky of Vermont, which there comes down upon it; and on the right, the wooded steep side of Lafayette, or Great Haystack. Nothing can exceed the awful sublimity of the great wall on the left. The vast mountain side is clothed with scales of rock, as with a coat of mail, scarred here and there with the old avalanches—while, opposite, the forest side of Lafayette is striped down with the deep green of modern woods, which have grown in the paths of the "slides." At the northern extremity of the great room, you come to view "the Old Man of the Mountain." It is on your left, up, say fifteen hundred feet, a perfect profile of an aged man, jutting out boldly from the sheer precipice, with a sort of turban on the head and brow; nose, mouth, lip, chin, and fragment of neck, all perfect and to the life—and with a little fancy, you supply the *cheek* and *ear*. It looks off south-east. It needs no imagination to complete it. It is perfect as if done by art. But it is up where art never climbed.

We have given but meager specimens of the writings of Mr. Rogers. He needs to be read carefully, article by article, to enable the reader to appreciate his genius. He made the most trite subject rich and beautiful by the magic of his pen. He wrote with strange facility, seemed never at a loss for subject, language, or ideas. He was always fresh, always attractive, and a vein of genial humor ran through almost all his articles. If not humor, then certainly biting sarcasm. He could never tolerate "platitudinous commonplace." But agitation wore upon him—or perhaps it would be more correct to ascribe his sorrow to the *results* of his agitating career. He was without a certain and sufficient support, and children were gathered at his feet. Never was there a more loving-hearted father, never a more devoted husband. His heart was sorrowful for them. Friends with whom he was associated in the anti-slavery reform, treated him, as he thought, with cruelty, and his heart began to be shattered.

A look of sorrow was always upon his face. He was a man of fine appearance. A large, noble brow, clear, intelligent, beautiful eyes, a profusion of dark gray hair, and that sad, ever sad, shadow over all, were his characteristics. It was a face which once seen, lingers forever in the memory.

About this time, he lost nearly all the little property which he could call his own, through the failure of a friend to whom it was entrusted. An illness fastened upon him which never deserted him for a day until he died. For many weeks, however, he continued to write for his favorite journal, and these contributions are among the finest he ever wrote. His faith in the ultimate triumph of the right did not desert him in the darkest hour. It was a time when church and state seemed to be in league against freedom. Mob law stalked unabashed through the land. The friends of the poor, crushed slave, were few. There were private griefs, too, in his heart. And at last, disease laid its disheartening hand upon him. But he was calm, gentle, and patient through it all. He declared to the friends who gathered about his couch that his illness would terminate in death. Seeing one of his family weep, he said that he was happy, and wished his friends to be happy also. At last, his hand, which had been so strong for the right, grew too feeble to hold the pen, but even after that he dictated article after article for the press. He possessed, almost to the day of his death, a strong desire to hear constantly of the progress of the great cause to which he had sacrificed his life. He asked eagerly for the welfare of his old associates, who were almost hopelessly opposing themselves to the war feeling which at that time overspread the country.

His greatest comfort during his illnesss was music, of which he once said:

"Oh! this music is one of God's dearest gifts. I do wish men would make more of it. How humanizing it is—and how purifying—elevating and ennobling to the spirit! And how it has been prostituted and perverted! That accursed drum and fife—how they have maddened mankind! And the deep bass boom of the cannon, chiming in, in the chorus of the battle—that trumpet, and wild, charging bugle—how they set the military devil into a man, and make him into a soldier! Think of the human family, falling upon one another, at the inspiration of music! How must God feel at it! To see those harp strings he meant should be wakened to love bordering on divine, strung and swept to mortal hate and butchery."

During the few days which preceded his death, Mr. Rogers suffered the most excruciating pains. "Oh, dear," said he, "*this* is the closing up of my terrible labors!" Terrible, indeed, were they, for his life, for the past few years, had been one continual conflict with the bigoted, the heartless, and the thoroughly depraved. A friend who leaned over the hot brow of the dying man, whispered into his ear that it must be a consoling thought that he had not labored in vain. "O yes," he answered, "it sustains me unspeakably—the reflection that I have done right." Though his agony was great, yet the light of reason did not flicker until death led him away.

The sixteenth day of October, 1846, was his last. His family friends were gathered around him, when he asked one of his daughters to sing to him Lover's beautiful "*Angel's Whisper.*" The sweet tones of the familiar voice filled the room, and he seemed to be in a rapture of bliss. When the last notes had died away, some one approached him, gently, and asked if Jesse Hutchinson, who was in the next room, should come in. But no answer came from his dying lips. The little band knew that the dread hour had come—no, not dread, but happy, happy hour, which should conduct his weary heart to rest.

In a few minutes, the look of sorrow, which, for a long time, had dwelt constantly upon his countenance, fled away, and a beautiful, seraphic smile rested calmly in its place. He was dead.

It was Friday when he died, and on the following Sabbath, a few friends gathered in his dwelling, forever bereft of his kindly presence, to consign his mortal remains to the grave. The spot of his burial was just that which he would have chosen—a quiet corner of the village grave-yard, beneath the branches of a cluster of oaks. The snow fell drearily into his open grave—very drearily to the bereaved ones who stood sobbing around it. But *he* was wrapt in the sunshine of his heavenly Father's love!

Thus lived and died a man whose name will never be forgotten, at least till American slavery has passed into oblivion. He was one of the earliest of the anti-slavery agitators of this country, and one of the purest. But it may be doubted if he was fitted to be a successful agitator at the time when he lived. He had a splendid intellect and a great heart, but the latter was too delicately made to enable him to walk calmly on amid the venomous attacks of enemies, and the not always gentle treatment of professed friends. And yet, he agitated right well, and his sayings will never die. To-day, they live in the deeds of those who, years ago, were roused from inaction by them—and to-day they are read by those who never read them before, and they will continue to bear fruit until the freed negro—his brethren likewise all free—shall weep tears of gratitude over his quiet New Hampshire grave.

THEODORE PARKER.

A FEW miles out of Boston, just far enough to escape the dust and confusion of the town, there is a dwelling which would attract the eye of a genuine lover of nature, and natural beauty. It is not characterized by splendor and ostentation, for no pompous cotton merchant or retired rumseller occupies it. It is plain and yet beautiful, unpretentious and yet spacious. It is surrounded by shrubs, and trees, and flowers of every hue, and the most delightful fragrance in the summer time. Should you chance some early May morning to wander past this pleasant spot, very likely in the garden you will see a man in a plain smock frock, hard at work. He is rather short in stature, rather slender in frame, and if you catch a glance of his eye, you will at once entertain a serious doubt if the man be by profession a gardener. Let him lift the wide straw hat from his perspiring brow to catch a cool breeze, and you know at once that he is no common cultivator of the soil. Theodore Parker is before you. The beautiful dwelling is his, and his own hands have contributed to the loveliness which surrounds it.

Theodore Parker is one of the noblest *men* this age can boast. No sham ever yet could find a lodgment in his brain or heart. He abhors the false, and loves the true and manly. Not a particle of vulgar gentility, not a grain of aristocratic feeling was ever in him, or ever can get into him. He esteems a man just according to his moral and intellectual worth, for what he does, or aims to do. He loves men because they *are* men; not because they are white, or rich, or can trace their genealogy back five hundred years. An outrage upon the rights of a poor negro in the streets of Boston, stirs the blood as quickly in his heart, as if it had been committed upon the person of the governor of the commonwealth. A wrong perpetrated upon a wretched drunkard's wife or child, awakes the thunder of his eloquence, when, if inflicted upon the strong or rich, he would have kept silent. It is this gigantic manhood in Theodore Parker which forces us to love and admire him. In spite of his infidelity, which so often startles and shocks us, we sit down involuntarily at his feet to listen to his great words, his courageous utterances against the most heartless and cruel oppression. We receive not one word of his infidelity. To us, Christ is not merely the greatest man that ever lived, but is vastly more; to us, the bible is not a book crammed with errors—the miracles exaggerations; and yet, to many of those who would crucify Mr.

Parker, we indignantly cry: "It is not for *you* to denounce this man; you who in your lives each day trample Jesus Christ and the bible under your feet; you who would refuse a cup of cold water to your 'Lord and Master,' ran there in his veins a drop of African blood!"

The manliness of Mr. Parker is apparent in his daily life. A shoemaker upon his bench, if heart-noble, is to him richer than Abbot Lawrence, with his acres of cotton-mills; a country farmer, in his fragrant clover fields, though of limited knowledge, if he be possessed of a generous heart and firm integrity, is in his eyes of greater worth than Daniel Webster, using his great intellect to perpetuate oppression.

No man will deny that Mr. Parker is one of the most remarkable men of our time, and that his influence is exceedingly powerful.

He is now between forty and fifty years old—we have forgotten his exact age—and is probably enjoying the most vigorous part of his existence. He was born in Lexington, where the first blood of the revolution was spilt, and it would seem as if the stories of that heroic time must have made a deep impression upon his mind and heart, for the Lexington spirit flashes from his eyes, and throbs in every pulse of his heart. His father was a farmer, and Theodore prepared himself for college as best he could. He worked on the farm, taught school winters, but studied incessantly. One day he swung the scythe from sunrise to sunset upon his father's meadow, and the next entered Harvard College. While there, he improved his opportunities, made use of every moment, and graduated a finished scholar. This was not enough. He could not content himself with the knowledge possessed by an ordinary college graduate. The literature of Europe and the east was locked away from him, and so he sat down and mastered the French language, till it was as familiar to his tongue as "household words." He then studied German, and enjoyed the pleasure of reading the great German authors and poets in their own language. The Italian, the Spanish, the Persian, and indeed all still more difficult languages were made his own, until the civilized world, and parts half civilized, were within his reach. After due preparation Mr. Parker entered the ministry, and was settled as pastor over a Unitarian church in West Roxbury, Massachusetts. He first excited the suspicions of the religious world by the delivery of a sermon in South Boston, upon the occasion of the ordination of the Rev. Mr. Shackford, in the early part of the year 1841. We will make a single quotation from this sermon, which will indicate its character:

"It has been assumed at the onset, it would seem, with no sufficient reason, without the smallest pretense on its writer's part, that all of its authors were infallibly and miraculously inspired, so that they could commit no error of doctrine or fact. Men have been bid to close their eyes at the obvious difference between Luke and John; the serious disagreement between Paul and Peter, to believe, on the smallest evidence, accounts which shock the moral sense and revolt the reason, and tend to place Jesus in the same series with Hercules and Apollonius of Tyana.

* * * "An idolatrous regard for the imperfect scripture of God's word is the apple of Atalanta, which defeats theologians running for the hand of divine truth. But the current notions respecting the infallible inspiration of the bible have no foundation in the bible itself."

This sermon created a good deal of excitement among the Unitarian body, especially the conservatives. They were not satisfied that a man holding such views should have the reputation of being a Unitarian clergyman in good standing. At this time Mr. Parker left the country for Europe, where he remained for three years, making the acquaintance of some of its most learned and philanthropic men. Among others, we may mention the name of Thomas Carlyle, who is to this day his warm friend and admirer. In the autumn of 1844 he returned, and exchanged pulpits with the Rev. Mr. Sargent, of Boston, a Unitarian clergyman. The conservative Unitarians were exceedingly indignant that Mr. Sargent should admit such a heretic into his pulpit, and they commenced a persecution against him, which obliged him to resign his charge. The Rev. Mr. Clarke, another Boston clergyman, soon after offered his pulpit to Mr. Parker, which resulted in great excitement, and a loss of members to the church. The following extract from a sermon preached by Mr. Parker, about this time, will show the nature of his heresy:

"The Jehovah of the Old Testament was awful and stern—a man of war, hating the wicked. The sacerdotal conception of God at Rome and Athens was lower yet. No wonder, then, that men soon learned to honor Jesus as a god, and then as God himself. Apostolical and other legends tell of his divine birth, his wondrous power that healed the sick, palsied, and crippled, deaf and dumb, and blind; created bread, turned water into wine, and bid obedient devils come and go—a power that raised the dead. They tell that nature felt with him, and at his death the strongly sympathizing sun paused at high noon, and for three hours withheld the day; that rocks were rent, and opening graves gave up their sainted dead, who trod once more the streets of Zion, the first fruits of them that slept; they tell, too, how disappointed death gave back his prey, and, spirit-like, Jesus, restored in flesh and shape the same, passed through the doors shut up, and in a bodily form was taken up to heaven before the face of men! Believe men of these things as they will; to me they are not truth and fact, but mythic symbols and poetry; the psalm of praise with which the world's rude heart extols and magnifies its King. It is for his truth and his life, his wisdom, goodness, piety, that he is honored in my heart; yes, in the world's heart. It is for this that in his name churches are built, and prayers are prayed; for this that the best things we know we honor."

The result of the utterance of such sentiments was the excommunication of Mr. Parker from the Unitarian body. He had powerful friends everywhere in the region of Boston; he had warm sympathizers in the Unitarian church, but they were not of sufficient numerical strength to be of service. His church in West Roxbury was crowded; his Boston admirers came out every Sunday, in large numbers, to hear him. At last they were determined that he should be entirely independent, and therefore invited him to preach to them in the Melodeon. He accepted their invitation, and was settled as their pastor, in the old Puritan fashion. There are no rites or ceremonies connected with his society; he does not administer baptism or communion, and there is in fact no church organization. About a year since his congregation hired the Music Hall, the finest interior in Boston, and now every Sunday an audience of three thousand people, comprising many of the most refined, intellectual, and wealthy people in Boston, convene to hear "the infidel preacher." His salary, we believe, is three thousand dollars. He lives a few miles out of town in the summer, or has a residence there, as well as in the city of Boston.

The personal appearance of Theodore Parker is not remarkable, and yet the observing man will discover indications of his wonderful genius in his face. He is slightly under the average height of men, rather spare in flesh, has a partially bald head, a fine, compact brow, and a flashing eye. His features are rather small, and his organization is of the finest mould. There is a delicacy in his nervous system, which is indicated by the fineness of his hair; just that amount of delicacy which is necessary to make a nervous and intense writer and speaker. A man with the nervous system of a Tom Hyer cannot become a great orator. He cannot himself feel intensely, cannot understand the subtler methods of reaching the souls of men.

People who have read the sermons of Mr. Parker are usually disappointed in hearing him preach or lecture. He is not an accomplished orator; in an ordinary discourse he is altogether too lifeless, too devoid of gesture. But he has a voice of exceeding beauty, and he can, when he chooses, charm an audience by his striking and fascinating gestures and manner. Occasionally in his sermons, from the bold and magnificent, from the intensely passionate, he suddenly glides into the calmly beautiful. The contrast at such times is almost overpowering, and the heart of the listener is touched, as by the voice of an angel. The pictures of strange and quiet loveliness, which nestled among the grand mountains of his discourses, are not surpassed in poetic beauty in the writings of any living clergyman. The fact is, Theodore Parker is a poet. He has the intense and consuming fire; he has also the gentleness and the love of the true poet. He is no rhymer, for the reformer of these times has not time for measured sentences, when the land is in danger of ruin.

A majority of the sermons of Mr. Parker contain nothing offensive to the most devout christian. His reputation is founded not so much upon his heresies, as upon his genius and philanthropy. It is the fact that he is a fearless and powerful defender of the wronged, which gives him a place in the hearts of millions who have no sympathy with his religious views.

In classic eloquence, in burning invective, in astonishing power, we know of few men of this or any other age, who equal Mr. Parker. What can surpass in eloquence the following passage, which we extract from a sermon preached by him, just after the passage of the fugitive slave law:

"Come with me, my friends, a moment more, pass over this Golgotha of human history, treading reverent as you go, for our feet are on our mothers' graves, and our shoes defile our fathers' hallowed bones. Let us not talk of them; go farther on, look and pass by. Come with me into the Inferno of the nations, with such poor guidance as my lamp can lend. Let us disquiet and bring up the awful shadows of empires buried long ago, and learn a lesson from the tomb.

"Come, old Assyria, with the Ninevitish dove upon thy emerald crown! what laid thee low? 'I fell by my own injustice. Thereby Nineveh and Babylon came with me also to the ground.'

"Oh, queenly Persia, flame of the nations, wherefore art thou so fallen, who troddest the people under thee, bridgedst the Hellespont with ships, and pouredst thy temple-wasting millions on the western world? 'Because I trod the people under me, and bridged the Hellespont with ships, and poured my temple-wasting millions on the western world, I fell by my own misdeeds!'

"Thou muse-like Grecian queen, fairest of all thy classic sisterhood of states, enchanting yet the world with thy sweet witchery, speaking in art and most seductive song, why liest thou there, with beauteous yet dishonored brow, reposing on thy broken harp? 'I scorned the law of God; banished and poisoned wisest, justest men; I loved the loveliness of flesh, embalmed it in the Parian stone; I loved the loveliness of thought, and treasured that in more than Parian speech. But the beauty of justice, the loveliness of love, I trod them down to earth! Lo, therefore have I become as those barbarian states—as one of them!'

"Oh, manly and majestic Rome, thy seven-fold mural crown all broken at thy feet, why art thou here? It was not injustice brought thee low; for thy great book of law is prefaced with these words—justice is the unchanged, everlasting will to give each man his right! 'It was not the saint's ideal; it was the hypocrite's pretense! I made iniquity my law. I trod the nations under me. Their wealth gilded my palaces—where thou mayst see the fox and hear the owl—it fed my courtiers and my courtesans. Wicked men were my cabinet counselors, the flatterer breathed his poison in my ear. Millions of bondmen wet the soil with tears and blood. Do you not hear it crying yet to God? Lo, here have I my recompense, tormented with such downfall as you see! Go back and tell the new-born child who sitteth on the Alleghanies, laying his either hand upon a tributary sea, a crown of thirty stars about his youthful brow—tell him that there are rights which states must keep, or they shall suffer wrongs! Tell him there is a God who keeps the black man and the white, and hurls to earth the loftiest realm that breaks his just, eternal law! Warn the young empire, that he come not down dim and dishonored to my shameful tomb! Tell him that justice is the unchanging, everlasting will to give each man his right. I knew it, broke it, and am lost. Bid him know it, keep it, and be safe!'"

The reader well remembers the case of the fugitive Simms, who was dragged back from the streets of Boston, past old Faneuil Hall, to hopeless slavery. The court house itself was in chains, and the spirit of Liberty afraid to draw its breath. Theodore Parker, the infidel, dared, from his pulpit, to rebuke the city for its acquiescence in such a deed, and it is a rebuke which will live as long as Boston does. The passage below, which we quote from it, is one of the most intensely powerful in the English language:

"Where shall I find a parallel with men who will do such a deed—do it in Boston? I will open the tombs and bring up most hideous tyrants from the dead. Come, brood of monsters, let me bring you up from the deep damnation of the graves wherein your hated memories continue for all time their never-ending rot. Come, birds of evil omen! come, ravens, vultures, carrion crows, and see the spectacle! come, see the meeting of congenial souls! I will disturb, disquiet, and bring up the greatest monsters of the human race! Tremble not, women; tremble not, children; tremble not, men! They are all dead! They cannot harm you now! Fear the living, not the dead!"

"Come hither, Herod, the wicked. Thou that didst seek after that young child's life, and destroyedst the innocents! Let me look on thy face! No, go! Thou wert a heathen! Go, lie with the innocents thou hast massacred. Thou art too good for this company!

"Come, Nero! thou awful Roman emperor, come up! No, thou wast drunk with power! schooled in Roman depravity. Thou hadst, besides, the example of thy fancied gods. Go, wait another day. I will seek a worser man.

"Come hither, St. Dominic! come, Torquemada!—fathers of the Inquisition! merciless monsters, seek your equal here. No; pass by. You are no companions for such men as these. You were the servants of atheistic popes, of cruel kings. Go to, and get you gone. Another time I may have work for you,

—now, lie there, and persevere to rot. You are not yet quite wicked and corrupt enough for this comparison. Go, get you gone, lest the sun turn back at sight of ye!

"Come up, thou heap of wickedness, George Jeffries! thy hands deep purple with the blood of thy murdered fellow-men. Ah! I know thee, awful and accursed shade! Two hundred years after thy death, men hate thee still, not without cause. Look me upon thee! I know thy history. Pause and be still while I tell it to these men. . . . . Come, shade of a judicial butcher. Two hundred years, thy name has been pilloried in face of the world, and thy memory gibbeted before mankind. Let us see how thou wilt compare with those who kidnap men in Boston. Go, seek companionship with them. Go, claim thy kindred, if such they be. Go, tell them that the memory of the wicked shall rot; that there is a God; an eternity; ay, and a judgment, too, where the slave may appeal against him that made him a slave, to Him that made him a man.

"What! Dost thou shudder? Thou turn back! These not thy kindred! Why dost thou turn pale, as when the crowd clutched at thy life in London street? It is true, George Jeffries and these are not thy kin. Forgive me that I should send thee, on such an errand, or bid thee seek companionship with such—with Boston hunters of the slave! Thou wert not base enough! It was a great bribe that tempted thee! Again, I say, pardon me for sending thee to keep company with such men! Thou only struckest at men accused of crime; not at men accused only of their birth! Thou wouldst not send a man into bondage for two pounds! I will not rank thee with men, who, in Boston, for ten dollars, would enslave a negro now! Rest still, Herod! Be quiet, Nero! Sleep, St. Dominic, and sleep, O Torquemada, in your fiery jail! Sleep, Jeffries, underneath 'the altar of the church' which seeks, with christian charity, to hide your hated bones!"

In one of Mr. Parker's sermons on "Immortal Life," occurs the following beautiful passage:

"I would not slight this wondrous world. I love its day and night. Its flowers and its fruits are dear to me. I would not willfully lose sight of a departing cloud. Every year opens new beauty in a star; or in a purple curtain fringed with loveliness. The laws, too, of matter seem more wonderful the more I study them, in the whirling eddies of the dust, in the curious shells of former life, buried by thousands in a grain of chalk, or in the shining diagrams of light above my head. Even the ugly becomes beautiful, when truly seen. I see the jewel in the bunchy toad. The more I live, the more I love this lovely world; feel more its Author in each little thing; in all that is great. But yet, I feel my immortality the more. In childhood, the consciousness of immortal life buds forth feeble, though full of promise. In the man, it unfolds its fragrant petals, his most celestial flower, to mature its seed throughout eternity. The prospect of that everlasting life, the perfect justice yet to come, the infinite progress before us, cheer and comfort the heart. Sad and disappointed, full of self-reproach, we shall not be so forever. The light of heaven breaks upon the night of trial, sorrow, sin; the sombre clouds which overhung the east, grown purple now, tell us the dawn of heaven is coming in."

The last quotation which we will make, is full of a sad eloquence. The preacher is speaking of the heroes of the present day, those men who have the courage and the principle to advocate unpopular reforms:

"I know their trials, I see their dangers, I appreciate their sufferings, and since the day when the Man on Calvary bowed his head, bidding persecution farewell with his 'Father, forgive them, for they know not what they do,' I find no such saints and heroes as live now! They win hard fare, and hard toil. They lay up shame and obloquy. Theirs is the most painful of martyrdoms. Racks and fagots soon waft the soul to God, stern messengers but swift. A boy could bear that passage, the martyrdom of death. But the temptation of a long life of neglect, and scorn, and obloquy, and shame, and want, and desertion by false friends; to live blameless, though blamed, cut off from human sympathy, that is the martyrdom of to-day. I shed no tears for such martyrs. I shout when I see one; I take courage, and thank God for the real saints, prophets and heroes of to-day. In another age, men shall be proud of these puritans and pilgrims of this day. Churches shall glory in their names, and celebrate their praise in sermon and in song."

One of the greatest sermons preached by Mr. Parker—that upon the death of Daniel Webster—is so widely known that we will but mention it here as one of the most brilliant sermons ever delivered from the American pulpit. The land was full of adoration of the dead statesman, and it required a profound courage to face it with the truth. The sermon met with opposition, in some places bitter opposition, but the country at large hailed it as a great, searching, and profound review of the character of one of the idols of the American people.

Whatever charges may be sustained against Theodore Parker, as a theologian, no man will accuse him of ever fawning before the powerful and the despotic—no man will accuse him of deserting the weak and oppressed. He is faithful to his brother-men—let him at least have all honor for this.

FREDERICK DOUGLASS.

The remarkable man who is the subject of this sketch, was born a slave in Maryland. His exact age is not known, though it is supposed that he is between thirty and forty years old. His mother died when he was quite young. His father was a white man, according to rumor, his own master. He was early compelled to witness and experience the bitterness of a life of bondage. Speaking of a time when he was quite young, he says:

"I have often been awakened at the dawn of day by the most heart-rending shrieks of an own aunt of mine, whom her master used to tie up to a joist, and whip upon her naked back till she was literally covered with blood. No words, no tears, no prayers, from his gory victim, seemed to move his iron heart from its bloody purpose. The louder she screamed the harder he whipped; and where the blood ran fastest there he whipped longest. He would whip her to make her scream, and whip her to make her hush; and not until overcome by fatigue, would he cease to swing the blood-clotted cowskin. I remember the first time I ever witnessed this horrible exhibition. I was quite a child, but I well remember it. I never shall forget it whilst I remember anything. It was the first of a long series of such outrages, of which I was doomed to be a witness and a participant. It struck me with awful force. It was the blood-stained gate, the entrance to the hell of slavery, through which I was about to pass. It was a most terrible spectacle. I wish I could commit to paper the feelings with which I beheld it."

For years the poor slave, as a field hand, served a sad apprenticeship to slavery. He was sold from master to master, and transferred from the whip of one overseer to that of another. But it was impossible by experience to reconcile him to his condition. Naturally possessed of brilliant powers of mind, with a fiery yet noble nature, he could not remain contentedly a miserable chattel on a Maryland plantation. As yet, he had thought little of liberty, for the love of it which is in every human creature's heart, had not kindled in his. Still there were strange, murmuring thoughts constantly haunting his brain. A melancholy was in his heart. He says, very strikingly as well as beautifully, of the songs which the slaves are so noted for singing:

"I did not, when a slave, understand the deep meaning of those rude and apparently incoherent songs. I was myself within the circle; so that I neither saw nor heard as those without might see and hear. They told a tale of woe which was then altogether beyond my feeble comprehension; they were tones loud, long, and deep; they breathed the prayer and complaint of souls boiling over with the bitterest anguish. Every tone was a testimony against slavery, and a prayer to God for deliverance from chains. The hearing of those wild notes always depressed my spirit, and filled me with ineffable sadness. I have frequently found myself in tears while hearing them. The mere recurrence to those songs, even now, afflicts me; and while I am writing these lines, an expression of feeling has already found its way down my cheek. To those songs I trace my first glimmering conception of the dehumanizing character of slavery. I can never get rid of that conception. Those songs still follow me, to deepen my hatred of slavery, and quicken my sympathies for my brethren in bonds. If any one wishes to be impressed with the soul-killing effects of slavery, let him go to Colonel Lloyd's plantation, and, on allowance-day, place himself in the deep pine woods, and there let him in silence analyze the sounds that shall pass through the chambers of his soul, and if he is not thus impressed, it will only be because there is no flesh in his obdurate heart."

From the field Douglass was transferred to the town. His joy was great at being permitted to live in Baltimore. He was allowed clean and decent clothing, for he was going to live with city people. His city mistress was a mild, pleasant woman, and he says that his soul was filled with rapture when he first saw her kind face, and experienced her gentle treatment. She taught him how to read, or rather, taught him his letters, and he, without further aid, completed his education. By persevering and secret toil, he managed to acquire the art of reading. One of the first books he met with was Sheridan's Speeches, and they served well to stir his heart, to awaken and intensify his longing for liberty. Months and years flew on, and in the meantime he changed masters. The desire for freedom grew strong in his heart, but it was not till after he had felt in his own person one of the bitterest portions of the slave's experience, that the desire attained its full intensity. We will quote his own account of this passage in his life:

"On one of the hottest days of the month of August, 1833, Bill Smith, William Hughes, a slave named Eli, and myself, were engaged in fanning wheat. Hughes was clearing the fanned wheat from before the fan, Eli was turning, Smith was feeding, and I was carrying wheat to the fan. The work was simple, requiring strength rather than intellect; yet, to one entirely unused to such work, it came very hard. About three o'clock of that day I broke down; my strength failed me; I was seized with a violent aching of the head, attended with extreme dizziness; I trembled in every limb. Finding what was coming, I nerved myself up, feeling it would never do to stop work. I stood as long as I could stagger to the hopper with grain. When I could stand no longer I fell, and felt as if held down by an immense weight. The fan of course stopped; every one had his own work to do; and no one could do the work of the other and have his own go on the same time.

Mr. Covey was at the house, about one hundred yards from the treading-yard where we were fanning. On hearing the fan stop, he left immediately, and came to the spot where we were. He hastily inquired what the matter was. Bill answered that I was sick, and there was no one to bring wheat to the fan. I had by this time crawled away under the side of the post and rail fence, by which the yard was enclosed, hoping to find relief by getting out of the sun. He then asked where I was. He was told by one of the hands. He came to the spot, and, after looking at me awhile, asked me what was the matter. I told him as well as I could, for I scarce had strength to speak. He then gave me a savage kick in the side, and told me to get up. I tried to do so, but fell back in the attempt. He gave me another kick, and again told me to rise. I again tried, and succeeded in gaining my feet; but stooping to get the tub with which I was feeding the fan, I again staggered and fell. While down in this situation, Mr. Covey took up the hickory slat with which Hughes had been striking off the half-bushel measure, and with it gave me a heavy blow upon the head, making a large wound, and the blood ran freely; and with this again told me to get up. I made no effort to comply, having now made up my mind to let him do his worst. In a short time after receiving this blow my head grew better. Mr. Covey had now left me to my fate."

After this, Douglas had the courage to resist another brutal attack from Covey, and triumphed. He began now to seriously contemplate running away from the bondage so hateful to him. His soul, animated by the same spirit which once dwelt in the bosom of Patrick Henry, could not brook chains, could not still its own pulses at the bidding of a white master. He has given in graphic language the conflict of hopes and fears in his heart, when contemplating escape by flight from the evils which surrounded him :

"At every gate through which we were to pass we saw a watchman—at every ferry a guard—on every bridge a sentinel, and in every wood a patrol. We were hemmed in upon every side. Here were the difficulties, real or imagined—the good to be sought, and the evil to be shunned. On the one hand, there stood slavery, a stern reality, glaring frightfully upon us, its robes already crimsoned with the blood of millions, and even now feasting greedily upon our own flesh. On the other hand, away back in the dim distance, under the flickering light of the north star, behind some craggy hill or snow-covered mountain, stood a doubtful freedom—half frozen—beckoning us to come and share its hospitality. This in itself was sometimes enough to stagger us; but when we permitted ourselves to survey the road, we were frequently appalled. Upon either side we saw grim death, assuming the most horrid shapes. Now it was starvation, causing us to eat our own flesh; now we were contending with the waves, and were drowned; now we were overtaken, and torn to pieces by the fangs of the terrible bloodhound. We were stung by scorpions, chased by wild beasts, bitten by snakes, and finally, after having nearly reached the desired spot—after swimming rivers, encountering wild beasts, sleeping in the woods, suffering hunger and nakedness—we were overtaken by our pursuers.

and, in our resistance, we were shot dead upon the spot! I say, this picture sometimes appalled us, and made us

> 'Rather bear those ills we had,
> Than fly to others that we knew not of.'"

But, thanks to a kind Providence, he attempted, and successfully, to fly from his oppressors. The mode of his flight he prudently says little about, for fear of injuring the chances for escape of thousands still in bondage. He settled down in New Bedford, got married, and went quietly at work. As yet no one had discovered the wonderful genius which dwelt beneath his dark skin. He had enjoyed wretched opportunities for information; his education was necessarily exceedingly limited, and after he came to reside in New Bedford, he was obliged to support himself and wife by manual labor, and of course had little time to devote to mental toil.

In the month of August, 1841, an anti-slavery meeting was held in Nantucket. Some of the most eloquent anti-slavery orators were present, and in an humble place sat Frederick Douglas, beside a dear friend. He was known to but few, and they knew him simply as a poor fugitive. Not one man of all those present had the remotest idea that in the person of the poor negro they beheld an orator. At length a friend urged him to get up and tell his story. It was common in anti-slavery meetings for fugitives, in their broken, illiterate way, to tell of their sufferings, that northern men and women might know the character of negro slavery. Urged vehemently, Douglass ascended the platform, and with a trembling voice commenced. But in a few moments fear of his audience vanished, and he poured forth a torrent of burning eloquence, such as the majority present never before had heard. His voice and action were natural, his language was intensely eloquent, and his whole bearing that of a great orator. The audience was astounded; it seemed almost miraculous, that an ignorant slave should possess such powers.

Few living orators surpass Frederick Douglass in declamatory eloquence. He is not so argumentative, so logical, as many of his cotemporaries, but few living men can produce a more powerful impression upon an audience than he. His manner is wonderfully eloquent, and his language is copious and impressive. He stands before an audience *a natural orator*, like the African Cinque, who, without the aid of the schools, pours forth with burning zeal the thoughts which crowd his brain. His voice is good, his form is manly and graceful, and his hot words leap forth clothed with beauty and power. He is bold in his imagery; his pictures are at times gorgeously beautiful, but are always full of a tropical heat. It is perhaps his principal fault—his tendency to paint too deeply, sometimes to exaggeration.

Mr. Douglass is a powerful writer, but we confess that we think he erred in attempting to maintain a weekly journal. We do not mean that his paper is not an excellent, and often an eloquent one, but nature intended Douglass for an orator—not to be an editor. As an orator, he has few superiors in this or any other country, and it seems to us that he cannot do full justice to himself as an orator while attempting to edit a newspaper.

It is impossible for us to give the reader any true idea of the eloquence of Mr. Douglass by quoting from his reported speeches. His best ones never were reported, and even if they were, without his presence, his impassioned manner, they would convey an inadequate idea of his oratorical powers. Nevertheless, we will give a few brief extracts from his speeches. The first is upon

THE SLAVE.

The slave is a man, "the image of God," but "a little lower than the angels;" possessing a soul eternal and indestructible; capable of endless happiness or immeasurable woe; a creature of hopes and fears, of affections and passions, of joys and sorrows; and he is endowed with those mysterious powers by which man soars above the things of time and sense, and grasps with undying tenacity the elevating and sublimely glorious idea of a God. It is *such* a being that is smitten and blasted. The first work of slavery is to mar and deface those characteristics of its victims which distinguish *men* from *things*, and *persons* from *property*. Its first aim is to destroy all sense of high moral and religious responsibility. It reduces man to a mere machine. It cuts him off from his Maker, it hides from him the laws of God, and leaves him to grope his way from time to eternity in the dark, under the arbitrary and despotic control of a frail, depraved, and sinful fellow-man.

As the serpent-charmer of India is compelled to extract the deadly teeth of his venomous prey before he is able to handle him with impunity, so the slave-holder must strike down the conscience of the slave, before he can obtain the entire mastery over his victim.

It is, then, the first business of the enslaver of men to blunt, deaden, and destroy the central principle of human responsibility. Conscience is to the individual soul and society what the law of gravitation is to the universe. It holds society together; it is the basis of all trust and confidence; it is the pillar of all moral rectitude. Without it suspicion would take the place of trust; vice would be more than a match for virtue; men would prey upon each other like the wild beasts; earth would become a *hell.*

Nor is slavery more adverse to the conscience than it is to the mind.

This is shown by the fact that in every state of the American Union, where slavery exists, except the state of Kentucky, there are laws *absolutely* prohibitory of education among the slaves. The crime of teaching a slave to read is punishable with severe fines and imprisonment, and in some instances with *death itself!*

Nor are the laws respecting this matter a dead letter. Cases may occur in which they are disregarded, and a few instances may be found where slaves may have learned to read; but such are isolated cases, and only prove the rule. The great mass of slaveholders look upon education among the slaves as utterly subversive of the slave system. I *well* remember when my mistress first announced to my master that she had discovered that I could read. His face colored at once, with surprise and chagrin. He said that "I was ruined, and my value as a slave destroyed; that a slave should know nothing but to obey his master; that to give a negro an inch would lead him to take an ell; that having learned how to read I would soon want to know how to write; and that, by and by, I would be running away." I think my audience will bear witness to the correctness of this philosophy, and to the literal fulfillment of this prophecy.

Here is an eloquent extract upon

MAN'S RIGHT TO LIBERTY.

Indeed, I ought to state, what must be obvious to all, properly speaking, there is no such thing as *new* truth; for truth, like the God whose attribute it is, is eternal. In this sense, there is, indeed, nothing new under the sun. Error may be properly designated as *old* or *new*, since it is but a misconception, or an incorrect view of the truth. Misapprehensions of what truth is have their beginnings and their endings. They pass away as the race move onward. But truth is "from everlasting to everlasting," and can never pass away.

Such is the truth of man's right to liberty. It existed in the very idea of man's creation. It was *his* even before he comprehended it. He was created in it, endowed with it, and it can never be taken from him. No laws, no statutes, no compacts, no covenants, no compromises, no constitutions, can abrogate or destroy it. It is beyond the reach of the strongest earthly arm, and smiles at the ravings of tyrants from its hiding-place in the bosom of God. Men may hinder its exercise—they may act in disregard of it—they are even permitted to war against it; but they fight against heaven, and their career must be short, for Eternal Providence will speedily vindicate the right.

The existence of this right is self-evident. It is written upon all the powers and faculties of man. The desire for it is the deepest and strongest of all the powers of the human soul. Earth, sea, and air—great nature, with her thousand voices, proclaims it.

In the language of Addison we may apostrophize it:

> "Oh Liberty! thou goddess, heavenly bright,
> Profuse of bliss, and pregnant with delight!
> Thou mak'st the glowing face of nature gay,
> Giv'st beauty to the sun, and pleasure to the day."

I have said that the right to liberty is self-evident. No argument, no researches into mouldy records, no learned disquisitions, are necessary to establish it. To assert it, is to call forth a sympathetic response from every human heart, and to send a thrill of joy and gladness round the world. Tyrants, oppressors, and slaveholders are stunned by its utterance; while the oppressed and enslaved of all lands hail it as an angel of deliverance. Its assertion in Russia, in Austria, in Egypt, in fifteen states of the American Union, is a crime. In the harems of Turkey, and on the southern plantations of Carolina, it is alike prohibited ; for the guilty oppressors of every clime understand its *truth*, and appreciate its electric power.

A portion of the citizens of Rochester invited Mr. Douglass, in 1852, to deliver a Fourth of July oration. He complied with the request, and gave a speech full of passionate, indignatory eloquence. We make two or three extracts from it :

THE WHITE MAN'S FOURTH OF JULY.

Fellow-citizens, pardon me; allow me to ask, why am I called upon to speak here to-day? What have I, or those I represent, to do with your national independence? Are the great principles of political freedom and of natural justice, embodied in that declaration of independence, extended to us? and am I, therefore, called upon to bring our humble offering to the national altar, and to confess the benefits, and express devout gratitude for the blessings resulting from your independence to us?

Would to God, both for your sakes and ours, that an affirmative answer could be truthfully returned to these questions. Then would my task be light, and my burden easy and delightful. For *who* is there so cold that a nation's sympathy could not warm him? Who so obdurate and dead to the claims of gratitude, that would not thankfully acknowledge such priceless benefits? Who so stolid and selfish, that would not give his voice to swell the hallelujahs of a nations's jubilee, when the chains of servitude had been torn from his limbs? I am not that man. In a case like that, the dumb might eloquently speak, and the "lame man leap as an hart."

But such is not the state of the case. I say it with a sad sense of the disparity between us. I am not included within the pale of this glorious anniversary! Your high independence only reveals the immeasurable distance between us. The blessings in which you this day rejoice, are not enjoyed in common. The rich inheritance of justice, liberty, prosperity, and independence, bequeathed by your fathers, is shared by you, not by me. The sunlight that brought life and healing to you, has brought stripes and death to me. This Fourth of July is *yours*, not *mine*. *You* may rejoice; *I* must mourn. To drag a man in fetters into the grand, illuminated temple of liberty, and call upon him to join you in joyous anthems, were inhuman mockery and sacrilegious irony. Do you mean, citizens, to mock me, by asking me to speak to-day? If so, there is a parallel to your conduct. And let me warn you that it is dangerous to copy the example of a nation whose crimes, towering up to heaven, were thrown down by the breath of the Almighty, burying that nation in irrecoverable ruin! I can to-day take up the plaintive lament of a peeled and woe-smitten people!

"By the rivers of Babylon, there we sat down. Yea, we wept when we remembered Zion. We hanged our harps upon the willows in the midst thereof. For there they that carried us away captive required of us a song; and they who wasted us required of us mirth, saying, Sing us one of the songs of Zion. How can we sing the Lord's song in a strange land?

If I forget thee, O Jerusalem, let my right hand forget her cunning. If I do not remember thee, let my tongue cleave to the roof of my mouth." * * * * * *

To me the American slave-trade is a terrible reality. When a child, my soul was often pierced with a sense of its horrors. I lived on Philpot-street, Fell's Point, Baltimore, and have watched from the wharves the slave-ships in the basin, anchored from the shore, with their cargoes of human flesh, waiting for favorable winds to waft them down the Chesapeake. There was at that time a grand slave-mart kept at the head of Pratt-street, by Austin Woldfolle. His agents were sent into every town and county in Maryland, announcing their arrival through the papers, and on flaming "*handbills*" headed Cash for Negroes. These men were generally well dressed, and very captivating in their manners. Ever ready to drink, to treat, and to gamble. The fate of many a slave has depended upon the turn of a single card; and many a child has been snatched from the arms of its mother, by bargains arranged in a state of brutal drunkenness.

The flesh-mongers gather up their victims by dozens, and drive them, chained, to the general depot at Baltimore. When a sufficient number have been collected here, a ship is chartered for the purpose of conveying the forlorn crew to Mobile, or to New Orleans. From the slave-prison to the ship, they are usually driven in the darkness of night; for, since the anti-slavery agitation, a certain caution is observed.

In the deep, still darkness of midnight, I have been often aroused by the dead, heavy footsteps, and the piteous cries of the chained gangs that passed our door. The anguish of my boyish heart was intense, and I was often consoled, when speaking to my mistress in the morning, to hear her say that the custom was very wicked; that she hated to hear the rattle of the chains, and the heart-rending cries. I was glad to find one who sympathized with me in my horror.

Fellow-citizens, this murderous traffic is, to-day, in active operation in this boasted republic. In the solitude of my spirit, I see clouds of dust raised on the highways of the south; I see the bleeding footsteps; I hear the doleful wail of fettered humanity, on the way to the slave-markets, where the victims are to be sold like *horses*, *sheep* and *swine*, knocked off to the highest bidder. There I see the tenderest ties ruthlessly broken to gratify the lust, caprice and rapacity of the buyers and sellers of men. My soul sickens at the sight.

* * * * * * *

What, to the American slave, is your Fourth of July? I answer: a day that reveals to him, more than all other days in the year, the gross injustice and cruelty to which he is the constant victim. To him, your celebration is a sham; your boasted liberty, an unholy license; your national greatness, swelling vanity; your sounds of rejoicing are empty and heartless; your denunciations of tyrants, brass-fronted impudence; your shouts of liberty and equality, hollow mockery; your prayers and hymns, your sermons and thanksgivings, with all your religious parade and solemnity, are, to him, mere bombast, fraud, deception, impiety and hypocrisy—a thin vail to cover up crimes which would disgrace a nation of savages. There is not a nation on the earth guilty of practices more shocking and bloody, than are the people of these United States at this very hour."

Several years since, a few transatlantic friends of Mr. Douglass raised the necessary funds to purchase his freedom from his master, for, according to the laws of the United States, the brilliant orator was *the property* of a Maryland trafficker in human flesh! But for this, Mr. Douglass, to-day, would be in imminent danger of seizure and reënslavement. His genius would avail him nothing—were he a Cicero or Demosthenes, a human brute would have the legal right to horsewhip him into subjection.

To those foolish people who contend that the African race is essentially a brute race, and far inferior to any other existing, we commend Frederick Douglass. He is perfectly competent to defend his race, and is *himself* an argument that cannot be refuted, in favor of the capability of the negro race for the highest degree of refinement and intellectuality. The more such men his race can produce, the sooner the day of its freedom will come. The sooner will the free blacks of the north rise to an equality with the whites. That singular and horrible prejudice against color, which pervades all classes, and which not even the religion of the day has affected, will vanish, when, as a class, the negroes are not only industrious and virtuous, but distinguish themselves for their love of learning and the fine arts. We mean no excuse for the negro-hating population of this country, but simply state a fact which black men should ponder. Every negro who acts well his part, is assisting his race to rise from its degrading enthrallment.

ICHABOD CODDING.

Ichabod Codding is well known in the free states as one of the earliest, most faithful and eloquent advocates of anti-slavery reform in America, and he deserves a place in this series of sketches of distinguished agitators. He gave himself up to the cause of freedom when he was in his youth, and when, to be known as an anti-slavery advocate, was to endure obloquy and scorn—to risk not only reputation, but life. He is, according to our thinking, one of the most powerful advocates of reform in the country. His talents are varied; he is persuasively eloquent, as an orator, but is socially still more eloquent. We never met a more talented conversationist, and his power in social circles is exceedingly great. His manners are bland and winning, and yet he is strong and rigid in his positions. The reformer who is endeavoring to impress society with certain great truths, is often, too often, harsh and repulsive in his manners and conversation. He is like a rock against which the billows may dash forever without making an impression—but he is cold and bleak. Mr. Codding unites with firmness a great deal of geniality and suavity of manner. His enemies soon love him when they know him. His conversation is fascinating, yet is utterly devoid of art. Its naturalness is one of its most charming characteristics. He is intensely earnest, overflows with anecdote and humor, and seems never to lack bright and genial thoughts, striking sentences, and *apropos* anecdotes. As an orator, he is surpassed by few living men. It is impossible, however, to compare him with his cotemporaries, for he is only like himself. His social characteristics follow him to the platform. He is at times vehement in his eloquence there, but oftener calmly in earnest—clear, frank and winning. One of his best speeches is not characterized by a continuous stream of eloquence, but here and there bubbles up with grand, or beautiful passages, and the whole speech has a web of logic stronger than steel.

In his personal appearance, Mr. Codding, at first sight, appears to be rather rough—and it is true that he has nothing of the fop in his composition. He is of medium height, has a fine, compact forehead, fine, dark hair, a large, homely mouth, but eyes of eloquent beauty. He has a rare voice, and reads finely. Mr. Codding was born in Bristol, Ontario county, New York, in the year 1811. His father died a short time previous to his birth, and he came into the world fatherless, and an inheritor of poverty. His mother was left in moderate circumstances, and all the members of the family who were old enough, were obliged to work. Before he was twelve years old, his educational advantages were slight. When seventeen, he became deeply interested in the cause of temperance. He had heard something of certain movements in the east, but had neither seen pledges, nor read addresses. A little society of thirteen members was formed upon the total abstinence basis. It is a little singular that this original teetotal society had not a member who was professedly a christian, or who was of age. Not long after, however, the society changed its constitution so as to conform to those of new societies which afterward sprang up upon the basis of the old pledge. A few, however, would not recede, and among these was Codding. He delivered addresses upon the subject in many places. Before he was twenty-one years old, he had delivered over one hundred temperance speeches. He also took up the subject of corporeal punishment in schools, opposing the customary use of the rod, with a good deal of zeal.

For three years, Codding was teacher in the English department of Canandaigua academy, at the same time pursuing higher and collegiate studies himself. The since well-known S. A. Douglas, the little giant, was studying at Canandaigua, while he was there. He was then, as now, devoted to politics—read the political newspapers eagerly and carefully, and was much more of a politician than a scholar. Before leaving Canandaigua academy, Mr. Codding was, probably, as accomplished a scholar as ordinary college graduates: he was such in the opinion of competent judges.

When twenty-three years old, he entered Middlebury College, in Vermont. While a freshman, he delivered a temperance speech in the town, which created a good deal of excitement, and he was waited upon by a committee who complained of his speech. In his junior year, needing money, and being familiar with the studies of the term, he got leave of absence to teach, or engage in a benevolent agency. He had for some time felt deeply interested in the cause of the slave, and engaged himself for the term to the Vermont Anti-slavery Society, to lecture. He went out into the towns, and was met by mobs of ruffians, in many instances, and excitement attended his lectures everywhere. The story was widely circulated that he was a member of Middlebury College, and the faculty, fearing that he was adding to their unpopularity, got together, and declared that he was away without liberty, and they therefore censured him. Of this shameful act he was not apprised, and knew nothing of it till he returned to college. Upon meeting his fellow-students, the noble young advocate of liberty found that he was in disgrace. He went to work in a manly fashion to make potent the injustice of the faculty. He demanded a college meeting—got his facts ready for the press, and threatened the officers with their publication in the public journals, unless they would rescind their vote of censure. They finally gave him a letter of explanation in which it was fully admitted that he was *not* away from college without leave. He was now upon his former standing, but their cruel conduct stung him to the heart, and having established his innocence of the charges against him, he left the college forever.

He immediately engaged himself as a public lecturer to the American Anti-slavery Society, and spent the winter in Vermont. In the spring he had orders to go to Massachusetts. The very first place he lectured in, he was mobbed. It was in the town of Brighton, and on the Sabbath. It was a beautiful, sunny, summer afternoon, and at the hour of five, the people assembled in the church to hear Mr. Codding deliver his address upon American slavery. He entered the house where the stillness of a New England Sabbath prevailed. But out of doors a wild mob was fast gathering, and their harsh shouts contrasted strangely with the still beauty of the Sabbath. Two of the boldest of the mob entered the church. Mr. Codding was in the midst of an opening prayer, when they rushed to the pulpit and seized him, dragged him down into the aisle, intending to pull him out into the street, and then wreak their vengeance upon him. But the audience, by this time, were roused to a state of excitement, and two young men who had known Codding at college being present, seized upon the intruders, overcame them, and binding them with handkerchiefs, forwarded them into the front slip, and forced them to hear *one* anti-slavery lecture, at least!

The next winter, Mr. C. was sent into Maine, and he had the honor of addressing the members of the legislature for three hours upon the Texas question. It was one of the greatest speeches he ever made, and its effect was astonishing. It was afterward said that it made above forty members over into abolitionists. In Brunswick, he was mobbed. In Calais, he commenced a course of lectures, but a few lawyers got the people together to vote him out of town. He attended the meeting, demanded the right to speak on the resolutions against him, which had been introduced, and having got the floor, used his time to good purpose. A set of desperadoes called "the Indians," from the fact that, dressed as Indians, they committed acts they dared not commit in their real characters, were present, and by appealing to their natural prejudices against lawyers, Mr. Codding arrested their attention, and got the meeting adjourned till the next night, when he met resolution after resolution, defeated each one, triumphed over the lawyers, and delivered his course of lectures without disturbance. While in Maine, Mr. Codding, for a time, edited an anti-slavery journal—the first established there. He was, after leaving Maine, with Judge Jay, mobbed in Bedford, New York. After being two years in Maine, and laying the foundation of the liberty party in that state, he received an invitation to visit Connecticut, which he accepted. He remained in Connecticut three years, making in all parts of the state the warmest friends. With S. M. Booth, he established the *Christian Freeman*, now the *Republican*. In 1842, he went west, to Illinois and Wisconsin. He delivered a great course of lectures in Chicago, and in Waukesha, Wisconsin, he established the first anti-slavery paper in that state—the journal now edited by Mr. Booth, at Milwaukee. He also preached for a time to a Congregational church in Waukesha, and afterwards to independent congregations in Joliet and Lockport, Illinois.

While once delivering a lecture in Southern Illinois, Mr. Codding was seized by his neckerchief, and a pistol was presented at his breast by an infuriated beast in the shape of a man, but the calm fearlessness of Mr. Codding overcame him, and at his bidding the pistol dropped to the floor. He was at one time lecturing, when a perfect volley of eggs was thrown at him, and he drenched with them. One eye was much hurt by a missile, yet he preserved his humor through this treatment, and with excellent good nature, he said:

> "Well, boys, I am fond of eggs, but I would like to have them done up in a little different style. May be, in the haste of your generosity, you did not take that into consideration!"

The "boys" roared with laughter at his reply to the peculiar arguments.

The finest specimens of Mr. Codding's oratory are unreported, and live only in the memories of those who listened to them. We will, however, make one extract from an address delivered by him before a mass convention in Illinois, and which was afterward published in a pamphlet form:

> "'Train up a child in the way he should go.' This commandment comes home to the heart of the slave father: he looks around upon the little children that God has given him; he hears the voice of God, and how it harmonizes with the response in his own bosom! Oh, how he burns with internal fire to educate their moral and intellectual nature, and fit them for usefulness here and for that state of being that shall come after. He obeys by commencing to teach his child to read; the slaveholder comes in and says, 'Not a letter shall that child learn.' The slave replies, 'God commands me to do it.' The slaveholder retorts, 'I will show you to whom that child belongs; I own it as I own the pig in the sty;' and the master proves his superior authority by triumphing over the express command of Jehovah. What a principle is here! The chattel principle

spurns all those commandments, and absolutely prevents their fulfillment. This is slaveholding in its essential characteristics. I beg this audience will not understand me to be speaking of its abuse. I am talking of the *seed principle*—it is NOT its abuse. *Itself* is the greatest of all abuses; it is the *giant evil*, and overshadowing crime. The principle, then, is settled, that chattel slavery, absolutely, so far as the slave is concerned, does overrule the direct command of God, and asserts more than God dare assert! If the principle is settled that God cannot rule over *all*, then it is settled that he cannot rule over any. If I say, here is a portion of the human family over which God may not reign—it is settled thus with regard to the slave, it is settled with regard to all men; and if God reigns over others, it is by express permission of the chattel principle. It must be seen, then, that if God has no right to rule over any, he is no God: this would be *No-godism*—ATHEISM; and whoever negatively, indirectly or positively puts forth an influence to sustain this monstrous system for one moment, is so far forth guilty of promoting downright atheism. Startle not; I have no time nor heart to say pretty things. Every man who apologizes for slavery is warring against God's throne, and the foundation principles of his church and his ministry.

"Before I make the application of this principle to the pro-slavery ecclesiastics of our time, suppose we take up, and for a moment, in the light of this principle, look at the atonement. Now, all christians will acknowledge that Jesus Christ has become the end of the law for righteousness; but, if God has no right to reign over this universe, he has no right to affix a penalty to this law, and therefore we need no atonement. You sweep the universe from his jurisdiction, what need of a gospel? The foundation rock is taken away, and the gospel plan has become as baseless as a vision.

"Again: 'God commandeth all men *now* everywhere to repent.' Suppose a minister should take this for his text, and during the discourse should make no allusion to the little particle *now*, do you not see that the theme is robbed of its point, and shorn of its power? The principal, as well as the practical reason announces that we should at *once* repent of all sin, and come into immediate harmony with God. Now to seize on one of God's rational creatures, by virtue of superior brute force, and doom him to a wretched life of unpaid toil, is the crowning exhibition of human guilt. MAN, created a little lower than the angels—endowed with all the mysterious, incomprehensible attributes of an immortal soul—with a mind capable of grasping the infinite and the unknown—with a destiny that shall reach through the cycles of eternity,—to go up mid-way heaven—grapple with Deity—seize *such* a being—hurl him to the dust—herd him with four-footed beasts and creeping things, and write upon his brow 'Chattel, *property*, BEAST OF BURDEN!' This is the acme of guilt, standing unrivaled in its detestable preëminence. If this be not a sin, you will search the catalogue of crime in vain to find one; and if any sin in that catalogue should be repented of immediately, in the name of God and humanity, should not this? Now, says the apologist for slavery, 'I believe slavery ought to be abolished, but the idea of immediate abolition is wild;' and he calls us Jacobins! Now, I contend that when you take the ground that this infamous system may be continued *for one moment*, you array yourself against a great and cardinal principle of the gospel—the doctrine of immediate repentance. But let the principle once be settled that we are under no obligation to repent of sin *to-day*, there is no proof that we shall be to-morrow, and if not to-morrow, then never. Hence, the principle settled that we are under no obligation to repent *now*, the principle is settled that there are no moral obligations in the universe; therefore, no authoritative law—no God. Hence, he that arrays himself against the gospel, against the divine law, would blot out the Deity from the universe.

"Once more, hear that anti-abolitionist: 'You are right in principle, but it will do no good to urge it.' What have we here! The infidel declaration that there is nothing in truth adapted to move mind. But the doctrine taught everywhere in the bible is, that 'the right with the might shall be,' that every honest blow struck in harmony with God and his universe, every breath of prayer, every voice of pleading, is an accretion upon the heart of universal truth; yes, and let it cheer the true-hearted; every nail driven into the temple of truth is FAST, and never to be extracted. This temple shall yet be completed.

> 'There's a good time coming, boys,
>   A good time coming;
> We may not live to see the day,
> But earth shall glisten in the ray,
>   Of the good time coming.'

Let it once be said there is no such adaptation in truth; hope dies from the world, and darkness that can be felt settles down upon the prospects of mankind. Call in your missionaries;

down with your pulpits; hush the thunders of the press; cease all moral effort, for it is uttered from Heaven, and believed among men, that there is no adaptation in truth to accomplish the purposes of benevolence; let us then go down by the cold streams of Babylon, and hang our harps upon the willows in utter despair.

"But thanks be to God! it is not so; let me tell all that hear me, *there is no real effort lost;* it is an impossibility; it is a libel upon God. Thus does anti-abolition dethrone God, nullify his commandments, abrogate matrimony, mock at the atonement, scout immediate repentance, and profanely declare that truth is not 'mighty through God to the pulling down the strong-holds of sin.'

"Now, all must admit that whoever puts forth an influence by his theories, his indifference, his apologies or open advocacy, to sustain slavery, is guilty of sustaining as bare-faced a system of infidelity as ever mocked God. Do you not see that all anti-abolitionists are thus implicated? I am sorry to be obliged to say that the leading influences of the church and the ministry in this country are in this fearful position. For uttering such sentiments as these, the cry has been given abroad by some ministers, and others, that I am an infidel in my tendencies. Such a charge was made against me recently in the city of Chicago, by several clergyman. Oh, I could bear it all; but when I see these great and overgrown ecclesiastical bodies standing upon the prostrate form of crushed humanity, and when I see great-hearted men driven to infidelity by seeing these churches and ministers, who profess to be the pink of piety, plead for this blighting curse, and strengthen the hands of the oppressor, it is too much; I must speak out; I must assign them their true position. You say that I am excited. I am. I never can discuss these great principles, involving all that pertains to this deep, mysterious nature of ours, without becoming excited; but God grant it may not lead me to take ground for slavery! I have endeavored to compress my remarks into as brief a space as possible. I leave it to my audience to say whether I have maintained my proposition. I have, so to speak, merely endeavored to throw out the bones of the argument. I have already declared that the leading influences of the church and ministry in America are in a position to support the system of slavery as I have described it. In exemplifying this position, I may seem unnecessarily severe. I have no time to get on a Sabbath-day face or adopt a holy tone. I know no better way than get right, and speak right on as I feel. I confess it seems utterly impossible that any of these religious bodies should yield an influence to support *such* a system. I persuade myself sometimes in my closet that it cannot be so; but, alas! the delusion soon gives place to reality. Talk not of *robbery*—I cannot descend to mention it in the same connection with slavery. Common robbery merely takes the *earned;* slavery takes the EARNER; common robbery takes only the *property;* slavery takes the PROPRIETOR; common robbery clutches the *thing;* slavery lays rude hands upon the MAN. Why, the slave cannot say *my* hands, *my* feet, *my* body—*my* SOUL, without using a figure of speech! All he has belongs to another. Legislators and constitution-makers talk gravely about the rights of property. I pray you, sir, what is the foundation right of all property—the grand, indestructible

Gibraltar upon which all rights are based? My right to myself. That gone, you have swept away all that is great and awful in man. Now, when we lay at the feet of the leading ecclesiastics of the age the awful charge of conniving at this atheistical principle, and of strengthening the hands of these man-hyenas who practice on it, we are warned off as laying hands on the sacred and the holy. I cannot help it. For when I discover the massive moral power of these large and influential bodies pressing with ponderous weight upon the prostrate forms and crushed hearts of my Father's children, and hear their suppressed sighs and groans, and see them striving, and struggling, and surging beneath the awful incubus, and all in vain, I must and will cry out, GET OFF—IN GOD'S NAME, GET OFF!"

Certain enemies of Mr. Codding, especially in the west, have endeavored to injure his influence by base falsehoods respecting his religious sentiments. We cannot do better than quote a few paragraphs from a letter written by the Hon. Francis Gillette, from the west, and which was published two years since:

"From Beloit I passed down into Northern Illinois, to Lockport, a village situated on the Des Plaines river and Illinois canal, thirty-five miles south of Chicago. In that place and its vicinity I spent several days with Mr. Codding, a gentleman whom very many of the readers of the 'Republican' remember with a lively interest, as, for some years a very eloquent and effective advocate of reform in this state, and those who had the pleasure of his personal acquaintance, as a truly fraternal and genial man. It is now ten years since Mr. Codding went from this state to visit some relatives in the vicinity of his present abode, with no thought but to return and resume his labors here; but he became so much interested in the great moral harvest-field of the west, that he finally yielded to pressing solicitations, and concluded to devote himself to that fresh and inviting field of labor. As a public speaker and an itinerating lecturer, no one of his many eastern friends and admirers will be surprised to learn that, in Illinois and Wisconsin, through which he has often passed and repassed, on missions of humanity and mercy, he is spoken of and admired by many, even, who differ from him in sentiment, as the Whitfield of the west, before whose truthful tongue and flashing eye the chosen and fitted champions of the opposition have quailed and slunk away never to encounter him again. In his person and manners he appears but slightly changed by the last ten years, time having brushed him lightly with his hoary wing. I found this admirable man, who, could he put his great soul into his wallet, could occupy a princely mansion and a most genteel city pulpit stuffed with the softest and downiest *cotton*, occupying his "own hired house," a very humble dwelling, quite retired from the village of Lockport, which, he told me, he had taken with a view of securing that retirement which is so favorable to study, and dividing his ministerial labors between two societies, neither of which is large—one in Lockport, and the other in Joliet, a village five miles south.

"Though regularly ordained some years since, after the strictest modes of Congregationalism, and cordially fellowshiped as sound in the faith, I understand that Mr. Codding is now regarded by the vigilant sentinels of sectarian orthodox, as having apostatized from the true standard, and they have raised against him the cry of heretic. I was unable to ascertain the exact points of his heterodoxy, though, as I was informed, it was gravely alleged, 'as a stone of stumbling and rock of offense,' to many, who *would not be thought* lacking in true piety, that men and women even, who had been 'stayers at home' from public worship, and others, not a few, who had been Universalists, Unitarians, and I know not what other suspicious ones, were seen to attend on his ministrations. Possibly it may be true of Mr. Codding, as of some other persons in this marvelous age of the world, that his most alarming heresy consists in the rejection of that most unadorable trinity of slave-mongers, lower-law theologians, and hunker demagogues; and especially the denial of that new article which has recently been adopted into their creed, viz: that slave-catching is both a political and saintly duty, without which there can be no salvation to the Union. He does insist that a democracy which crushes liberty is a despotism, and that a religion without humanity is not christianity. He teaches that the worst heterodoxy is that which violates the divine law, *in practice*, and that sect-making is not christianizing society, but, on the contrary, filling it with discord and bigotry, thus impeding the progress of peace on earth and good will to men. In addition to the performance of his parochial labors, he occasionally goes out on a lecturing tour, his great aim still being to be diligent in his Master's vineyard, and devote all his noble powers to the elevation and advancement of his race."

It is impossible by description or quotation to give the reader a just idea of Mr. Codding as a writer or speaker. He must be seen and heard to be appreciated. He is now in the full maturity of his powers, and though he perhaps lacks something of the impetuosity of his youth, he has more of wisdom and charity for his foes. We consider him, in many respects, a model reformer. He scarcely ever indulges in bitter denunciations of slaveholders — scarcely ever makes enemies, unless it be among the most depraved class of people. All over the north there are men opposed to him, in his political, anti-slavery views, who, nevertheless, respect and love him. Yet he does not ever flinch a hair from rigid adherence to principle.

HARRIET BEECHER STOWE.

We have no new information to communicate to the reader respecting the history of Mrs. Stowe, neither do we hope to make any profound criticisms upon her remarkable volume, and yet we cannot, in such a series of sketches as this, wholly pass her by. And so, though hundreds, here and in Europe, have written about her, praised her, blamed her, criticised her great work with acuteness, *we* will venture to make her the subject of an article.

Mrs. Stowe was born in Litchfield, Connecticut, and is a little more than forty years of age. She received an excellent education and a great deal of energy of character from her parents. They removed to Boston when she was young, and there she enjoyed very superior advantages in the pursuit of knowledge. She commenced her career of usefulness as an assistant teacher in the female school of an elder sister in Boston. Her father subsequently went to the west, to preside over Lane Seminary, and Mrs. Stowe, with her sister, went to Cincinnati, where they opened a school for the education of young ladies. Lane Seminary is near Cincinnati, and in the course of a few years, which were devoted to teaching, Harriet Beecher was sought and won by Calvin E. Stowe, professor of biblical literature in the seminary, and one of the most accomplished scholars in the country. The married couple took up their residence in one of the buildings connected with the seminary, and devoted to the use of the professors. For a long term of years this was the home of Mr. and Mrs. Stowe. It is not necessary for us to give a history of the anti-slavery excitement which at one time threatened to ruin Lane Seminary. It is well known that Cincinnati was for a long time the theater of violent agitation upon the question of negro slavery. In and around it the bitterest, the most unprincipled enemies of anti-slavery doctrines lived—and also the warmest and most courageous advocates of liberty for all men. For years, to be an abolitionist in Cincinnati, was to be scorned, hissed at, and threatened with death. Mob law set aside the constitution, and screamed out threats of vengeance upon meek, Christ-like men, who, with a courage exceedingly rare at this day, asserted the truth, that "all men should be free." Anti-slavery presses were destroyed again and again, and the buildings of Lane Seminary were often in imminent danger of being destroyed, because of the anti-slavery reputation of its scholars and professors. Mrs. Stowe could not well fail to see the inherent wickedness of an institution which could only be defended by drunken mobs with brick-bats and tar and feathers.

The diabolical persecution of the abolitionists won them many warm friends, and sympathy for their principles grew rapidly in thousands of hearts. Situated as Cincinnati is, the friends of the slave in its vicinity soon found that they could show their love for him in a more excellent way than by talking. Poor fugitives from oppression were constantly crossing the Ohio river, and the abolitionists banded together and built an "underground railroad" to Canada. Mrs. Stowe could not, if she had wished, escape from a knowledge of the negro character. She was often appealed to by some weary, half-starved, lashed, slave-mother for food and shelter. She saw time after time the shy, painful look of the fugitive—witnessed his joy at escape, or his sorrow at the thought of loved ones left behind in bondage. In the course of many years she gained, not only a knowledge of negro character, but of the terrible atrocities which are perpetrated upon slaves by brutal masters. She also had opportunities for knowing the character of slave-holders and slave-catchers, for hundreds of them were at any time to be found and met in Cincinnati. There are many who wonder how Mrs. Stowe could gain the knowledge of negro character, and of the character of men like Tom Loker and Mr. Shelby, so abundantly displayed in her story. We certainly cannot be surprised that an exceedingly observing woman, after a residence of fifteen or twenty years in a city commanding the trade of slave states, and through which thousands of slaves escaped during that time, should learn the character of the slaves and their owners and catchers. Besides, Mrs. Stowe made several visits into the neighboring slave states, and became acquainted with slave-masters and mistresses—had opportunities to see the peculiar institution at home, and its effects upon society. For years she calmed her fervid spirit, and kept to herself her thoughts upon the great iniquity. But the tears of the panting fugitive, the thrilling stories of hair-breadth escapes, were never forgotten by her; they were all in her heart. At length with her husband she returned to the east.

The congress of the United States saw fit, at the bidding of the slave-power, to make every man in the free states *a slave-catcher.* The scenes which followed the enactment of that terrible law caused the story of *Uncle Tom's Cabin* to be written. Night after night Mrs. Stowe wept bitter tears over them, and she resolved to write a story of slavery: the world knows the rest.

Of Mrs. Stowe's personal appearance we have little to say. We think no one could mistake her for an ordinary woman. There is a look of conscious power in her face. There is strength of character

expressed in it. She is not a beautiful woman, and yet her eyes are not often surpassed in beauty. They are dark and dreamy, and look as if some sorrowful scene ever haunted her brain. In dress she is very plain and homely; in manners gentle, without a particle of false gentility.

Previous to commencing in the *National Era* her great story of *Uncle Tom*, Mrs. Stowe had written comparatively brief sketches and tales, which were gathered into a little volume entitled "*The Mayflower*," a quaint and exceedingly appropriate name. Those who have read the little book could not have been surprised when they read her subsequent and more popular volume. For, though the brevity of the little stories and sketches in the earlier volume precluded the possibility of eminent success in the portraiture of individuals, or of great popularity for the book, yet they were executed with wonderful skill. To us, after a fresh reading of the volume, with our eyes yet wet with tears of sympathy, and our sides not yet done aching with laughter, *Uncle Tom* seems no marvelous advance upon the *Mayflower*. The one was fragmentary—the other whole, complete. There are passages in the first, almost or quite equal to anything in the last. There are stories, though short, which are told most admirably. In them we see Mrs. Stowe's wonderful skill at sketching character. She describes the old Puritan in such a vivid style, that he appears to the reader as if painted on canvas by a master artist. There is, too, the same tendency to humor in these little sketches as in *Uncle Tom's Cabin*—also the same inimitable pathos. We cannot do better than to copy one of her sketches. Those of our readers who have read it once, will delight to do so again, and those who have never read it, will thank us for copying it here. It is entitled

"LITTLE EDWARD."

Were any of you born in New England, in the good old catechising, church-going, school-going, orderly times? If so, you may have seen my Uncle Abel; the most perpendicular, rectangular, upright, downright, good man that ever labored six days and rested on the seventh.

You remember his hard, weather-beaten countenance, where every line seemed drawn with "a pen of iron and the point of a diamond;" his considerate, gray eyes, that moved over objects as if it were not best to be in a hurry about seeing; the circumspect opening and shutting of his mouth; his down-sitting and up-rising, all performed with conviction aforethought—in short, the whole ordering of his life and conversation, which was, according to the tenor of the military order, "to the right about face—forward, march!" Now if you supposed, from all this triangularism of exterior, that this good man had nothing kindly within, you were much mistaken. You often find the greenest grass under a snow-drift; and, though my uncle's mind was not exactly of the flower-garden kind, still there was an abundance of wholesome and kindly vegetation there.

It is true, he seldom laughed and never joked, himself, but no man had a more serious and weighty conviction of what a good joke was in another; and when some exceeding witticism was dispensed in his presence, you might see Uncle Abel's face slowly relax into an expression of solemn satisfaction, and he would look at the author with a sort of quiet wonder, as if it was past his comprehension how such a thing could come into a man's head.

Uncle Abel, too, had some relish for the fine arts; in proof of which I might adduce the pleasure with which he gazed at the plates in his family bible, the likeness whereof is neither in heaven, nor on earth, nor under the earth. And he was also such an eminent musician, that he could go through the singing-book at one sitting, without the least fatigue, beating time like a windmill all the way.

He had, too, a liberal hand, though his liberality was all by the rule of three. He did to his neighbor exactly as he would be done by; he loved some things in this world very sincerely: he loved his God much, but he honored and feared him more; he was exact with others, he was more exact with himself, and he expected his God to be more exact still.

Everything in Uncle Abel's house was in the same time, and place, and manner, and form from year's end to year's end. There was old Master Bose, a dog after my uncle's own heart, who always walked as if he were studying the multiplication-table. There was the old clock, forever ticking in the kitchen corner, with a picture on its face of the sun forever setting behind a perpendicular row of poplar trees. There was the never-failing supply of red peppers and onions, hanging over the chimney. There, too, were the yearly hollyhocks and morning-glories, blooming about the windows. There was the "best room," with its sanded floor, the cupboard in one corner, with its glass doors, the evergreen asparagus bushes in the chimney, and there was the stand, with the bible and almanac on it, in another corner. There, too, was Aunt Betsey, who never looked any older, because she always looked as old as she could; who always dried her catnip and wormwood the last of September, and began to clean house the first of May. In short, this was the land of continuance. Old time never took it into his head to practice either addition, or subtraction, or multiplication on its sum total.

This Aunt Betsey aforenamed, was the neatest and most efficient piece of human machinery that ever operated in forty places at once. She was always everywhere, predominating over, and seeing to everything; and though my uncle had been twice married, Aunt Betse'ys rule and authority had never been broken. She reigned over his wives when living, and reigned after them when dead, and so seemed likely to reign on to the end of the chapter. But my uncle's latest wife left Aunt Betsey a much less tractable subject than ever before had fallen to her lot. Little Edward was the child of my uncle's old age, and a brighter, merrier little blossom never grew on the verge of an avalanche. He had been committed to the nursing of his grandmamma till he had arrived at the age of *in*discretion, and then my old uncle's heart so yearned for him that he was sent for home.

His introduction into the family excited a terrible sensation. Never was there such a contemner of dignities, such a violator of high places and sanctities, as this very Master Edward. It was all in vain to try to teach him decorum. He was the most outrageously merry elf that ever shook a head of curls; and it was all the same to him whether it was "*Sabba' day*" or any other day, he laughed and frolicked with everybody and everything that came in his way, not even excepting his solemn old father; and when you saw him, with his fair arms around the old man's neck, and his bright blue eyes and blooming cheek pressing out beside the bleak face of Uncle Abel, you might fancy you saw spring caressing winter. Uncle Abel's metaphysics were sorely puzzled by this sparkling, dancing compound of spirit and matter; nor could he devise any method of bringing it into any reasonable shape, for he did mischief with an energy and perseverance that was truly astonishing. Once he scoured the floor with Aunt Betsey's very best Scotch snuff; once he washed up the hearth with Uncle Abel's most immaculate clothes-brush; and once he was found trying to make Bose wear his father's spectacles. In short, there was no use, except the right one, to which he did not put everything that came in his way.

But Uncle Abel was most of all puzzled to know what to do with him on the Sabbath, for on that day Master Edward seemed to exert himself to be particularly diligent and entertaining. "Edward!—Edward must not play Sunday!" his father would call out; and then Edward would hold up his curly head, and look as grave as the catechism; but in three minutes you would see "pussy" scampering through the "best room," with Edward at her heels, to the entire discomposure of all devotion in Aunt Betsey and all others in authority.

At length my uncle came to the conclusion that "it wasn't in natur' to teach him any better," and that "he could no more keep Sunday than the brook down in the lot." My poor uncle! he did not know what was the matter with his heart, but certain it was, he lost all faculty of scolding, when Little Edward was in the case, and he would rub his spectacles a quarter of an hour longer than common, when Aunt Betsey was detailing his witticisms and clever doings.

In process of time our hero had compassed his third year, and arrived at the dignity of going to school. He went illustriously through the spelling-book, and then attacked the catechism; went from "man's chief end" to the "requirin's and forbiddin's" in a fortnight, and at last came home inordinately merry, to tell his father that he had got to "amen." After this, he made a regular business of saying over the whole every Sunday evening, standing with his hands folded in front, and his checked apron folded down, occasionally glancing round to see if pussy gave proper attention. And, being of a practically benevolent turn of mind, he made several commendable efforts to teach Bose the catechism, in which he succeeded as well as might be expected. In short, without further detail, Master Edward bade fair to become a literary wonder.

But alas for poor Little Edward! his merry dance was soon over. A day came when he sickened, Aunt Betsey tried her whole herbarium, but in vain: he grew rapidly worse and worse. His father sickened in heart, but said nothing; he only stayed by his bedside day and night, trying all means to save with affecting pertinacity.

"Can't you think of anything more, doctor?" said he to the physician, when all had been tried in vain.

"Nothing," answered the physician.

A momentary convulsion passed over my uncle's face. "The will of the Lord be done," said he, almost with a groan of anguish.

Just at that moment a ray of the setting sun pierced the checked curtains, and gleamed like an angel's smile across the face of the little sufferer. He woke from troubled sleep. "Oh, dear! I am so sick!" he gasped, feebly. His father raised him in his arms; he breathed easier, and looked up with a grateful smile. Just then his old playmate, the cat, crossed the room. "There goes pussy," said he; "Oh, dear! I shall never play with pussy any more."

At that moment a deadly change passed over his face. He looked up in his father's face with an imploring expression, and put out his hands as if for help. There was one moment of agony, and then the sweet features all settled into a smile of peace, and "mortality was swallowed up of life."

My uncle laid him down, and looked one moment at his beautiful face. It was too much for his principles, too much for his consistency, and "he lifted up his voice and wept."

The next morning was the Sabbath—the funeral day—and it rose with "breath all incense and with cheek all bloom." Uncle Abel was as calm and collected as ever, but in his face there was a sorrow-stricken appearance touching to behold. I remember him at family prayers, as he bent over the great bible and began the psalm, "Lord, thou has been our dwelling-place in all generations." Apparently he was touched by the melancholy splendor of the poetry, for after reading a few verses he stopped. There was a dead silence, interrupted only by the tick of the clock. He cleared his voice repeatedly, and tried to go on, but in vain. He closed the book and kneeled down to prayer. The energy of sorrow broke through his usual formal reverence, and his language flowed forth with a deep and sorrowful pathos which I shall never forget. The God so much reverenced, so much feared, seemed to draw near to him as a friend and comforter, his refuge and strength, "a very present help in time of trouble."

My uncle rose, and I saw him walk to the room of the departed one. He uncovered the face. It was set with the seal of death, but oh! how surpassingly lovely! The brilliancy of life was gone, but that pure, transparent face was touched with a mysterious, triumphant brightness, which seemed like the dawning of heaven.

My uncle looked long and earnestly. He felt the beauty of what he gazed on; his heart was softened, but he had no words for his feelings. He left the room unconsciously, and stood in the front door. The morning was bright; the bells were ringing for church; the birds were singing merrily, and the pet squirrel of Little Edward was frolicking about the door. My uncle watched him as he ran first up one tree, and then down and up another, and then over the fence, whisking his brush, and chattering just as if nothing was the matter.

With a deep sigh Uncle Abel broke forth: "How happy that *cretur'* is! Well, the Lord's will be done!"

That day the dust was committed to dust, amid the lamentations of all who had known Little Edward. Years have passed since then, and all that is mortal of my uncle has long since been gathered to his fathers, but his just and upright spirit has entered the glorious liberty of the sons of God. Yes, the good man may have had opinions which the philosophical scorn, weaknesses at which the thoughtless smile; but death shall change him into all that is enlightened, wise, and refined; for he shall awake in "His" likeness, and be satisfied.

There are persons who pretend to believe that Mrs. Stowe's story of *Uncle Tom* is not a work of remarkable genius and power. Its success, they say, arose from the desire of the people of the northern states and Europe to hear harrowing tales of negro slavery. We confess that for such critics we have little charity. Their prejudices lead them astray—or they are incapable of making a just criticism. What is the reason that anti-slavery tales, written and published long before that by Mrs. Stowe, did not meet with great success? Several had been published, but though moderately well written, the public did not go enthusiastic over them. But when a tale of slavery came to be written in a masterly manner, full of pathos, humor and eloquence, it attracted the attention of the public. Friends of the slave first read it, and, discovering that it was, aside from its teachings, the most remarkable story of the time, they called the attention of the great world of indifferent men and women to the fact. The story flew on the wings of the wind. Millions cried over it, who had never before bestowed a thought upon the negro slave; it met with a success, such perhaps as no other single volume, since the art of printing was invented, can boast. And can men with brains be persuaded that a volume not remarkable for its power of exciting the sympathies of the people accomplished this? Let superannuated women believe it, and no others. *Uncle Tom's Cabin* is one of the most remarkable volumes of the century, and its authoress will go down to posterity, not merely as a philanthropist, but as a great writer, possessed of a most brilliant genius. The leading critics of Europe have already recorded this as their decision, as well as all the competent and unprejudiced ones in this country. There are scattered through the volume some of the finest pictures in the English language. When Eliza heard that her boy was sold, she "crept stealthily away." How vividly in the following extract is her agony portrayed:

"'Pale, shivering, with rigid features and compressed lips, she looked an entirely altered being from the soft and timid creature she had been hitherto. She moved cautiously along the entry, paused one moment at her mistress' door, raised her hands in mute appeal to heaven, and then turned and glided into her own room. It was a quiet, neat apartment, on the same floor with her mistress. There was the pleasant, sunny window, where she had often sat singing at her sewing; there a little case of books, and various little fancy articles, ranged by them, the gifts of Christmas holidays; there was her simple wardrobe in the closet and in the drawers; here was, in short, her home; and, on the whole, a happy one it had been to her. But there, on the bed, lay her slumbering boy, his long curls falling negligently around his unconscious face, his rosy mouth half open, his little fat hands thrown out over the bed-clothes, and a smile spread like a sunbeam over his whole face.

"'Poor boy! poor fellow!' said Eliza; 'they have sold you! but your mother will save you yet!'

"No tear dropped over that pillow; in such straits as these, the heart has no tears to give—it drops only blood, bleeding itself away in silence."

It is impossible in our limited space to give by extracts any adequate idea of the graphic power of the story, and it is unnecessary, for everybody has read it. But there are passages which we often delight to read—and a few of them, gems, we must again look at. The episode of the slave-mother, cheated by a brutal master of her husband, and inveigled aboard a steamboat going down the Ohio, is one of these passages:

"The woman looked calm as the boat went on, and a beautiful, soft, summer breeze passed like a compassionate spirit over her head—the gentle breeze that never inquires whether the brow is dusky or fair that it fans. And she saw sunshine sparkling on the water, in golden ripples, and heard gay voices, full of ease and pleasure, talking around her everywhere; but her heart lay as if a great stone had fallen on it. Her baby raised himself up against her, and stroked her cheeks with his little hands; and, springing up and down, crowing and chatting, seemed determined to arouse her. She strained him suddenly and tightly in her arms, and slowly one tear after another fell on his wondering, unconscious face; and gradually she seemed, but little by little, to grow calmer, and busied herself with tending and nursing him."

The wretched mother lays her babe down to sleep, and a devil in human form steals *that*, too, from her:

"'Lucy,' said the trader, 'your child's gone; you may as well know it first as last. You see, I know'd you could n't take him down south; and I got a chance to sell him to a first-rate family, that 'll raise him better than you can.'

"But the woman did not scream. The shot had passed too straight and direct through her heart for a cry or tear. Dizzily she sat down. Her slack hands fell lifeless by her side. Her eyes looked straight forward, but she saw nothing. All the noise and hum of the boat, the groaning of the machinery, mingled dreamily to her bewildered ear; and the poor, dumb-stricken heart had neither cry nor tear to show for its utter misery. She was quite calm."

But the following paragraphs are the finest in this tragical episode; indeed, it is as touching a description as we ever saw. Note how the beauty of the night, its mysterious solemnity, and the agony of the one poor heart are commingled :

"Night came on—night, calm, unmoved, and glorious, shining down with her innumerable and solemn angel eyes, twinkling, beautiful, but silent. There was no speech nor language, no pitying voice nor helping hand, from that distant sky. One after another the voices of business or pleasure died away; all on the boat were sleeping, and the ripples at the prow were plainly heard. Tom stretched himself out on a box, and there, as he lay, he heard, ever and anon, a smothered sob or cry from the prostrate creature—'O! what shall I do! O Lord! O good Lord, do help me!' and so, ever and anon, until the murmur died away in silence.

"At midnight Tom waked with a sudden start. Something black passed quickly by him to the side of the boat, and he heard a splash in the water. No one else saw or heard anything. He raised his head—the woman's place was vacant! He got up, and sought about him in vain. The poor bleeding heart was still at last, and the river rippled and dimpled just as brightly as if it had not closed above it."

We must quote also the inimitable description of

"LITTLE EVA."

Her form was the perfection of childish beauty, without its usual chubbiness and squareness of outline. There was about it an undulating and aerial grace, such as one might dream of for some mythic and allegorical being. Her face was remarkable less for its perfect beauty of feature than for a singular and dreamy earnestness of expression, which made the ideal start when they looked at her, and by which the dullest and most illiteral were impressed, without exactly knowing why. The shape of her head and the turn of her neck and bust were particularly noble, and the long golden-brown hair that floated like a cloud around it, the deep, spiritual gravity of her violet-blue eyes, shaded by heavy fringes of golden brown — all marked her out from other children, and made every one turn to look after her, as she glided hither and thither on the boat. Nevertheless, the little one was not what you would have called either a grave child or a sad one. On the contrary, an airy and innocent playfulness seemed to flicker like the shadow of summer leaves over her childish face, and around her buoyant figure. She was always in motion, always with a half smile on her rosy mouth, flying hither and thither, with an undulating and cloud-like tread, singing to herself as she moved, as in a happy dream. Her father and female guardian were incessantly busy in pursuit of her, but when caught, she melted from them again like a summer cloud; and as no word of chiding or reproof ever fell on her ear for whatever she chose to do, she pursued her own way all over the boat. Always dressed in white, she seemed to move like a shadow through all sorts of places, without contracting spot or stain; and there was not a corner or nook, above or below, where those fairy footsteps had not glided, and that visionary golden head, with its deep blue eyes, fleeted along.

The fireman, as he looked up from his sweaty toil, sometimes found those eyes looking wonderingly into the raging depths of the furnace, and fearfully and pityingly at him, as if she thought him in some dreadful danger. Anon the steersman at the wheel paused and smiled, as the picture-like head gleamed through the window of the round-house, and in a moment was gone again. A thousand times a day rough voices blessed her, and smiles of unwonted softness stole over hard faces as she passed; and when she tripped fearlessly over dangerous places, rough, sooty hands were stretched involuntarily out to save her and smooth her path.

Here is something entirely different, and yet executed with wonderful skill, as any one can attest who has lived in New England. It is a picture of

"A NEW ENGLAND FARM-HOUSE."

Whoever has traveled in the New England states will remember, in some cool village, the large farm-house, with its clean-swept, grassy yard, shaded by the dense and massive foliage of the sugar-maple; and remember the air of order and stillness, of perpetuity and unchanging repose, that seemed to breath over the whole place. Nothing lost, or out of order; not a picket loose in the fence, not a particle of litter in the turfy yard, with its clumps of lilac bushes growing up under the windows. Within he will remember wide, clean rooms, where nothing ever seems to be doing or going to be done, where everything is once and forever rigidly in place, and where all household arrangements move with the punctual exactness of the old clock in the corner. In the family "keeping-room," as it is termed, he will remember the staid, respectable old book-case, with its glass doors, where Rollin's History, Milton's Paradise Lost, Bunyan's Pilgrim's Progress, and Scott's Family Bible, stand side by side in decorous order, with multitudes of other books, equally solemn and respectable. There are no servants in the house, but the lady in the snowy cap, with the spectacles, who sets sewing every afternoon among her daughters, as if nothing ever had been done, or were to be done —she and her girls, in some long-forgotten fore part of the day, "*did up the work*," and for the rest of the time, probably, at all hours when you would see them, it is "*done up.*" The old kitchen floor never seems stained or spotted; the tables, the chairs, and the various cooking utensils, never seem deranged or disordered; though three and sometimes four meals a day are got there, though the family washing and ironing is there performed, and though pounds of butter and cheese are in some silent and mysterious manner there brought into existence.

And here is something very, very beautiful. The gentle Eva is passing calmly and quietly to her home in heaven:

"St. Clare smiled. You must excuse him, he could n't help it—for St. Clare could smile yet. For so bright and placid was the farewell voyage of the little spirit—by such sweet and fragrant breezes was the small bark borne toward the heavenly shores, that it was impossible to realize that it was death that was approaching. The child felt no pain—only a tranquil, soft weakness, daily and almost insensibly increasing; and she was so beautiful, so loving, so trustful, so happy, that one could not resist the soothing influence of that air of innocence and peace which seemed to breathe around her. St. Clare found a strange calm coming over him. It was not hope—that was impossible; it was not resignation; it was only a calm resting in the present, which seemed so beautiful that he wished to think of no future. It was like that hush of spirit which we feel amid the bright, mild woods of autumn, when the bright hectic flush is on the trees, and the last lingering flowers by the brook; and we joy in it all the more because we know that soon it will all pass away."

The unbounded popularity of *Uncle Tom's Cabin*, provoked such violent and false accusations on the part of its enemies, that Mrs. Stowe was almost obliged to prepare a key, which should *prove* that she had not exaggerated in her story. In a letter to friends in Scotland, she speaks thus of the labor of preparing it:

"When the time came for me to fulfil my engagement with you, I was, as you know, confined to my bed with a sickness, brought on by the exertion of getting the Key to Uncle Tom's Cabin through the press during the winter. The labor of preparing that book, simply as an intellectual investigation, was severe; but what a risk of life and health it was to me, no one can appreciate but myself.

"Nothing could have justified me, with my large family of children, in making such an effort, in the state of health in which I then was, except the deep conviction which I had, and still have, that I was called of God's providence to do it.

"In every part of the world, the story of Uncle Tom had awakened sympathy for the poor American slave, and, consequently, in every part of the world, the story of his wrongs had been denied; and it had been asserted that it was a mere work of romance, and I was charged with being the slanderer of the institutions of my own country.

"I knew that, if I shrunk from supporting my position, the sympathy which the work had excited would gradually die out, and the whole thing would be looked upon as a mere romantic excitement of the passions, without any adequate basis of facts.

"Feeble and reduced as I was, it became absolutely necessary that I should take this opportunity, when the attention of the world was awakened, to prove the charges which I had made.

"Neither could such a work be done slightly; for every statement was to be thrown before bitter and unscrupulous enemies, who would do their utmost to break the force of everything which was said.

"It was, therefore, necessary that not an assertion should be made without the most rigorous investigation and scrutiny; and, worn as I then was with the subject, with every nerve sensitive and sore, I was obliged to spend three months in what were to me the most agonizing researches.

"The remembrance of that winter is to me one of horror. I could not sleep at night, and I had no comfort in the daytime. All that consoled me was, that I was bearing the same kind of suffering which Christ bore, and still bears, in view of the agonies and distresses of sin in this world."

The "Key" was eminently successful in sustaining the *truth* of the story of Uncle Tom. It was an awful exposure to the world of American slavery, and one which Mrs. Stowe would gladly have avoided, but it was forced upon her in self-defense. That it and the book to which it is an accompaniment may fly swiftly upon their errand of mercy, to beg for the poor slave the sympathy and love of every humane heart, is our heartfelt desire.

ELIHU BURRITT.

Elihu Burritt is forty-three years old, and was born in the village of New Britain, Connecticut, a few miles south-west of the city of Hartford. His parents were very poor, and a common school education was all that they could give their children. The father was an ordinary man—honest, virtuous and respectable, though excessively poor. The mother, however, was remarkable for her many virtues. She was a woman of fine intellect, lofty courage, ardent piety, and brought up her children most admirably. Such mothers seem always to have uncommon children. Besides the subject of this sketch, she had another son, Elijah Burritt, whose name is not unknown to fame, and who perished on the prairies of the far south, a victim to an insatiable thirst for adventure and knowledge.

Elihu, like the majority of New England boys, laid the foundation for his after greatness, in a district school-house. While yet a boy, he had visions of future greatness. Though the roof beneath which he slept was humble, though his position was lowly, yet in his heart there were great and noble aspirations.

Engraved by J.C. Buttre

Elihu Burritt

We have heard him speak of some of his boyish dreams of future usefulness, and he would be dull, indeed, who could not gather from them the fact that at a very early age, he looked forward to a career by no means insignificant. At a certain age, he was filled with a martial spirit. Nor is this a singular fact, as it arose from an ardent admiration of heroism. He saw, as he grew older, that true heroism does not consist in 'cutting men's throats, but in braving the scorn, ridicule and hatred of wicked men, and doing great deeds of humanity. But at one time in his life, when he was young, he read much of warlike men, and the sound of the drum stirred his heart, as if he had been a soldier. We heard him once, by the fire-side, tell how he, when a boy, rose one morning long before sunrise, to accompany, on foot, a few kindred spirits to a neighboring town, to witness a "regimental training." The long walk, through lonesome woods and valleys, was filled with martial tales and dreams of future heroic, martial deeds. The marching and counter-marching of the soldiers, the spirited music, the sham-fighting, all made a deep impression upon him. For he saw not mere red-coated men—saw not *sham* conflicts, but his imagination transformed the real into the unreal, and he gazed upon a regiment of heroes, ready to spill their last drop of blood in the cause of freedom! In a little time, he learned that all is not what it seems, but an ardent admiration for the truly heroic, characterizes him to-day.

At an early age, Mr. Burritt commenced to learn the trade of a blacksmith, in his native town. While learning his trade, he prosecuted his school studies with great industry. He soon, alone and unaided, took up a Latin grammar, and made himself familiar with that language. He then took up the Greek, then the Italian, and, in the course of a few years, could read more or less readily in nearly fifty languages. The last year which Mr. Burritt spent in New Britain, before seeking his fortune abroad, he kept a refreshment-shop in the village. Being unsuccessful, he left it, and, as he was desirous of enjoying the privileges of an antiquarian library, he removed to Worcester, Massachusetts, where he worked industriously at his trade and books. His linguistical acquirements soon gave him notoriety. In the mean time, his fertile brain was filled with great plans for the future. He once went to Boston with a view to take ship to some distant countries, where he could, with better advantage, pursue his study of the languages. The world should rejoice that he, about this time, renounced his passion for linguistical knowledge, and devoted himself with intense earnestness to the advocacy of peace, temperance, and anti-slavery. He established a weekly journal in Worcester, called the "*Christian Citizen*," in which he poured out the wealth of his heart and brain. His powerful articles soon attracted the attention of the good and great, and his journal had a wide circulation. We think that some of the miscellaneous writings of Mr. Burritt are among the finest things in the English language; and as those who have read them once, will not dislike to read them a second time, we copy two or three of them here. Here is the best description, in a few lines, of the iron horse, we ever saw:

"I love to see one of these huge creatures, with sinews of brass and muscles of iron, strut forth from his smoky stable, and, saluting the long train of cars with a dozen sonorous puffs from his iron nostrils, fall back gently into his harness. There he stands, champing and foaming upon the iron track, his great heart a furnace of glowing coals; his lymphatic blood is boiling in his veins; the strength of a thousand horses is nerving his sinews; he pants to be gone. He would 'snake' St. Peters across the desert of Sahara, if he could be fairly hitched to it; but there is a little, sober-eyed, tobacco-chewing man in the saddle, who holds him in with one finger, and can take away his breath in a moment, should he grow restive or vicious. I am always deeply interested in this man, for, begrimmed as he may be with coal, diluted in oil and steam, I regard him as the genius of the whole machinery; as the physical mind of that huge steam-horse."

The little sketch which follows is, it seems to us, is one of the most touching ever written:

"BURY ME IN THE GARDEN."

There was sorrow there, and tears were in every eye; and there were low, half-suppressed sobbings heard from every corner of the room; but the little sufferer was still; its young spirit was just on the verge of departure. The mother was bending over it in all the speechless yearnings of parental love, with one arm under its pillow, and with the other, unconsciously drawing the little dying girl closer and closer to her bosom. Poor thing! in the bright and dewy morning it had followed out before its father into the field; and while he was there engaged in his labors, it had patted around among the meadow-flowers, and had stuck its bosom full, and all its burnished tresses, with carmine and lily-tinted things; and returning tired to its father's side, he had lifted it upon the loaded cart; but a stone in the road had shaken it from its seat, and the ponderous, iron-rimmed wheels had ground it down into the very cart-path—and the little crushed creature was dying.

We had all gathered up closely to its bedside, and were hanging over the young, bruised thing, to see if it yet breathed, when a slight movement came over its lips and its eyes partly opened. There was no voice, but there was something beneath its eyelids which a mother alone could interpret. Its lips trembled again, and we all held our breath—its eyes opened a little farther, and then we heard the departing spirit whisper in that ear which touched those ashy lips: "Mother! Mother! don't let them carry me away down to the dark, cold grave-yard, but bury me in the garden—in the garden, mother."

A little sister, whose eyes were raining down with the meltings of her heart, had crept up to the bedside, and taking the hand of the dying girl, sobbed aloud in its ears: "Julia! Julia! can't you speak to Antoinette?"

The last, fluttering pulsation of expiring nature struggled hard to enable that little spirit to utter one more wish and word of affection: its soul was on its lips, as it whispered again: "Bury me in the garden, mother—bury me in the ——" and a quivering came over its limbs, one feeble struggle, and all was still.

The last sketch which we quote is, perhaps, the best:

THE NATURAL BRIBGE.

The scene opens with a view of the great Natural Bridge in Virginia. There are three or four lads standing in the channel below, looking up with awe to that vast arch of unhewn rocks, which the Almighty bridged over those everlasting butments "when the morning stars sang together." The little piece of sky spanning those measureless piers, is full of stars, although it is mid-day. It is almost five hundred feet from where they stand, up those perpendicular bulwarks of limestone, to the key rock of that vast arch, which appears to them only of the size of a man's hand. The silence of death is rendered more impressive by the little stream that falls from rock to rock down the channel. The sun is darkened, and the boys have unconsciously uncovered their heads, as if standing in the presence-chamber of the Majesty of the whole earth. At last, this feeling begins to wear away; they begin to look around them; they find that others have been there before them. They see the names of hundreds cut in the limestone butments. A new feeling comes over their young hearts, and their knives are in their hands in an instant. "What man has done, man can do," is their watchword, while they draw themselves up, and carve their names a foot above those of a hundred full-grown men who have been there before them.

They are all satisfied with this feat of physical exertion, except one, whose example illustrates perfectly the forgotten truth that there is no royal road to intellectual eminence. This ambitious youth sees a name just above his reach, a name that will be green in the memory of the world, when those of Alexander, Cæsar, and Bonaparte shall rot in oblivion. It was the name of Washington. Before he marched with Braddock to that fatal field, he had been there, and left his name a foot above all his predecessors. It was a glorious thought of the boy, to write his name side by side with that of the great father of his country. He grasps his knife with a firmer hand; and, clinging to a little jutting crag, he cuts a niche into the limestone, about a foot above where he stands; he then reaches up and cuts another for his hands. 'Tis a dangerous adventure; but, as he puts his feet and hands into those niches, and draws himself up carefully to his full length, he finds himself a foot above every name chronicled in that mighty wall. While his companions are regarding him with concern and admiration, he cuts his name in rude capitals, large and deep, into that flinty album. His knife is still in his hand, and strength in his sinews, and a new-created aspiration in his heart. Again he cuts another niche, and again he carves his name in larger capitals. This is not enough. Heedless of the entreaties of his companions, he cuts and climbs again. The gradations of his ascending scale grow wider apart. He measures his length at every gain he cuts. The voices of his friends wax weaker and weaker, till their words are finally lost on his ear. He now, for the first time, casts a look beneath him. Had that glance lasted a moment, that moment would have been his last. He clings with a convulsive shudder to his little niche in the rock. An awful abyss awaits his almost certain fall. He is faint with severe exertion, and trembling, from the sudden view of the dreadful destruction to which he is exposed. His knife is worn half-way to the haft. He can hear the voices, but not the words of his terror-stricken companions below. What a moment! What a meager chance to escape destruction! There is no retracing his steps. It is impossible to put his hands into the same niche with his feet and retain his slender hold a moment. His companions instantly perceive this new and fearful dilemma, and await his fall with emotions that "freeze their young blood." He is too high, too faint, to ask for his father and mother, his brothers and sisters, to come and witness or avert his destruction. But one of his companions anticipates his desire. Swift as the wind, he bounds down the channel, and the situation of the fated boy is told upon his father's hearth-stone.

Minutes of almost eternal length roll on, and there are hundreds standing in that rocky channel, and hundreds on the bridge above, all holding their breath, and awaiting the fearful catastrophe. The poor boy hears the hum of new and numerous voices both above and below. He can just distinguish the tones of his father, who is shouting with all the energy of despair: "William! William! don't look down! Your mother, and Henry, and Harriet, are all here, praying for you! Keep your eye toward the top!" The boy didn't look down. His eye is fixed like a flint toward heaven, and his young heart on Him who reigns there. He grasps again his knife. He cuts another niche, and another foot is added to the hundreds that remove him from the reach of human help from below. How carefully he uses his wasting blade! How anxiously he selects the softest places in that vast pier! How he avoids every flinty grain! How he economizes his physical powers, resting a moment at each gain he cuts! How every motion is watched from below! There stand his father, mother, brother and sister, on the very spot where, if he falls, he will not fall alone.

The sun is now half-way down the west. The lad has made fifty additional niches in that mighty wall, and now finds himself directly under the middle of that vast arch of rocks, earth, and trees. He must cut his way in a new direction, to get from under this overhanging mountain. The inspiration of hope is dying in his bosom; its vital heat is fed by the increasing shouts of hundreds, perched upon cliffs and trees, and others who stand with ropes in their hands, on the bridge above, or with ladders below. Fifty gains more must be cut before the longest rope can reach him. His wasting blade strikes again into she limestone. The boy is emerging painfully, foot by foot, from under that lofty arch. Spliced ropes are ready, in the hands of those who are leaning over the outer edge of the bridge. Two minutes more, and all will be over. The blade is worn to the last half-inch. The boy's head reels; his eyes are starting from their sockets. His last hope is dying in his heart; his life must hang upon the next gain he cuts. That niche is his last. At the last faint gash he makes, his knife, his faithful knife, falls from his little nerveless hand, and, ringing along the precipice, falls at his mother's feet. An involuntary groan of despair runs like a death-knell through the channel below, and all is as still as the grave. At the height of nearly three hundred feet, the devoted boy lifts his hopeless heart, and closes his eyes to commend his soul to God. 'Tis but a moment—there! one foot swings off! he is reeling—trembling—toppling over into eternity! Hark! a shout falls on his ear from above. The man who is lying with half his length over the bridge, has caught a glimpse of the boy's head and shoulders. Quick as thought, the noosed rope is within reach of the sinking youth. No one breathes. With a faint, convulsive effort, the swooning boy drops his arms into the noose. Darkness comes over him, and with the words, GOD! and MOTHER! whispered on his lips, just loud enough to be heard in heaven--the tightening rope lifts him out of his last shallow niche. Not a lip moves while he is dangling over that fearful abyss; but when a sturdy Virginian reaches down and draws up the lad, and holds him up in his arms before the tearful, breathless multitude, such shouting—such leaping and weeping for joy—never greeted the ear of a human being so recovered from the yawning gulf of eternity.

The pieces which we have quoted will not, perhaps, give the reader a proper idea of Mr. Burritt's usual style in his reformatory writings. He is an earnest, powerful, enthusiastic writer. It may seem strange, that an enthusiast should understand the power of well-arranged facts and figures, but Mr. Burritt does, and uses his knowledge to great advantage.

About eight years ago Mr. Burritt left this country for England. We believe he was invited by the friends of peace in that country, at any rate he started on his way like a poot pilgrim, bent on doing good in an humble manner. He entered England quietly, and in a plain dress, with a knapsack over his shoulder, wandered over the country to see its beautiful landscapes, and to do good. One of his objects was to establish little peace societies, which he denominated "Leagues of Brotherhood." The first of these he organized in the little village of Penshore, and in the course of a few months a large number were flourishing throughout England. By degrees the fame which had attached itself to him in America for his knowledge of the languages, and his powers as a writer, spread to England, and his society was sought by great personages. But great men were avoided by Mr. Burritt, unless they could be made to advance the great cause to which all his energies were devoted. Everything centered there. In his little upper room in Broad-street, London, the American blacksmith worked incessantly, night and day, to advance the interests of the League of Brotherhood. He allowed himself no intermission from the contemplation of the one great subject. His only relaxation was that of lecturing in the provincial towns upon it. His "one idea" was not popular among the fashionable classes in England, and *he* was not popular with them. But the philanthropic, the wise and good esteemed him more and better. His success in England, though apparently small, was after all encouraging. He won over to the cause of peace a large class of English men and women, who before had not examined the subject. And though the state of Europe at present is not peaceful, that does not prove that Mr. Burritt's mission there was a failure. For several years he has advocated the establishment of an ocean penny postage between all the great countries of the world. This is, at present, his favorite subject, and he is devoting himself mainly to its advocacy.

Mr. Burritt has a striking personal appearance. He is rather tall, his frame is by no means puny, though the narrowness of his chest gives him a frail look. His arms and hands, which are large and stout, remind one of the fact, that he for years swung the hammer upon the anvil. His face is long, forehead large and sloping, his eyes are blue, and his mouth is one of the finest ever man possessed. In his movements Mr. Burritt is awkward, as in his pronunciation. His manners are somewhat of the same stamp. This arises from his seclusion and absent-mindedness. He is, however, exceedingly social at times, and has great conversational talents. He has the power of attracting the close attention of all about him, to the subject he is discussing.

He is no orator, in the ordinary meaning of the word, but he is sometimes intensely eloquent. He has extraordinary energy, great power of concentration of thought and feeling, and when he is thoroughly aroused, he makes up for the lack of the natural graces of oratory in burning, impressive, intense eloquence. His words may be uttered in a homely style, but his thoughts are magnificent, and his enthusiasm is almost sublime. He often, as it were, magnetizes his audiences by his remarkable and lofty enthusiasm. The same is true of him in conversational circles.

By long continued study Mr. Burritt has acquired a worn and weary appearance. He looks much older than he really is, and his nervous system is injured.

Several years ago, Mr. Fowler, the phrenologist, took a cast of Mr. Burritt's head, and he speaks as follows of his moral organs:

"He has a high head, and narrow at the base; or, a great development of the moral organs, with small selfish propensities. His labors are eminently labors of love. In every good work he acts a leading part. He is exerting a most excellent influence, and doing immense good. His talents are controlled by higher faculties. He is a true philanthropist. Long may he live to shed benign influences on his race.

"He has very large social organs, and hence those strong personal friends he makes, and also that expansive love for his fellow man, which he evinces. He abominates war, and would 'take Quebec by ships of PROVISIONS, instead of ships of war,' and bind our race in one great bundle of love, by indissoluble bonds of fraternal affection.

"His ambitious organs are likewise large, yet they take an intellectual and moral direction. They simply fit him to take a leading part, and sustain him in his public capacity, but do not raise Elihu Burritt above his cause. On the other hand, he is rather modest, yet firm and dignified, and well qualified to lead off the public mind. May such men be multiplied till they stay the popular tide of evil and depravity, in high places and low, which now abounds."

Mr. Fowler quotes the following paragraphs from an authentic source, in reference to Mr. Burritt's ancestry and relatives:

"His maternal grandfather, Hinsdale, was a remarkable man, intrusted with town offices, a great reader, and with only ordinary advantages, possessed himself of an extraordinary fund of knowledge.

"Burritt's brother, author of that excellent astronomical treatise, the 'Geography of the Heavens,' inherits a like insatiable thirst after knowledge, and facility in acquiring it, besides being extensively erudite.

"A sister and a maternal nephew are also endowed with a similar power of memory and passion for reading, as well as capability of storing their minds with knowledge.

"One of this learned family, I think Elihu's brother, literally killed himself by study, in which he progressed with astonishing rapidity. This wonderful love of learning, and capability of retaining it, will undoubtedly be found to have been handed down to the Hinsdales, and throughout the various branches of their descendants, as far as it can be traced."

There are many more noisy reformers in the world than Elihu Burritt, but we know of few who are acquiring a purer and nobler reputation than his. He is by no means without faults, but his long and wearisome labors for his fellow-men shall not be fruitless, nor will his name ever be forgotten.

WILLIAM LLOYD GARRISON.

It is difficult, at the present time, to do full justice to William Lloyd Garrison. It remains for the future historian of this generation to accord to him the position which a prejudiced people cannot now allow him to occupy. There are so many millions who now hate Garrison, so many thousands of comparatively good men who dislike him, who consider him at least rash and headstrong, that he cannot hope, for many years, to be judged candidly and generously. We have no more doubt that fifty years hence the name of Garrison will be revered by the American nation, than we have of the ultimate overthrow of human slavery in this country. We look upon him as the great puritan of anti-slavery. Like one of the grand old Puritans, he is stern, solemnly enthusiastic, terribly severe upon wrong-doers, and unswerving from his idea of what is right. We think, also, like some of the Puritans, he is bigoted, as men with their thoughts directed intensely upon one object, are apt to be, but the future generation will look upon his severity of character, his bigotry, as we look upon the same faults in the grand men who laid the foundations of this republic—as spots upon the reputation of one of the noblest men that ever lived. Mr. Garrison is, we believe, a native of Massachusetts. At a very early age he was placed in a printing office, in Newburyport, by his mother, who was a poor widow, and a pious, worthy woman. In the short space of twelve months he was master of his trade, and at once went to work to assist his mother, in addition to supporting himself. At an early age he was fond of books, magazines, and newspapers, and read them with great avidity. He joined a club, and being invited to deliver an oration before it, he did so, to the gratification of all who listened to it. He was also at this time a contributor to the columns of the Newburyport *Herald*, furnishing for it several well-written essays, which attracted considerable attention. When he was twenty-one years old, he published his first poem in that journal. Shortly after, he set up a new paper, with the name of "*The Free Press*," which was edited with so much vigor and earnestness of purpose, that it was well received by the more advanced class of readers at the north. He, however, soon removed to Vermont, where he published and edited the "*Journal of the Times.*" This was as early as 1828, and he advocated in his paper "the gradual emancipation of every slave in the republic." He also advocated with much zeal and power the cause of temperance. In September, 1829, he removed to Baltimore, for the purpose of editing the

"*Genius of Universal Emancipation*" there. While performing the duties of his office, a Newburyport merchant fitted out a small vessel, and filled it in Baltimore with slaves for the New Orleans market. It was a Yankee speculation in the flesh and blood of his fellow-men, and Mr. Garrison commented with great and deserved severity upon the transaction in his newspaper. The consequence was, he was prosecuted in the courts, before slave-holding jurors, who were interested in getting him silenced, or at least severely rebuked. He was sentenced to pay a very heavy fine, and to be imprisoned until he paid it. He had not so much money, and never hoped even to be possessed of so much, and therefore calmly entered his dungeon. It was his first terrible experience of the cruelty of southern despotism. For administering a just rebuke to a man who had been making merchandize of his fellow-men, he was sent to hopeless confinement, and that, too, in free America! Can the reader wonder why Garrison is so bitter in his denunciations of slavery? While in his dungeon he composed the following beautiful and spirited verses:

"High walls and huge *the body* may confine,
And iron gates obstruct the prisoner's gaze,
And massive bolts may baffle his design,
And vigilant keepers watch his desirous way.

"Yet scorns the immortal *mind* this base control!
No chains can bind it and no cell enclose;
Swifter than light it flies from pole to pole,—
And in a flash from earth to heaven it goes.

"It leaps from mount to mount—from vale to vale,
It wanders plucking honeyed fruits and flowers;
It visits home to hear the fireside tale,
Or in sweet converse pass the joyous hours.
'Tis up before the sun, soaring afar—
And in its watches wearies every star."

Arthur Tappan volunteered to pay Mr. Garrison's fine, and he was thereupon released. He now gave up the attempt to publish an anti-slavery journal in Baltimore, though he did entertain the idea of publishing one in Washington. When he established the "*Liberator*" in Boston, in January, 1831, he said:

"In the month of August I issued proposals for publishing "*The Liberator*" in Washington city; but the enterprise, though hailed approvingly in different sections of the country, was palsied by public indifference. * * * During my recent tour for the purpose of exciting the minds of the people by a series of discourses on the subject of slavery, every place that I visited gave fresh evidence of the fact that a greater revolution in public sentiment was to be effected in the free states, and particularly in New England, than at the south. I found contempt more bitter, opposition more active, detraction more relentless, prejudice more stubborn, and apathy more frozen than among slave owners themselves. Of course there were individual exceptions to the contrary. This state of things afflicted but did not dishearten me. I determined at every hazard to lift up the standard of emancipation in the eyes of the nation, within the sight of Bunker Hill, and in the birth-place of liberty. * * * I am aware that many object to the severity of my language; but is there not cause for severity? I will be as harsh as truth, and as uncompromising as justice. On this subject I do not wish no think, or speak, or write with moderation. No, no! Tell a man whose house is on fire to give a moderate alarm; tell him to moderately rescue his wife from the hands of the ravisher; tell the mother to gradually extricate her babe from the fire into which it has fallen; but urge me not to use moderation in a cause like the present! I am in earnest. I will not equivocate—I will not excuse—I will not retreat a single inch—and I will be heard. The apathy of the people is enough to make every statue leap from its pedestal, and to hasten the resurrection of the dead."

But the most thrilling event perhaps of his life was the occurrence of the mob in Boston, in October, 1835. At that time George Thompson, from England, was in this country, and he, with Mr. Garrison, were engaged to address the Female Anti-Slavery Society, at its annual meeting in that city. Public excitement against the abolitionists was intense, and before the time appointed for the convention, the lessee of Congress Hall, fearing the destruction of his property, decided that the meeting must be held elsewhere. It was subsequently arranged to convene in the Anti-Slavery Hall, in Washington-street, on Wednesday, October 21st, at three o'clock, in the afternoon and addresses were expected on the occasion. Fearing lest his presence might be productive of injury to the cause, Mr. Thompson withdrew from the city before the day appointed. On that morning a placard was circulated to the intent that "the infamous foreign scoundrel, Thompson, would hold forth in the Anti-Slavery Hall in the afternoon, and that the present was a fair opportunity to snake him out; that a purse of one hundred dollars had been raised by a number of *patriotic* individuals, to reward the person who should first lay violent hands upon him, so that he might be brought to the tar kettle before dark." By such measures, and by editorials in influential papers, the worst passions of the inhabitants were aroused to the highest pitch of fury. Early in the afternoon a crowd began to gather around the building, and a little before three Mr. Garrison appeared, got through the crowd, and took his seat, expecting to address the ladies of the society, of which quite a large number had assembled. As the time drew near the crowd increased, and with it increased the intensity of the tumultuous excitement. Mr. Garrison now stepped towards the door of the hall, through which some had entered and commenced making disturbance, and very cautiously requested them to withdraw, stating that it was a ladies' meeting, and no gentlemen were expected to be present but the speakers. This had no effect, however, and Mr. Garrison then mentioned to the president of the society that since his own presence would evidently increase the tumult, it would be advisable for him to leave, to which she assented. With an intimate friend he now withdrew to the anti-slavery office, which was separated from the hall by a thin partition only, and commenced writing to an acquaintance an account of the riot. The mob soon increased to thousands, filling the hall; the danger became imminent that they would break through into the office and destroy the publications of the society. The lower panel of the door was now broken through by one of the ringleaders, who, looking in, exclaimed, "There he is—that's Garrison; out with the scoundrel!" Upon this, the person with him walked out, locked the door after him, and put the key in his pocket. The mayor, having at length cleared the hall of the crowd, begged the ladies to desist, and assured them that he could no longer protect them from insult and violence, upon which they adjourned to the house of one of their number to finish their business.

The mayor then addressed the rioters; told them that the anti-slavery meeting was broken up; that Mr. Thompson was not there, and urged them to disperse. But having got rid of these objects they felt the more liberty to give exclusive attention to Mr.

Garrison, and yelled his name, loudly crying, "We must have him! lynch him! lynch him!" The mayor, seeing that he had lost all control over the mob, besought Mr. Garrison to make his escape at the rear of the building, since he could not get through the crowd to the street. Just at this juncture his devotion to his principles were so self-forgetting as to demand special notice. A non-resistant brother near him, seeing the danger, declared his determination to renounce these views upon the spot, and use forcible measures for his preservation. But Mr. Garrison earnestly protested against such a course in the following language: "Hold, my dear brother; you know not what spirit you are of; do you wish to become like one of these violent and bloodthirsty men, who are seeking my life? Shall we give blow for blow, and array sword against sword? God forbid! I will perish sooner than raise my hand against any man, even in self-defense, and let none of my friends resort to violence for my protection. If my life be taken the cause of emancipation will not suffer," &c. Even in this hour of extremest peril, his devotion to principles which in the hour of quiet he believed right, rose with the danger almost to the sublime. While all around was in an uproar, and his friends were shivering with fear, his faith in an Omnipotent arm was strongest. Preceded by a friend, at the peril of his life, he dropped from the window to the ground, and attempted to escape through Wilson's Lane, but was circumvented by the mob. Again he retreats up stairs, and was secreted for a few minutes behind a pile of boards, but being discovered by the ruffians, his friends effected an escape. They now dragged Garrison to the window, evidently intending to pitch him that distance to the ground, but upon second thought, concluded not to kill him outright, they placed a rope around his body, apparently designing to drag him through the streets. Reaching the ground by a ladder, he disengaged himself from the rope, and was seized by two or three of the most powerful of the rioters and dragged along bareheaded. Blows were aimed at his head, and at length his clothing was nearly torn from him. Insulted by the jeers of the mob, in a denuded condition, he reached State-street, in front of the city hall, and now there was a tremendous rush to prevent his entering that building. With the help of his posse and friends, the mayor finally succeeded in getting him to his office, where he was reclothed by individuals from the post-office, immediately below.

The mayor and his advisers there declared that the only safety lay in committing him to jail as a disturber of the public peace! A hack was brought to the door for the purpose, but the scene that ensued defies description. The surging mob rushed upon the carriage with ungovernable fury, and attempted every kind of violence. The windows were broken in, the attempt was made to overset the vehicle, but the driver wielded his whip with such dexterity, first upon the horses and then upon the rioters, that he got clear, and drove for the prison. Failing to reach there in advance of the ruffians, he drove circuitously about, and by a back passage Mr. Garrison was at length beyond the reach of danger, within the iron gratings. Even here his spirit was unfettered, and upon the walls of his cell he inscribed the following lines:

"When peace within the bosom reigns,
 And conscience gives the approving voice,
Though bound the human form in chains,
 Yet can the soul aloud rejoice.

 'Tis true, my footsteps are confined—
 I cannot range beyond this cell;
But what can circumscribe my mind?—
 To chain the winds attempt as well!

"Confine me as a prisoner—but bind me not as a slave.
Punish me as a criminal—but hold me not as a chattel.
Torture me as a man—but drive me not as a beast.
Doubt my sanity—but acknowledge my immortality."

After a mock examination he was released from prison, but, at the earnest request of the authorities, he left the city until the tumult had subsided. Thus ended a mob in that city containing the "Cradle of Liberty," which first rocked for freedom to the tune of "Hail Columbia," the echo of which made tyrants tremble. Throughout the whole transaction, Mr. Garrison retained that coolness and presence of mind which, evinced upon the battle field, in pursuit of that poor bubble, glory, wins for its aspirants undying fame, earth's immortality. The same devotion to human liberty which Garrison here manifested, when displayed by the actors in the drama of the American revolution, caused a thrill of animation the world over; but when evinced in behalf of the downtrodden African, it assumes the name of fanaticism.

Mr. Garrison has been severely criticised as an ambitious man; we know of no better method of disproving it, than to remark, that aspirants for honor are apt to strike out for themselves other paths of distinction than those leading through scenes like the above. There are a few noble thoughts from Whittier which are in point here, and which give the opinion of that sound man and earnest poet in regard to Mr. Garrison's character. They were addressed

TO WILLIAM LLOYD GARRISON.

Champion of those who groan beneath
  Oppression's iron hand,
In view of penury, hate and death,
  I see thee fearless stand;
Still bearing up thy lofty brow,
  In the steadfast strength of truth,
In manhood sealing well the vow
  And promise of thy youth.

Go on!—for thou hast chosen well;
  On in the strength of God!
Long as the human heart shall swell
  Beneath the tyrant's rod.
Speak in a slumbering nation's ear,
  As thou hast ever spoken,
Until the dead in sin shall hear—
  The fetter's link be broken!

I love thee with a brother's love—
  I feel my pulses thrill,
To mark thy spirit soar above
  The cloud of human ill;
My heart hath leaped to answer thine,
  And echo back thy words,
As leaps the warrior's at the shine
  And flash of kindred swords!

They tell me thou art rash and vain—
  A searcher after fame;
That thou art striving but to gain
  A long-enduring name;
That thou hast nerved the Afric's hand,
  And steeled the Afric's heart,
To shake aloft his vengeful brand,
  And rend his chain apart.

Have I not known thee well, and read
  Thy mighty purpose long,
And watched the trials which have made
  Thy human spirit strong?
And shall the slanderer's demon breath
  Avail with one like me,
To dim the sunshine of my faith,
  And earnest trust in thee?

Go on!—the dagger's point may glare
 Amid thy pathway's gloom—
The fate which sternly threatens there,
 Is glorious martyrdom!
Then onward, with a martyr's zeal—
 Press on to thy reward—
The hour when man shall only kneel
 Before his Father—God.

But since we have commenced quoting, we will will give a specimen of his fierce, denunciatory style of writing, which appeared in an editorial upon the Union. It is also a good opportunity to show his *peculiar* position upon the slavery question:

"Tyrants! confident of its overthrow, proclaim not to your vassals, that the American Union is an experiment of freedom, which, if it fail, will forever demonstrate the necessity of whips for the backs, and chains for the limbs of the people. Know that its subversion is essential to the triumph of justice, the deliverance of the oppressed, the vindication of the brotherhood of the race. It was conceived in sin, and brought forth in iniquity; and its career has been marked by unparalleled hypocrisy, by high-handed tyranny, by a bold defiance of the omniscience and omnipotence of God. Freedom indignantly disowns it, and calls for its extinction; for within its borders are three millions of slaves, whose blood constitutes its cement, whose flesh forms a large and flourishing branch of its commerce, and who are ranked with four-footed beasts and creeping things. To secure the adoption of the constitution of the United States, first, that the African slave-trade—till that time a feeble, isolated, colonial traffic—should, for at least twenty years, be prosecuted as a national interest, under the American flag, and protected by the national arm; secondly, that a slaveholding oligarchy, created by allowing three-fifths of the slaveholding population to be represented by their task-masters, should be allowed a permanent seat in congress; thirdly, that the slave system should be secured against internal revolt and external invasion, by the united physical force of the country; fourthly, that not a foot of national territory should be granted, on which the panting fugitive from slavery might stand, and be safe from his pursuers, thus making every citizen a slave-hunter and slave-catcher. To say that this 'covenant with death' shall not be annulled—that this 'agreement with hell' shall continue to stand—that this 'refuge of lies' shall not be swept away—is to hurl defiance at the eternal throne, and to give the lie to Him that sits thereon. It is an attempt, alike monstrous and impracticable, to blend the light of heaven with darkness of the bottomless pit, to unite the living with the dead, to associate the Son of God with the Prince of Evil. Accursed be the American Union, as a stupendous, republican imposture!"

It is not to be wondered at that such a writer should be accused of harshness and severity. English cannot be rendered with greater force and energy than he combines it to express his views upon this subject. But hear him criticise his critics:

"I am accused of using hard language. I admit the charge. I have not been able to find a soft word to describe villainy, or to identify the perpetrator of it. The man who makes a chattel of his brother—what is he? The man who keeps back the hire of his laborers by fraud—what is he? They who prohibit the circulation of the bible—what are they? They who compel three millions of men and women to herd together like brute beasts—what are they? They who sell mothers by the pound, and children in lots to suit purchasers—what are they? I care not what terms are applied to them, provided they do apply? If they are not thieves, if they are not tyrants, if they are not men-stealers, I should like to know what is their true character, and by what names they may be called. It is as mild an epithet to say that a thief is a thief, as to say that a spade is a spade. Words are but the signs of ideas. 'A rose by any other name would smell as sweet.' Language may be misapplied, and so be absurd or unjust; as for example, to say that an abolitionist is a fanatic, or that a slaveholder is an honest man. But to call things by their right names is to use neither hard nor improper language. Epithets may be rightly applied, it is true, and yet be uttered in a hard spirit, or with a malicious design. What then? Shall we discard all terms which are descriptive of crime, because they are not always used with fairness and propriety? He who, when he sees oppression, cries out against it—who, when he beholds his equal brother trodden under foot by the iron hoof of despotism, rushes to his rescue—who, when he sees the weak overborne by the strong, takes sides with the former, at the imminent peril of his own safety—such a man needs no certificate to the excellence of his temper, or the sincerity of his heart, or the disinterestedness of his conduct. Or is the apologist of slavery, he who can see the victim of thieves lying bleeding and helpless on the cold earth, and yet turn aside, like the callous-hearted priest and Levite, who needs absolution."

Upon the same subject he says again :

"Let us speak plain; there is more force in names
Than most men dream of; and a lie may keep
Its throne a whole age longer, if it skulk
Behind the shield of some fair-seeming name.
Let us call tyrants, *tyrants*, and maintain
That only freedom comes by grace of God,
And all that comes not by his grace must fall;
For men in earnest have no time to waste
In patching fig-leaves for the naked truth.

"Let us call tyrants, *tyrants;* not to do so is to misuse language, to deal treacherously with freedom, to consent to the enslavement of mankind. It is neither an amiable nor a virtuous, but a foolish and pernicious thing, not to call things by their right names. 'Woe unto them,' says one of the world's great prophets, 'that call evil good, and good evil; that put darkness for light, and light for darkness; that put bitter for sweet, and sweet for bitter.'"

His own power in stinging criticism is well displayed, and there is an expression of severe purity and uprightness upon it. In his social relations he is said to be an exceedingly amiable man, a kind and loving husband and father. His purity of character is irreproachable. Not a whisper was ever raised by his worst enemy against his private character.

As an orator he does not occupy a very high position. He lacks the graces of oratory—is too severe in his style of speaking. Yet in spite of these disadvantages he often speaks with tremendous power. It is by simple force of the ideas he utters. He uses an iron logic, and his earnestness is so intense that it arrests the attention of the hearer as effectually as the natural graces of oratory. We think there is no humor in his writings or speeches—he is too solemnly in earnest for that; but as a man and companion he by no means lacks geniality of character.

We presume that there is no living American who is such a victim to the adverse prejudices of the people as William Lloyd Garrison, but we have faith to believe that in the future his name will be glorious, when those of the majority of his cotemporaries will have been forgotten.

JOHN B. GOUGH.

The history of the temperance reformation in the United States is intimately associated with that of a few prominent individuals. At an early period in the enterprise, we shall find the account of the Washingtonian movement, in which John Hawkins appeared, heading the reform ranks, himself but just escaped the drunkard's grave. His star was hardly in its zenith, when a new one of greater magnitude appeared in the eastern part of Massachusetts, the rays of which have reached every portion of the United States, lit the extinguished lamp of hope in ten thousand bosoms, and has since gone to kindle the flames of reform in the Old World. John B. Gough was born in Sandgate, county of Kent, England, in August, 1817. His father had been a soldier in the Peninsular war, and at the birth of this son was living upon a small pension at home. Accustomed to the severe discipline of the army, his nature possessed few attractions for a youth like John; yet it is interesting to trace thus early in his life the strength of his imagination, which held him breathless by the hour while his father was relating the story of the seige of Corunna, or the burial of Sir John Moore. His mother was a gentle, lovely woman, whose affections early twined themselves around her only son, and whose spirit, like a guardian angel, followed him down through every grade of vice, and finally exerted more influence than anything else to induce him to a life of temperance and sobriety.

The humble circumstances of his parents did not admit of a very extensive education for their son, yet in the school which he attended he seems to have acquired a distinction equivalent to that of a monitor. His unusual abilities, however, manifested themselves at a very early period, for his skill in reading attracted the attention of Wilberforce, and he received from him a small book as a tribute to his talents. About this time he received a wound in his head, the effects of which he has felt through life. It was considered dangerous for weeks, but he recovered apparently, although he attributes his unfortunate relapse at a later period to the internal injury.

At the age of twelve years, in company with a family from his native place, he embarked for America; he describes the parting with his parents, and especially with his mother, in a manner very affecting. So loth was she to part with him, that she followed him to the vessel, though she could ill afford it, and finally, bathing him in tears, committed him to God, and left him. In the morning the vessel was far from land, and he was left alone, to win or lose in the game of life. After remaining eight weeks in New York city, he started with the family for Western New York. During his stay at this place, he became the subject of serious religious impressions, and joined the Methodist Episcopal church. Not thinking that he was doing well enough here, however, in two years, with the permission of his father, he left for New York. Here he apprenticed himself to learn the book-binding business, for two and one-quarter dollars per week, boarding himself. While here he was under very good influences, and united with the church in Allen-street. Circumstances afterward occurred, under which, he decided to leave that place for another, in which he was more exposed to temptation. Being still successful in saving a little, he sent for his friends to join him, from England, and after a time he was informed of the arrival of his mother and sister, whom he found, and together they engaged rooms and went to house-keeping. In the following winter they were reduced to the lowest degree of poverty, so as to suffer for the necessaries of life. He mentions with much gratitude the circumstances that some kind stranger gave him a three-penny loaf of bread, when in great want, and says that he went to the neighboring country to pick up fuel for their use, notwithstanding which they suffered severely from the cold.

In the spring of 1834, following, work improved, and their circumstances were relieved; still they occupied but one room, close beneath a hot roof, and their condition was deplorable. In the succeeding hot season he lost his mother, and he gives the history of that event in the following touching language:

"And now comes one of the most terrible events of my life, an event which almost bowed me to the dust. The summer of 1834 was exceedingly hot; and as our room was immediately under the roof, and had but one small window in it, the heat was almost intolerable, and my mother suffered much from this cause. On the 8th of July, a day more than unusually warm, she complained of debility, but as she had before suffered from weakness, I was not apprehensive of danger, and saying I would go and bathe, asked her to provide me some rice and milk against seven or eight o'clock, when I should return. That day my spirits were unusually exuberant. I laughed and sung with my young companions, as if not a cloud was to be seen in all my sky, when one was then gathering which was shortly to burst in fatal thunder over my head. About eight o'clock I returned home, and was going up the steps, whistling as I went, when my sister met me at the threshold, and seizing me by the hand, exclaimed, '*John, mother's dead!*' What I did, what I said, I cannot remember; but they told me afterward, I grasped my sister's arm, laughed frantically in her face, and then for some minutes seemed stunned by the dreadful intelligence. As soon as they permitted me, I visited our garret, now a chamber of death, and there, on the floor, lay all that remained of her whom I had loved so well, and who had been a friend when all others had forsaken me. There she lay, with her face tied up with a handkerchief:

> 'By foreign hands her aged eyes were closed;
> By foreign hands her decent limbs composed."

"Oh, how vividly came then to my mind, as I took her cold hand in mine and gazed earnestly in her quiet face, all her meek, enduring love, her uncomplaining spirit, her devotedness to her husband and children. All was now over; and yet, as through the livelong night I sat at her side, a solitary watcher by the dead, I felt somewhat resigned at the dispensation of Providence, that she was taken from the 'evil to come.'"

The burial, too, he thus eloquently describes:

"There was no 'pomp and circumstance' about that humble funeral; but never went a mortal to the grave who had been more truly loved, and was then more sincerely lamented, than the silent traveler toward Potter's Field, the place of her interment. Only two lacerated and bleeding hearts mourned for her; but as the almost unnoticed procession passed through the streets, tears of more genuine sorrow were shed than frequently fall, when

> 'Some proud child of earth returns to dust.

"We soon reached the burying-ground. In the same cart with my mother was another mortal whose spirit had put on immortality. A little child's coffin lay beside that of her who had been a sorrowful pilgrim for many years, and both now were about to lie side by side in the narrow house. When the infant's coffin was taken from the cart, my sister burst into tears, and the driver, a rough-looking fellow, with a kindness of manner that touched us, remarked to her, 'Poor thing, 'tis better off where 'tis.' I undeceived him in his idea as to this supposed relationship of the child, and informed him that it was not the child, but our mother for whom we mourned. My mother's coffin was then taken out and placed in a trench, and a little dirt was thinly sprinkled on it. So was she buried."

Nature had given to Mr. Gough a good musical voice, and considerable mimicking powers, which his companions now began to discover. Indeed, we may say, that from this time onward, his course was steadily down, down to the lowest depth of degradation in drunkenness. Habits of dissipation were steadily growing upon him, and though he received good wages, yet he squandered them in low company amid scenes of bacchanalian revelry. He now commenced performing the lower parts in comedies, at the Franklin theater, and singing comic songs, for which his talents fitted him admirably. About this time his employer was burnt out in New York, and Gough lost most of his clothes and movables. His employer proposed moving to Rhode Island, and invited Gough to go with him, which invitation he accepted. Soon after the removal he became acquainted with a company of actors from Providence, by whose request he became one of their number.

In this business his ventriloquial powers were called into action, and for a while he gave himself up to the stage almost entirely. His anticipations were soon after again doomed to disappointment through a failure in his remuneration.

After wandering about some time in a wretched condition, he obtained a situation as a comedian for a theater in Boston. This occupation he followed until the theater closed in 1837, when, as he says, he "was thrown, like a foot-ball, upon the world's great highway." Through the assistance of a kind woman he obtained decent board, and again was furnished employment at his old trade. All this he continued till he was a little more than twenty years of age, when his appearance became so shabby that his employer turned him out of work. Hearing, however, of a situation in Newburyport, he pushed for it with all haste, and for a time tried successfully to abstain from liquor; but the evil demon still followed him, and forming acquaintances with the members of an engine company, his old habits were resumed, and he became worse than ever. His case now seemed utterly hopeless, and work failing, he started on a coasting excursion in a fishing smack, when in a storm he nearly lost his life. Preserved by a change of weather almost miraculous, he narrowly escaped drowning a second time, by the hoisting of a small boat on board of the vessel, in the bottom of which

he lay intoxicated. The violence with which they hoisted one end of the boat threw him into the other, and it being so dark that the sailors failed to observe him, he barely saved his life by an outcry which alarmed the seamen, and they took him on board. By this voyage he obtained sufficient money to buy some furniture, and he married the sister of the captain with whom he had sailed. Again he became steady for a while, and went to church, and almost began to cherish a slight hope of reform; but the overpowering strength of that monster habit was too much for his resolutions, and again he went down lower than ever. Even the young men who had been half-decent companions in drinking, began to be ashamed of him, and avoid his society. The oblivion which followed these reflections was that of the wine cup. His nature, sensitive to the slightest suspicion of ill-treatment, could not endure the coldness of those who had laughed loudest at his sport when in better circumstances, and he sought relief in the intoxicating bowl. Through the exertions of a friend in Newburyport, an Englishman, he was again partially reclaimed only to fall again, and now his constitution began to be impaired by his debaucheries. He became so nervous that, drunk or sober, he was unable to do the finer parts of book binding and gilding. He resorted to the most miserable expedients to keep up an appearance of decency, but each successively was a more signal failure. His wife now left him on a visit to his sister, and he was, if possible, more free to carouse than ever. He bought a gallon of rum, and invited a fellow in to help him drink it, and for three days he subsisted upon rum alone, without a morsel of food.

But for thus abusing his system, retribution, though tardy, was terrible. We have followed him from one step to another, till now he was to encounter that fearful malady, delirium tremens. After having drank a great amount of liquor, his throat becoming more parched and his tongue more dry by each application of the stimulant, a horrible feeling, hitherto unknown to him, began to be experienced. He sought relief in the use of tobacco, but not being able to stand up to light a match, ignited it while lying upon the bed, lit his pipe and threw the match carelessly by. Very soon the narcotic effect of the tobacco displayed itself, and he slept till the neighbors, alarmed by the smell and smoke, came into the room and aroused him from a lethargy which in fifteen minutes more would have been fatal. Thus aroused, he went out and purchased a pint of rum, which he drank in half an hour, when he was seized by a violent attack of the disease above alluded to. For three days he was tortured seemingly with a visit from all the inhabitants of the infernal regions. Hideous faces stared from out beneath shaggy locks, horrid phantoms floated through the air, and clutched their bony fingers at his throat. Frightful sounds issued from every object, and demons from Pandemonium seemed holding a horrible jubilee about their suffering victim.

But strange as it may seem, he recovered, and tells us that upon surveying his features, haggard and pale, in a glass, he thought of his *mother!* After spending some time in reflection upon the prayers and tears which she had poured forth for him, the instruction which she had given him, he went out and took a glass of brandy; another and another followed till he was again intoxicated. Yet again he found employment as an actor, in which employment he continued, till from debauchery he was too worthless to be of service, when they reprimanded him so severely that he became angry, and upon the strength of it attended to the business. Thus it continued for a while, when he again sought his old avocation, and managed to conceal his drunkenness sufficiently to retain his situation. His wife becoming ill about this time, by the advice of friends, he purchased two quarts of rum, so as to have some in the house if needed, and he soon found use for it: after ten days his wife and child both died, and then he drank to forgetfulness. At times, however, in his deepest degradation, the spirit of his mother seemed to beckon him to reform. He thus beautifully alludes to it:

"And through the mists of memory my mother's face would often appear, just as it was when I stood by her knee and listened to the lessons of wisdom and goodness from her loving lips. I would see her mild, reproving face, and seem to hear her warning voice; and surrounded by my riotous companions, at certain seasons reason would struggle for the throne whence she had been driven, and I would, whilst enjoying the loud plaudits of companions,

> 'See a hand they could not see,
> Which beckoned me away.'"

We have reached the lowest point in his history—indeed, he or any man could have gone no lower. He was habitually intoxicated, keeping partially sober only when necessary to obtain the means for obtaining a supply of spirits. The most wretched outcast in Boston felt above him, and his life was a burden to himself. Had it not been for that instinctive clinging to an existence whose terrors we know, and the instinctive dread of future horrors we apprehend may be worse, he would doubtless have committed suicide. He felt, and in his bitterness exclaimed, that "no man cared for his soul." His prospects were utterly ruined, his reputation gone, his wife and child dead, and he realized that deep loneliness which none can feel but they who have been in his isolated position. His constitution was also greatly impaired by abuse and by the attack of delirium.

His was a most wretched and hopeless case. But a great work was yet before him—a work in which his natural powers of mind, hitherto partially developed, should have full scope upon the work of reform and humanity. Experience was to him a dear schoolmaster, but just the one needed to fit him for his great life's work. In order to paint those glowing pictures in after life so successfully as to draw the admiration of listening thousands, he must himself pass through the scenes which his pencil would portray. He must feel the deadly clasp of the tyrant from whose embrace he would free others, and experience for himself the utter wretchedness of the inebriate whom he would reclaim. To his own personal acquaintance with these things must we trace that startling reality which he made the soul, the life of his pictures, when a lecturer.

In the month of October, 1842, he was wandering hopelessly through the streets of Worcester, Massachusetts, reflecting upon his deplorable condition, when some one tapped him gently upon the shoulder, and said in a mild voice, as he looked around, "Mr. Gough, I believe." "That is my name," replied he; upon which the stranger entered into conversation with him about his dissipated habits, and questioned him kindly about his prospects for the future. Mr. Gough told him his circumstances, mentioned that he was tired of life, and cared not how soon he should die, or whether he should die drunk or sober; that since he despaired of ever being anything to the world, it was immaterial to him how or how soon he left it. Then, for the first time in years, words of true sympathy and encouragement greeted his ear, like the offer of assistance to a drowning man. All the better feelings of his nature were aroused, and a faint glimmering of light reached him. The stranger, Mr. Joel Stratton, of Worcester, told him of the pledge, how many had been saved by it from a doom as deep as his, and concluded by asking him to come to the temperance meeting at the hall the next evening, and join the society. Mr. Gough promised to do so, and the stranger having left him, he went for a glass of brandy, which he drank, and, following it by three more, went home in a thorough state of drunkenness. Still, when he became sober, he remembered his promise to attend the meeting, and determined to fulfill it; throughout the day he occasionally moistened his throat with that which would only render it the more parched, but when evening came he was tolerably sober. With his ragged dress covered by an old surtout buttoned to the chin, he started for the meeting. Seating himself with others in the same condition, he waited till an opportunity was given, and then for the first time related his experience as a drunkard. This was his first address, and was probably received like that of hundreds in like circumstances, but did not attract particular attention. Having signed the pledge with a firm resolve to be a man again, he summoned all his energies to the task of subduing that fierce appetite which had hitherto known no restraint. He went home and to bed, but not to sleep. He was so fully conscious of the strength of that foe against which he was to contend, that the dread of the fearful struggle would not allow of rest. All night he tossed in feverish excitement, and in the morning arose with a fierce fire in his brain and torturing thirst in his throat. He rallied all the resolution he was master of behind that pledge as the fortress of his sincerity; he knew that while the enemy could be kept from breaking over that, he was safe, and while that position was uncarried he felt a deep joy in the consciousness that he was a man, and that even he might succeed. On the following day he went to his workshop, reeling with weakness, and there received from a temperance friend a word of encouragement which cheered him to persevere and strengthened his hope. But the demon whose sway he had owned so long was not thus easy to lose his victim. As a natural effect of breaking off so suddenly the long continued use of so great a stimulus, he was thrown into a second attack of delirium tremens. In speaking of it afterward he thus describes it:

"Fearful was that struggle. God in his mercy forbid that any other young man should endure but a tenth part of the torture which racked my frame and agonized my heart. I seemed to have a knife with a hundred blades in my hand, every blade driven through the flesh of my hands, and all were so inextricably bent and tangled together that I could not withdraw them for some time; and when I did, from my lacerated fingers the bloody fibers would stretch out all quivering with life. A great portion of the time I spent alone; no mother's hand was near to wipe the big drops of perspiration from my brow; no kind voice cheered me in my solitude."

This attack lasted him a week, when he gradually recovered, his health improved, and he began to get about; but he was thin and pale, his features haggard and worn, and his whole system deeply debilitated. Yet his resolution never wavered, and the determination to conquer never faltered; he knew that, physically, the severest part of the struggle was over, and he resolved that his mental fortitude should hold out while life remained.

A short time after his recovery, he was invited to speak in a small school-house, on which occasion he delivered his first regular temperance address, fifteen minutes or more in length. His circumstances being yet much reduced, he was obliged to wear his overcoat as before, buttoned tightly to conceal his rags, and there being a rousing fire in the room, he was nearly roasted before he had finished. We have alluded to the incident in order to show more fully the unfavorable auspices under which he commenced his career as a public speaker.

But his talent was no longer to remain buried in the earth, for God had called him to a high and holy work, as the champion of reform. His brilliant talents as an orator began to attract attention, and at the earnest solicitation of friends he procured permission of absence from his employers, leaving a job partly finished, which he promised to complete in two weeks. But he never saw the books again; he had commenced a career which was to end only with his life, and book-binding was quitted forever. It was so long since he had worn a decent suit of clothes, that his awkwardness in them shall be told by himself:

"The pantaloons were strapped down over feet which had long been used to freedom, and I feared to walk in my usual manner, lest they should give at the knee. I feared, too, lest a strap should give and make me lop-sided for life; the swarthy cut coat was so neatly and closely fitted to the arms, and the shoulders, and the back, that when it was on, I felt in a fix, as well as a fit. I was fearful of anything but mincing motion, and my arms had a cataleptic appearance. Every step I took was a matter of anxiety, lest an unlucky rip should derange my smartness. Verily, I felt more awkward in my new suit than did I while roasting before the fire in my old one."

His engagements now rapidly increased, and he was called upon to address full houses everywhere in that vicinity. The star of his reputation had finally got above the clouds which obscured its rising; its light began to be seen, and its influence to be felt, when it was subject to a short eclipse. Upon his constitution, emerging from the debility of sickness and prostration, five months of constant lecturing had worn with great severity. That pain in his head which had returned periodically with more or less violence since the blow received in youth, now visited him with renewed severity, causing for a time a partial derangement. This occurred on the way to Worcester, while under an engagement to lecture in that vicinity. In addition to this cause was a constant hemorrhage from the stomach, with long continued nervous excitement, want of rest, and loss of appetite. Hardly conscious of what he was doing, instead of preparing for the evening lecture, he took the cars for Boston. Under this irresistible impulse he went to the theater, and then fell in with some of his old companions, who, noticing something out of the way, inquired what was the matter, and invited him to go in and get some oysters. He went, and being offered a glass of brandy, without a thought or reflection drank it off. The old appetite once aroused, was not satisfied without two or three glasses more, and in that state he retired to his hotel. In the morning he took the cars for Newburyport, thence back to Boston, and from there to Worcester, where he had an appointment; meeting with his friends, he frankly told them the whole; how as from a cloudless sky the bolt had fallen, and begged their forgiveness. It was not a time for them to give him up, and they rallied around him with encouragement and sympathy. Instead of being discouraged, he resolved to derive new benefit from the lesson received, and wage the warfare with more vigor than ever. His field of labor was now the larger towns in the New England states, in which he labored continually for a number of months. After this he was urged to speak in Boston, where he drew large houses, and finally the largest were insufficient to contain the crowds that were entranced by his oratory.

In the autumn of 1843 he was again married, and remained in Boston and the vicinity during that winter. In the May following, having received invitations to lecture in the largest cities of the middle and western states, he started in company with Mr. Grant on a tour more widely extended than he had hitherto attempted.

He was now fairly upon the stage as a speaker, and some account of his appearance may not be out of place. He is about medium height, slender, with a look of care upon his countenance. Time has prematurely furrowed his brow, and sorrow and hardships left their indelible footprints. His temperament is nervous and sanguine, and his constitution, naturally strong, has become weakened by disease.

As he takes his seat quietly upon the platform, a stranger would not select him for a man of great power, yet under the arching brow, shaded by careless locks of dark, flowing hair, his fine rolling eye cannot fail to excite a deep interest on the part of the beholder. Not until he rises to his address is one impressed with his wonderful talents. He commences deliberately and distinctly, seeming unconscious of his power, but as he becomes interested in his subject he grows more fervent and earnest, till at length he seems hurried only to keep pace with the rapid evolutions of his own mind; every thought becomes a bolt from the hot furnace of his brain, and wrought into sentences, they fall with the rapidity, and we might almost add, with the effect of lightning. The sympathetic influence is imperceptibly communicated to his audience, until at length they are entirely under his control. They are interested in whatever interests him; the man is forgotten, and nothing is felt but the passionate impulse of an absorbing mind. You surrender your judgment, emotions, sensibilities, in fact your whole being, to a dominion which is irresistible, and would wonder, if you could stop to wonder, at your own lack of self-government. Still he hurries you onward; now some scene of woe has received a coloring so vivid from the pencil of his imagination, that before you are aware, tears have answered to the fervor of his appeal; the next instant the whole scene is changed, and some grotesque figure stands forth in an attitude so ludicrous that you are convulsed with laughter. This strength of imagery is no better exhibited than in his comparison of the young man's danger from intemperance to the boat rushing down the cataract of Niagara. We give it in his own language:

"I remember riding near Niagara Falls, and I said to a gentleman, 'What river is that, sir?' 'That,' he said, 'is Niagara river.' 'Well,' said I, 'it is a beautiful stream, bright, and fair, and glassy: how far off are the rapids?' 'About a mile or two,' was the answer. 'Is it possible,' I said, 'that only a mile from us we shall find the water in such turbulence, as I presume it must be, near the falls?' 'You will find it so, sir.' And so I found it; and that first sight of the Niagara I shall never forget. Now launch your bark on that Niagara river; it is bright, smooth, beautiful, and glassy; there is a ripple at the bow; the silvery lake you leave behind you adds to your enjoyment; down the stream you glide; you have oars, sails, and helm prepared for every contingency, and you set out on your pleasure excursion. Some one comes out from the bank, 'Young men, ahoy!' 'What is it?' 'The rapids are below you.' 'Ha, ha! we have heard of the rapids below us, but we are not such fools to get into them. When we find we are going too fast to suit our convenience, then hard up the helm, and steer to the shore; when we find we are passing a given spot too rapidly, we will set the mast in the socket, hoist the sail and speed to land. We are not alarmed by the danger.' 'Young men, ahoy! The rapids are below you.' 'Ha, ha! we will laugh and quaff; all things delight us. What care we for the future! No man ever saw it. Sufficient unto the day is the evil thereof. We will enjoy life while we may, and catch pleasure as it flies. This is enjoyment; it is time enough to steer out of danger when we find we are swiftly sailing with the current.' 'Young men, ahoy!' What is it?' 'The rapids are below you!' Now you see the water foaming all around; see how fast you pass the point! Now turn! pull hard! quick, quick! Pull for your life! Pull till the blood starts from your nostrils, and the veins stand like whipcords upon the brow! Set the mast in the socket! Hoist the sail! Ha, ha! it is too late! Shrieking, cursing, howling, blaspheming, over you go! And thousands thus go over by the power of evil habit, declaring all the while, 'When I find out that it is injuring me, then I will give it up.'"

Here lies Mr. Gough's great strength; he is a perfect orator. Whatever his vivid imagination grasps, he paints before you with startling reality; the awkward appears intensely ludicrous, the homely scares you, the disagreeable becomes hateful, and the ugly fiendish. By a touch of the same magic wand, the interesting becomes beautiful, and the lovely is transformed into the angelic. His metaphors always seem the best adapted to the object which he would illustrate, and when he has finished the picture, perfection asks nothing more.

Mr. Gough's oratory has none of the classical finish of Burke, the stinging satire of Pitt, or the massive grandeur of Webster; but it flows onward like a strong mountain torrent, its surface now flashing with the star-light of wit, then dark with the heaving billows of passion, but always possessing a power irresistible. What early education omitted in his discipline, experience has recompensed; what he failed to acquire in the schoolhouse of boyhood, he learned in the school of life. To an originality of conception in thought, nature has added the perfect ability of a mimic, so that his scope is not limited to one subject or to one method of treating it. He possesses a fine musical voice which prepossesses one in his favor, and relieves the monotony too frequent in a discourse; altogether, he is one of the most fascinating speakers we have heard. Some parts of his orations, like that above quoted, appear well in print, but usually their beauty lies in his inimitable manner of delivery; he never writes an oration, but having acquired an off-hand habit, the natural consequence is a disconnectedness of style which would appear imperfect as a whole; nevertheless, we find in his speeches occasional passages which cannot easily be excelled in the language for touching pathos, or bewitching beauty. After all, descriptions do not touch him; he must be heard and seen to be appreciated. He came in a time when he was most needed, when the mere experience of the reformed inebriate was becoming threadbare. His stirring appeals aroused the flagging strength of the cause, and reänimated its adherents. Once only, the devices of fiends for a short time prevailed, and by means of a drugged mixture administered under the guise of friendship, he was drawn from the path of rectitude; but being reclaimed by his friends, he has ever since been a more uncompromising foe to rum drinking than ever. When the idea of totally restraining the traffic in intoxicating drinks was developed in the Maine law, it found in him a firm supporter and zealous advocate. To the great work of the temperance reformation he has consecrated his life, and for its welfare he hesitates not to sacrifice the best energies of his being. When intemperance shows its monster head he is ready to strike a blow at his life. He has now crossed the ocean, and is lecturing to the benighted millions of Europe, speaking words of encouragement to the fainting, and assisting the slave of the winecup in high places and in low to break the thralldom which enchains him, and become free. No one without his experience could have done his work; and we do not hesitate to rank him among the most distinguished of American reformers.

CHARLES G. FINNEY.

It is astonishing how many different appearances are given of an eminent person by different biographers. In reading Scott's or Alison's history of Napoleon, we should never dream that he was anything but a tyrannical usurper wading through seas of blood to the throne of the world; while in the account of Mr. Abbott we see but a stern and resolute patriot, who from the sense of duty unwillingly offered human sacrifices upon the altar of his country. We have noticed the same shade of difference in various representations of the subject of the present sketch. One of these was a late memoir of Dr. Nettleton, containing allusions to Mr. Finney, which we shall refer to again, remarking here that there is perhaps no man of the same religious eminence living, about whom society at large has as great variety of opinions as of President Finney. Political squabbles, though of not half the importance, have always taken a more vital hold of society in general than theological discussions, and it is owing perhaps to the reason that the true position of this distinguished theologian is no better known to the world. Having taken some pains to investigate and ascertain the facts in regard to his character, we hope to give it a fair delineation in the following paragraphs.

Charles G. Finney was born in Litchfield county, in the year 1792. Two years after, his parents, who were in moderate circumstances, removed to "the Black river country," New York, with their family, where Mr. Finney spent the years of his childhood. His character as a leader began to develop itself in youth; in sports his associates ranked him among the foremost, yet in school he was studious, and it is remarked by an early acquaintance, that mathematics was to him but a recreation. By the intense vigor of his intellect he was enabled to master easily what other boys did only by close application, and he found considerable time to wield the sledge at his father's anvil. Here he took his first lesson in moulding the hot iron to a desired shape, and here he first felt in his own breast the glowings of a fire which should send forth glowing truths, to arouse men from the slumbers of carnal security, and light the fires of reform. Here he learned the force of one strong arm under the control of a brave heart and clear intellect, and while his physical system was gaining muscular strength from continual action, his mind was as constantly acquiring an energy no less needed to prepare him for his great work. At the age of twenty he returned to Connecticut and commenced teaching a day-school and giving instruction in music, at which he gained considerable reputation. He subsequently returned to New York, and entered upon the study of law, which he completed honorably; was admitted to the bar, and practiced for a time in that state. Up to this period, though not wild, he had paid no particular personal attention to religious subjects. He was what is called a strictly moral man, but now being led to a more thoughtful contemplation of divine truth and the claims of God upon him, he perceived that his life had been one of rebellion and sin; and, yielding to the powerful convictions of the Divine Spirit, he submitted his whole being to God.

His plans and purposes now took a new direction, and he consecrated himself to the ministry. After studying theology one year at Auburn Seminary, at the age of thirty he commenced preaching as an Evangelist, in the larger cities of New York. It was during the powerful revival that attended this portion of his ministry that he and Dr. Asahel Nettleton came somewhat into collision.

Dr. Nettleton was nine years older than Mr. Finney, and had then been laboring as an evangelist for twenty-one years, principally in New York, Connecticut, and Massachusetts. He was a preacher of altogether a different character from Mr. Finney, being mild and persuasive, and had won the affections of the people among whom he had labored and doubtless been exceedingly useful. He was now worn with the excitement and toil of twenty years of activity, and was unable to go on with the work. To an impartial observer it would seem that God had raised up Mr. Finney for the express purpose of filling his place. Many hearts had become hardened by long continued repetition of the same truths in much the same style, and there was need of a new energy and power in the delivery of the truth, to make it effective. In saying this, we do not speak forgetfully of other means, and especially of the Divine influence, but God has ordered that the success of his kingdom shall depend to a certain extent upon human instrumentalities, and in the economy of grace they are as much needed as some inducements presented only by a divine power. The earnest fervor of Mr. Finney, accompanying his lucid expositions of the requirements of God's law, constituted him the man for the emergency, and he applied himself to the work with a zeal which won for him and his adherents the name of "Western Wild Fires." But, to refer to the biography before spoken of, which alludes to Mr. Finney in a manner quite unkind and uncourteous, to say the least: It characterizes the work of grace in which Mr. Finney was engaged as a "great religious excitement;" accuses him of "harshness and severity;" says that "multitudes were reported as subjects of renewing grace," and leaves upon every mind the impression that the greatest and worst part of truth had been left unsaid; it closes with this remark: "that very many of the reported converts were like the stony-ground hearers, who endured only for a time, few, I presume, will at this day be disposed to deny." Certainly, but is it not so in every revival? Are not "many called, but few chosen?" Is there any evidence that less were savingly converted than in the corresponding labors of Mr. Nettleton? The real cause of the difficulty is betrayed in the following rather careless sentence: "He (Dr. Nettleton) found that Mr. Finney was unwilling to abandon *certain measures* which *he* had ever regarded as exceedingly calamitous to the cause of revivals;" and because "certain measures" did not meet with the approbation of Dr. Nettleton, he was necessitated to use his influence against the whole work. In this opposition he was sustained by numbers who either objected to the same measures, or were of different theological sentiments, or, for some reason, disliked the man. We will further quote from a letter of Dr. Nettleton to a friend, written in January, 1827. It will show what results Dr. Nettleton found fault with, and who were really to blame for those results. He says, "We do not call in question the genuineness of those revivals, or the purity of the motives of those who have been the most active in them. You doubtless are reaping and rejoicing in their happy fruits; but the evils to which I allude are felt by the churches abroad, numbers of which have gone out to catch the spirit, and have returned, some grieved, others soured, and denouncing ministers, colleges, theological seminaries, and have set whole churches by the ears, and kept them in turmoil for months together."

Is the blame, then, to be attached to the principal preacher, or to the individuals who went home discontented and prejudiced? When, in a multitude of instances, the Almighty had set his seal to the work, is it to be considered spurious because a number of individuals could not extend to it their approbation? We find it stated on reliable authority, that "Dr. Nettleton afterward repented of his rashness," and although he had been aforetime very successful in his ministry, his usefulness seemed to die when he came out so bitterly against Mr. Finney. Dr. Lyman Beecher wrote to Dr. Nettleton, who had been sick about a year, that "his sickness seemed a judgment upon him for his opposition to Mr. Finney; if we are not able to keep up with the boys, why, let them go ahead; we will follow on and do what good we can." In alluding to the matter, President Finney remarks, "I never had much to do with him in any way."

The work in which Mr. Finney was engaged progressed rapidly, and great success attended his efforts. His knowledge of human law made him more acute in perceiving, and ready in interpreting the divine law. His first volume of sermons was published in 1835, but some or all of them must have been written eight or nine years before, at the time of these revivals. The impenitent man who could fail to be aroused by such appeals as fill these lectures, must have been already stupefied by that torpor which is the precursor of eternal death. By their vigor and thrilling earnestness, thousands who had never before given a thought to the subject of religion, were awakened, and renouncing the service of Satan, entered the christian church. There are before us no statistics of the actual addition to the different denominations, but it is certain that no revivals since the days of Edwards, were nearly as productive of benefit to the churches, in whose vicinity they occurred. In company with "Father Nash," as fellow-laborer, he discharged the duties of a successful evangelist in Rochester, Utica, Rome, Auburn, Buffalo, Troy, Boston, and New York city, and various other places of considerable importance.

In 1832, Mr. Finney was settled over the Chatham-street chapel, in New York city, where he discharged the duties of the pastoral office acceptably for two years. He then removed to the Tabernacle church, where he ministered for three years. In 1835, when he had been pastor of the Tabernacle one year, he was elected professor of theology, at Oberlin, Ohio, and after two years, finding the double duties too much for his health, he resigned the charge of the church in New York, and removed to Oberlin. In 1836, he published "Sermons on important subjects," and "Lectures to Christians," in 1837. In the course of the next four years he published three other works, entitled, "Sanctification," "Revival Letters," and "Skeletons upon the subject of Moral Government." From the time he left New York, he was engaged in professional duties at Oberlin, and preaching in different cities in the Union, for a number of years. In 1846 and 1847 he issued his comprehensive work upon Systematic Theology, in two octavo volumes. They are the second and third of the series. In reference to the absence of the first, Professor Finney, in his preface to the second volume, says, "I have begun with the second volume, as this was to be on subjects so distinct from what will appear in the first, that this volume might as well appear first, and because it seemed especially called for just now, to meet a demand of the church, and of my classes." Any comment from us upon these works might appear assuming, and perhaps arrogant. The public are aware of the nature of the subjects therein discussed, and of his mode of discussion. Professor Finney has brought to the work a maturity of mind, a strength of purpose, and a logical acumen which is seldom found. Professor Hodge, in his ill-fated review of them, says: "The work is, therefore, in a high degree logical. It is as hard to read as Euclid. Nothing can be omitted; nothing passed over slightly. * * * It is like one of those spiral stair-cases, which lead to the top of some high tower, without a landing from the base to the summit. The author begins with certain postulates, or what he calls first-class truths of reason, and these he traces out with singular clearness and accuracy to their legitimate conclusions. We do not see that there is a break or defective link in the whole chain; if you grant his premises, you have already granted his conclusions."

The article by Professor Hodge, in the Princeton Biblical Repository for June, 1847, is the most like an attempt to combat Mr. Finney of anything we have seen, and this is an attempt only in appearance. After admitting that his premises must be wrong, or his conclusions right, one would suppose that unless Professor Hodge could deny successfully the premises, he must feel the force of the arguments, and admit the conclusions and positions established thereby. But no, he does nothing of the kind; seeing no place upon all the battle-field where he could erect a battery, he retreats behind the overthrown castle of Old School Presbyterianism, and barks at the author. It is indeed a pastime for a curious man to compare the work reviewed with the Review, to see how infinitely behind the one the other is in logic, in power of reasoning, and in intellectual perception. Professor Finney, with surprising ease and clearness, traces out principles which his reviewer, after close application and untiring diligence, comprehends much as a schoolboy half perceives the beauty of an intricate geometrical demonstration. He is evidently just as far behind Mr. Finney in metaphysical disquisition and intellectual apprehension as the schoolboy is behind Euclid in mathematics; and the beauty of it is, that this truth is so obvious to every one. Professor Hodge acknowledges in the first place that he cannot see the principles upon which the work is founded, in fact that he does not believe there are any. We will quote: "Our task would be much easier if there were any one radical principle to which his several axioms could be reduced;" further on in the same page he begins to see dimly as follows: "We are not sure that Mr. Finney's doctrines may not be traced to two fundamental principles;" after writing eight pages, he is "assured that he has discovered the two principles," the key-stones of the arch; well, what does he in this case? Does he try to pull them out, and thus overthrow the structure? No, he stands laughing at it, and calls upon those who think as he does to help him laugh it down. The only real difference between them is shown by Mr. Finney, in an "Examination of the Review of Finney's Theology," published in the Oberlin Quarterly for August, 1847. We quote briefly from the "Examination:" "Professor Hodge asserts that 'it is no less obviously true that an inability which has its origin in sin, which consists in what is sinful, and relates to moral action, is perfectly consistent with continued obligation;'" "I deny that moral obligation extends to any act or state, either of soul or body, that lies wholly beyond both the direct and indirect control of the will, so that it is naturally impossible for the agent to be or do it.'" In referring to Professor Hodge, Mr. Finney says further: "He represents *reverence*, *gratitude*, and *devotion* as higher forms of virtue than benevolence;" "I had shown that these were attributes of benevolence, but he regards them manifestly as involuntary emotions. Reverence for God for or on account of his benevolence—gratitude to God for his benevolence—devotion to God for his benevolence, higher forms of virtue than the benevolence which we adore! Amazing! What will the church and the world say, when they are told that at Princeton they hold such views of the nature of true religion? What, good will to God and to being in general, that efficient principle that is the foundation and source of all doing good, one of the lowest forms of virtue! Tell it not in Gath. * * * If, as he says, the involuntary states of the intellect and the sensibility are more virtuous than the benevolence in which I hold that all true virtue strictly consists, I am utterly mistaken. And if, on the other hand, supreme, disinterested good will to God and man, including all its attributes and developments, is virtue, and, strictly speaking, the whole of virtue, then this writer is wholly in fault, and has not the true ideal of the christian religion before him when he writes." But we have not room to trace the skirmish any further; indeed, were it not the only semblance of an attack upon his system from an opposing school, we should only have alluded to it. Before leaving this subject, it will be proper for us to mention a paper written by Dr. Duffield, issued under the sanction of the Presbytery of Detroit, and "approved by the Synod of Michigan;" it is entitled "A Warning against Error," but should have been named conversely, an "Error against Warning," or a bundle of errors in despite of warning. We have read most of it, and after reading the "Reply" to it, which Mr. Finney published, we do not think it worth our while to quote a paragraph. It is a mere collection of pathos, grandmotherly tenderness of the churches, and misapprehensions of Mr. Finney's views, with a few pious ejaculations of horror at his awful impiety. We are not sufficiently posted up in metaphysics to define all the points of difference between Professor Finney's system and either the Old or New School; it differs somewhat from both. In the words of Professor Hodge, "Principles which have long been current in this country, he has had the strength of intellect and will to trace out to their legitimate conclusions, and has thus shown the borderers that there is no neutral ground." The work is doubtless the purest, clearest, and at the same time the most profound metaphysical disquisition we have ever seen—perhaps which has been written. To quote a specimen from it, would be like taking a stone out of an arch to exhibit the perfection of the structure, or like cutting a piece from a tight rope to show you how it looked when stretched, or like removing the central piece of a suspension bridge to exhibit its strength; remove a link, and the chain falls. Yet one time or other the world will ask, "If all this be true, if Mr. Finney's theological positions cannot be overthrown, why are they not adopted by the different schools of the land? If men can fulfill the commands of God, if he in this life expects them to do what he requires, if he is a reasonable being, and only requires things which it is possible for us to perform, why, O theologians, do you not tell us so? If God only expects us to love him with all our powers, why do you teach that he requires in us the perfect love of Adam before the fall? Is the credit of this or that particular school of more importance than the word of God? Are the traditions of men more binding than the Divine commands? If the Infinite is a tyrannical being, exacting of his creatures that which we are incapable of performing, let us know it *now*, and your further service will be dispensed with. But if, as some injudicious men strangely argue, the Almighty Agent who holds our life and destinies in his hand, if he is also a God of justice, requiring only that degree of service which we are capable of performing, why do you not preach that plainly, and hold out to us the inducements for doing it?"

But we have tarried too long upon a subject upon which we could not have said less without refusing to speak, and we turn to the narrative of his life. About four years since, Prof. Finney went to England, and in spite of the admonitions and "warnings" of American conservatives, was well received by the most eminent orthodox divines in the realm. We copy an account of his reception from the letter of an intelligent American, in the Puritan Recorder: "Mr. Finney's Lectures on Revivals, which as well as one or two other volumes of his works, had been published in England, and even translated into Welsh, prepared the way for his visit. When Dr. Campbell first invited him to come up to London from some provincial town where he was laboring, he did it as he does everything, with all his heart. He determined to have a full and fair experiment of the influence of such labors on such a population. His plans were zealously seconded by the working members of the church, who distributed at the commencement fifty thousand copies of an address inviting attendance. These were followed by thousands more; and huge placards were in some instances carried, according to the London fashion, on men's shoulders, through the streets. The result was a constant and increasing attendance on the Sabbath, and generally six evenings in the week, for about nine months, ranging from one thousand to three thousand two hundred. There was no confusion or undue excitement. At the close of the public evening services, all who wished to be more directly and familiarly addressed, were requested to remain; and the hundreds who complied with this invitation, were still further, subdivided at a later period in the evening, by an invitation to inquirers to remain. None were received to the communion under four or five months from the time of their hopeful conversion. In short, every precaution was taken to prevent the evils which were well understood to have attended these "special efforts" in America; and with such a man as Dr. Campbell at the helm, and in such a community as that which offered itself in the busy, worldly, wicked English metropolis, there was little danger of hurtful extravagance."

In reference to Prof. Finney's theological sentiments, this correspondent remarks: "Dr. Campbell's treatment of Mr. F. as, on the whole, sound in doctrine, notwithstanding many startling statements, though disapproved by some of the Congregational body, yet found an extensive concurrence. And it struck me as not a little remarkable, that even his Treatise on Theology, after a careful examination of three days by Mr. James, of Birmingham, and Dr. Bedford, of Worcester, was revised and edited by the latter, and published with Dr. B.'s preface in an elegant form by Mr. Tegg, the eminent London publisher. How much the revision amounted to I know not. The American edition would probably want considerable revision to suit the taste of New England theologians of any school." We beg leave to differ in this last sentiment of the writer, for had there been any feature in Mr. Finney's theology very objectionable to New England divines, they would not have invited him so earnestly to preach in their pulpits, immediately upon his return to America. The farewell exercises in London were of a very impressive and interesting character. A large tea-meeting was given, in which flattering testimonials were presented to Mr. and Mrs. F., and speeches were made in honor of their distinguished visitor. Upon reaching New York, Mr. F. was urged to labor for a time in the Tabernacle Church, of that city, which he did, and many were converted and added to the church. The Independent says of him: "The truths upon which he most insisted during his continuous stay of ten or twelve weeks in this city, were the entire sinfulness of man, his guilt and condemnation, his pinching need of Christ, the glorious provision of grace in the atonement, a free salvation by grace, and yet the absolute sovereignty of God in the dispensation of the Spirit, whose aid, by his voluntary perverseness, the sinner has rendered indispensable to his conversion, man's accountability, and the justice of God in the eternal condemnation of the wicked. These truths were often presented with great force of logic and vividness of illustration; but if we had any criticism to offer upon Mr. Finney, it would be, that at times he manifested a want of earnestness and concentrated power—a consequence of the prolix diffuseness of extemporaneous speaking—rather than a dangerous excess of these qualities."

Mr. Finney then went to Hartford, at the solicitation of Drs. Hawes, Bushnell, and Mr. Patton, and lectured with success for a number of weeks. He is a very earnest and energetic speaker, rigidly terse as a writer, and spends no time in tickling the ear by flowery illustrations or splendid metaphors.

He commences a discourse by digging down and showing the great principles which, like foundation stones, underlie the surface; upon these, truth after truth is piled like blocks of granite, which once placed can never be removed; gradually, but surely, rises the superstructure, and when completed, there is not one piece too much, nor is anything lacking. The argument completed, he proceeds to the application of the subject with a force and scrutiny which can neither be resisted or avoided. The Divine Law appears to the hearer like a great and equitable rule of action; he wonders that he never saw it in that light before; he sees himself a culprit, feeble and insignificant as a worm, but magnified by his offense to a rebel against the Ruler of worlds. There appears no way of escape; every avenue seems barred against him; "which way he flies is hell," yet fly he must, for behind him the Law, like a flaming sword, is darting its double edge of fire around his soul; in consternation and anguish he falls down exclaiming, "What shall I do?" when a voice, still and small like a zephyr, reaches him from Calvary: "Look unto me and live." How transcendentally beautiful now appears the love of God; hope kindles in the bosom of the offender, as he sees, behind the stern glance of the magistrate, the yearning face of a Father; with a heart overflowing with gratitude, the late rebel embraces the atonement of Christ, and is at peace with God. Something akin to this class of sensations, we have known to be produced in the minds of three thousand at once, by his vivid manner of presenting the truth; we could almost see them sway to and fro, as the trees of a forest when the wind sweeps over them in power. We intended to give a specimen from one of his discourses, but have not one convenient which does justice to the man. Indeed it is not by a remarkable concentration upon a dozen lines, that his discourses are made so effective; it is by the wonderful energy of thought and expression of the whole. His sermons are almost all extemporaneous, and therefore he changes rapidly from one point or thought to another, yet never loses sight of the main thread of discourse. Much of his address has a personal manner, which, though perhaps more powerful when spoken, does not appear as smoothly when written. He is a remarkable man, and one who, it would seem, would more suitably and effectively labor as an evangelist, than as instructor in a college. The result of his professional labors is more felt at the west than elsewhere, because that in the condition of their society, new measures or opinions are more readily received. Mr. Finney has been twice married, and both connections were happy in their domestic results. From a family of six children, two have passed away. Three of those remaining are filling stations of eminence and usefulness at the west, and the youngest is at home. Mr. Finney, now sixty-two years of age, is President of the Oberlin College, Professor of Theology at the same institution, and minister of the Congregational Church in that village. His church and congregation are reported as the largest in the United States.

JOSHUA R. GIDDINGS.

Giddings is one of the "old guard" of liberty. He is intimately connected with the anti-slavery reform in America—was one of its first and warmest supporters. He has been so long known as an uncompromising opponent of Negro slavery in the United States, that he is looked upon everywhere as a kind of moral hero, both among his friends and enemies, for the latter know full well, that it requires courage to support unwaveringly an unpopular cause. Not for an instant during the last fifteen years, has Mr. Giddings faltered—not for a moment has he harbored a thought of relinquishing his opposition to slavery.

Mr. Giddings is not a disciple of Lord Chesterfield: he knows not how to bandy compliments—is not a fashionable gentleman, according to the definition of the polite world. He is not by any means ungentlemanly or uncourteous, but he is plain, direct, and always forcible. His manner comports well with his appearance. He is of middle height, is thick-set, has a corrugated forehead, piercing eyes, and a hearty voice. Sometimes there is a half-scowl upon his face as if he were thinking of the many hard battles he has fought with the enemies of human freedom. Neither does Mr. Giddings make pretensions to profound scholarship. He does not believe in shams, and wishes to be taken for what he is, rather than for what he is not. He was not made in schools or colleges, but got his education by the fireside. He knows, however, the history of American slavery as thoroughly as any man in the country. He has by heart every feature of the system, every movement of its adherents, since the Union was formed. Stern in his adherence to his principles, enduring as the hardest granite, he is eminently fitted for his position. In the past years no man could hold Mr. Giddings' views upon slavery on the floor of Congress, without being made of stern stuff. No common man could, day after day, and year after year, endure the studied insults of southern orators and blackguards. Mere power of rhetoric could not make front against such a mighty opposing force. Nothing but iron integrity could do it. Mr. Giddings has been accused by some of lacking geniality, but we think not by those who know him well, and can appreciate the life he has led, and the constant series of attacks which he has encountered in congress for the last fifteen years or more. A man cannot stop to measure his words with an enemy charging upon him; he must fight as best he can, and how. Mr. Giddings is simply a hearty, solid, stern believer in human rights, and does not know how to grow mellow over his grog, after the genuine congressional fashion. He is anti-slavery at all times—out of congress as well as in it; it is his "one idea," to make war upon the institution, and for that reason he is accused by some of lacking geniality. He is a man of warm, generous feelings and humor, but he is distinguished chiefly by his clear common sense, and his dogged perseverance. Once right, all the powers of hell cannot swerve him from his path, and his sturdy intellect and philanthropic heart, are safe guides for him to follow. He is no orator. He does not understand the power of a graceful address, or if he does, cannot speak gracefully. His manners as an orator are far from pleasing, and yet he usually commands the attention of the house. He lacks an easy flow of language; the words sometimes are too rapidly uttered, and again too slowly. But there is so much force, so much power in his thoughts, that he is sure of being listened to as eagerly as if he were an orator.

Mr. Giddings was born the 6th of October, 1795, at Athens, New York. His ancestors emigrated from England, in 1650, to this country. His great grandfather left Connecticut, in 1725, for the state of New York, and in 1806, his father emigrated to Ashtabula county, Ohio, taking his son with him. They have remained there ever since. Young Giddings had not the advantage of a collegiate education, nor had he an academical education, for he only attended school in a common, district school-house. His father had been cheated out of a grant of lands, and was quite poor, and father and son worked industriously upon the farm. His father fought in the battles of the revolution, and his stories of the stirring times of '76 made a deep impression upon the mind of young Giddings—an impression which will never be effaced so long as he lives. It was by the humble fireside of his father that he learned to love and respect human rights. He was taught that human liberty is worth dying for—that all men possess the right to own themselves and manage their own affairs. Revolutionary blood runs in his veins, and the tales of the courage of the old revolutionary heroes in the dark days of the rebel colony, were calculated to fill him with a desire to imitate them in their virtues. In 1812 he took part in the war with Great Britain, and was engaged in one or two battles with the enemy. Shortly after he returned, he was invited to teach a district school near Ashtabula, and, though feeling diffident about his qualifications, he accepted the invitation, and succeeded admirably. He became desirous for more knowledge, for a more enlightened intellect, and for a time he put himself under the tuition of a neighboring clergyman. He then commenced studying law, and was admitted to the bar in 1817. He shortly after married, and settled down in his profession. In 1826 he was elected to the legislature of Ohio, and in 1836 he was first elected to congress, from Ashtabula district, and he has been continued there by his constituents ever since.

When he entered congress, the nation was engaged in prosecuting the Florida war, the principal object of which was to recover fugitive slaves. Seeing this, Mr. Giddings at once commenced a series of speeches, to show the manner in which the north was dragged into the support of a system odious to her alike by nature and education. Two years after he entered congress, the infamous gag-law was passed, whereby all discussion of slavery on the floor of the house was prohibited. Mr. Giddings, with a few other manly northern men present, were determined to test the power of the gag, and, as an experiment, discussed questions which indirectly involved the institution of slavery. The Florida war was before the house, and Mr. Giddings led off in an able speech upon it. He took the ground that slavery caused the war—that it was a shameful and slave-catching war. The slave-holding members called him to order for breaking the rules of the house, but the speaker decided that it was in order to discuss the causes of the war. This decision paved the way for the repeal of the odious restriction upon the right of speech.

In 1841, the celebrated "Creole" case was before the country. The slave ship "Creole," from Richmond, was, while at sea, taken possession of by the slaves on board, who guided it to British soil, where, by the laws of Great Britain, they were free. Our government, through the secretary of state, Daniel Webster, demanded pay for the slaves. Mr. Giddings felt outraged that the general government should in so offensive a manner involve the whole country in a sectional institution. He therefore drew up a set of resolutions denying the power of the president to make such demands in behalf of the people of this country, claiming that a majority of the citizens of the Union did not recognize the right of property in man. These resolutions were introduced into congress by him. A bomb-shell thrown among them could not have created a greater excitement or confusion. A scene ensued which beggars description. The "chivalry" of the south were ready to devour him with their poisonous fangs. He was publicly censured by congress, and he immediately resigned his seat and went home. His constituents told him to return, and to reässert the views embodied in his resolutions. They knew they were correct—that the federal government had no right to take under its protection the institution of slavery. He went back to his seat, and courageously reässerted his convictions upon the subject. The defenders of the "peculiar institution" thought it was not wise to attempt to censure him again, and now there is scarcely a man in the whole north but will agree that they were not only correct, but that it was proper to present them to congress at that time. On the question of the right of petition Mr. Giddings fought bravely and nobly, and lived to see the right not only asserted but maintained. Throughout his whole career he has been most bitterly assailed by southern members. We give a specimen from his speech on the annexation of Texas:

"Mr. Payne, of Alabama, interrupting Mr. Giddings, requested permission to propound a question.

"Mr. Giddings. An hour is a short time to make a speech; but, if the gentleman will occupy but a moment, he may propound his question.

"Mr. Payne desired the reporters to note what he said; and stated that about two years since, a man by the name of Torrey, a negro-stealer, brought a wagon and team to this district. While stealing some negroes they were arrested, and Torrey made his escape. Subsequently it was said, that a member on this floor claimed the wagon and team; and he now asked the gentleman from Ohio (Mr. Giddings) what interest he had in the property?

"Mr. Giddings. I am not at liberty to receive anything uttered on this floor as an insult. Indeed, nothing coming from a certain quarter *can* insult me.

"Mr. Payne. I call upon the gentleman from Ohio to answer my question; and if he does not, a committee ought to be appointed to inquire into the fact. (Cries of order, order.)

"Mr. Giddings. I have witnessed too many of these sudden outbursts of passion to be very seriously alarmed at them.

"Mr. Payne. A man that will deceive his own party, cannot be ashamed at anything. (Cries of order, order, all over the hall.)

"Mr. Giddings. These little innocent outpourings of the heart are perfectly harmless even from an *overseer*, when deprived of his whip. You may in such case look him in the face with safety. To you, Mr. Chairman, and to the members generally, whom I respect, I will say, this is the first intimation that I have ever had, that any member was suspected of being connected with the transaction alluded to."

This is a faint specimen of the thousand insults which have been heaped upon Mr. Giddings during his congressional career, until at last he has become so hardened against them, they excite little feeling in him, and he can laugh a blackguard coolly in the face.

One of the most eloquent speeches ever delivered by Mr. Giddings in congress was upon the Dayton and Sayers case. Some seventy or eighty slaves attempted to escape from the District of Columbia, in the schooner Pearl. The captain and mate were thrown into prison. Mr. Giddings visited them the day after their arrest, but his life was threatened unless he would leave, which he refused to do. He made the following statement at the time:

"I, Joshua R. Giddings, a member of the house of representatives, state: That, during the forenoon of yesterday, I visited the jail of this district. I was not acquainted with the keeper, and when I arrived I announced to him my name, and that I was a member of this body. That I further said to him that I wished to see the persons confined there on a charge of carying away slaves from this district. I told him that I wished to say to them that they should have the benefit of counsel and a legal trial, and their rights should be protected, and desired him to be present. He went with me to the passage that leads to the cells.

"While conversing with these men in the presence of the keeper, a mob came to the iron gate at the head of the stairway, and demanded that I should leave forthwith. The keeper informed them that he would not open the door until they retired. I was further informed that the mob had compelled the guard at the lower gate to deliver up the key to them; and in this way they had opened that gate, and by that means obtained access to the passage at the head of the stairs.

"After the mob had left the stairs and entered the lower passage, the keeper, and myself, and the Hon. E. S. Hamlin, who had visited the jail as attorney for the prisoners with me, came down to the lower gate, in front of which the mob was assembled. He opened the gate and I walked out. This morning I have been informed by a gentleman who is a stranger to me, but who says he was present, and heard the proposition made by individuals, to lay violent hands upon me as I came out of the prison, one of whom, he informed me, was a Mr. Slatter, a slave-dealer from Baltimore, whom he states to have been active in instituting others to acts of violence."

The affair created a great deal of excitement, and came up in congress. Certain slave-holding members, in a state of frantic passion, went so far as to desire the hanging of Mr. Giddings and his friends, and so expressed themselves in their speeches. They also threatened to expel any members who should, upon examination, be found to have anything to do with inciting the slaves to escape. Mr. Giddings' speech upon the subject was unusually eloquent and bold. We will copy a few paragraphs from it:

"Well, sir, what are the facts at which almost the whole slave-holding fraternity of this body has been thrown into such a ferment? Why, sir, it is said that some seventy-six men, women, and children, living in this district, possessing the same natural right to the enjoyment of life and liberty as gentlemen in this hall; feeling the galling chains of slavery chafing and festering into their flesh; themselves shut out from the social and intellectual enjoyments for which they were designed by their Creator; bound down in abject servitude, surrounded by moral darkness, robbed of their labor, and shut out even from the hope of immortality under the laws which we have enacted, and which we still refuse to modify or repeal; inspired with an ardent desire to enjoy the rights with which God has endowed our race, went on board a schooner lying at one of the wharves of this city, and set sail for 'a land of liberty.' When they reached the mouth of the river, adverse winds compelled them to cast anchor. Thus detained, we may imagine the anxiety that must have filled their minds. How that slave-mother pressed her tender babe more closely to her breast, as she sent up to the God of the oppressed her silent supplication for deliverance from the men-stealers who were on their track; for those bloodhounds in human shape were in hot pursuit, clothed with the authority of the laws enacted by congress, and now kept in force by this body, and they seized upon those wretched fugitives, and brought them back to this city, and thrust them into yonder prison, erected by the treasure of this nation. There they remained until Friday, the 21st instant, when nearly fifty of them, having been purchased by the infamous 'Hope H. Slatter,' who headed the mob at the jail on Tuesday, were taken in daylight from the prison to the railroad depot and from thence to Baltimore, destined for sale in the far south, there to drag out a miserable existence upon the cotton and sugar plantations of that slave-consuming region.

"The scene at the depot is represented as one which would have disgraced the city of Algiers or Tunis. Wives bidding adieu to their husbands; mothers, in an agony of despair, unable to bid farewell to their daughters; little boys and girls weeping amid the general distress, scarcely knowing the cause of their grief. Sighs, and groans, and tears, and unutterable agony characterized a scene at which the heart sickens, and from which humanity shrinks with horror. Over such a scene that fiend in human shape, Slatter, presided, assisted by some three or four associates in depravity, each armed with pistols, bowie-knife and club. Yes, sir, by virtue of our laws he held these mothers and children, their sisters and brothers, subject to his power, and tore them from all the ties which bind man kind to life, and carried them south, and doomed them to cruel and lingering deaths.

"Sir, do you believe that these members of our body who stubbornly refuse to repeal those laws are less guilty in the sight of a just and holy God than Slatter himself? We, sir, enable him to pursue his accursed vocation, and can we be innocent of those crimes? How long will members of this house continue thus to outrage humanity? How long will the people themselves remain partakers in this enormous wickedness, by sending to this hall men who can here speak of their association with these heaven-daring crimes in the language of ribald jesting? If other members sanction and approve such torture, far more than ordinary murder, *I will not.* It is unbecoming a christian people; it is unsuited to the age in which we live. Why, sir, what a spectacle do we present to the civilized world! Yesterday we assembled with the citizens of the district, in front of this capitol, to rejoice and sing in honor of the people of France, many of whom offered up their lives to attain the liberty which we ourselves enjoy.

"While we were thus collected together, and singing the soul-stirring Marseilles hymn, and shouting praises to our brethren, who, on the other side of the Atlantic, have achieved this freedom, and driven their monarch from his throne and country, a different scene was witnessed on the avenue before us, where some fifty slaves, destined for the southern market, were marched to the railroad depot. The clanking of their chains, their sighs and groans, mingling with our songs and shouts of praise *in favor of liberty*, ascended to heaven, and entered the ear of the God of the oppressed. Yes, sir, while we were thus professing our admiration of freedom, we who now sit in this hall, were at that moment sustaining a slave-market in this city, far more shocking to the feelings of humanity than can be found in any other part of the civilized world."

Mr. Giddings has been always at his post in Washington—has always been faithful to his constituents. He has at all times been ready to meet the south upon any subject involving the question of slavery; he has opposed all compromises with the "institution," and though hated, yet is respected by the slaveholding members of congress.

The sternness which characterizes Mr. Giddings's character, his persevering devotion to principle, has, as a matter of course, made him many enemies, north as well as south. Politicians generally hate men of principle; political leaders, or at least corrupt political leaders, do not like to meet with men who cannot be threatened, or bribed, or cheated. Mr. Giddings has too much spirit to bear a threat, too much principle to entertain a bribe, and too much common sense to be led astray by designing politicians.

WILLIAM CULLEN BRYANT.

Not merely as a poet, a politician, or an editor, is Mr. Bryant distinguished. He is widely known as a philanthropist. His sympathies are always with the unfortunate; and though from his retiring disposition he has had little to do with philanthropic *organizations*, yet he deserves the esteem of all lovers of humanity for his constant, unwavering devotion to the welfare of his race. Though editing a political journal, he has long advocated the cause of the slave with masterly ability, and an impressive sincerity. Long ago, when the abolitionists were subjected to the outrages of mobs, Mr. Bryant came out boldly in his journal in condemnation of the mob-spirit, though at that time it was popular to justify illegal attacks upon the anti-slavery reformers. Since then he has himself become nearly anti-slavery in his feelings and principles, and in his journal has not hesitated to rebuke his party friends, though high in office, for their zeal in extending the institution of slavery.

Mr. Bryant was born at Cummington, Massachusetts, on the 3d of November, 1794. His father was a physician of good education and respectable talents.

He early saw in his boy the germ of a brilliant genius, and spared no pains in his education. At a very early age, the boy wrote poetry. When but thirteen years old, he wrote two poems of considerable length, which were published in a book form. In 1810 he entered Williams' College, where he distinguished himself in the languages, and in polite letters. He remained there two years, when desiring to leave, he sought and obtained an honorable dismissal. He at once commenced the study of the law, and was admitted to practice at the bar in Plymouth, Mass., in the year 1815. He continued to practice his profession till 1825, when he removed to New York. His famous poem, perhaps his best, "Thanatopsis," was written in 1821, or at least published during that year in a volume with others. He was married in 1825, and one year after he assumed the proprietorship and editorship of the *New York Evening Post*, one of the oldest and most influential democratic journals in the country. He has ever since been connected with that paper, adding much to its usefulness and popularity. Of Mr Bryant's person and manners, we can say little, but will quote from the "*Homes of American Authors*," upon this head, premising that "Roslyn" is his country seat, a little away from New York:

"Mr. Bryant's habits of life have a smack of asceticism, although he is the disciple of none of the popular schools which, under various forms, claim to rule the present world in that direction. Milk is more familiar to his lips than wine, yet he does not disdain the 'cheerful hour' over which moderation presides. He eats sparingly of animal food, but he is by no means afraid to enjoy roast goose lest he should outrage the manes of his ancestors, like some modern enthusiasts. He 'hears no music,' if it be fantastical, yet his ear is finely attuned to the varied harmonies of wood and wave. His health is delicate, yet he is almost never ill; his life laborious, yet carefully guarded against excessive and exhausting fatigue. He is a man of rule, but none the less tolerant of want of method in others; strictly self-governed, but not prone to censure the unwary or the weak-willed. In religion he is at once catholic and devout, and to moral excellence no soul bows lower. Placable, we can, perhaps, hardly call him, for impressions on his mind are almost indelible; but it may with the strictest truth be said, that it requires a great offense or a great unworthiness to make an enemy of him, so strong is his sense of justice. Not amid the bustle and dust of the political arena, cased in armor offensive and defensive, is a champion's more intimate self to be estimated, but in the pavilion or the bower, where, in robes of ease, and with all professional ferocity laid aside, we see his natural form and complexion, and hear, in placid domestic tones, the voice so lately thundering above the fight. So we willingly follow Mr. Bryant to Roslyn; see him musing on the pretty rural bridge that spans the fish-pond; or taking the oar in his daughter's fairy boat; or pruning his trees; or talking over farming matters with his neighbors; or—to return to the spot whence we set out some time ago—sitting calm and happy in that pleasant library, surrounded by the friends he loves to draw around him, or listening to the prattle of infant voices, quite as much at home there as under their own more especial roof—his daughter's—within the same inclosure.

"In person, Mr. Bryant is quite slender, symmetrical, and well poised; in carriage, eminently firm and self-possessed. He is fond of long rural walks and of gymnastic exercises—on all which his health depends. Poetical composition tries him severely—so severely, that his efforts of that kind are necessarily rare. His are no holiday verses; and those who urge his producing a long poem are, perhaps, proposing that he should, in gratifying their admiration, build for himself a monument in which he would be self-enveloped. Let us rather content ourselves with asking 'a few more of the same,' especially of the later poems, in which, certainly, the poet trusts his fellows with a nearer and more intimate view of his inner and peculiar self, than was his wont in earlier times. Let him more and more give human voice to woods and waters; and, in acting, as the accepted interpreter of nature, speak fearlessly to the heart as well as the eye. His countrymen were never more disposed to hear him with delight; for, since the public demand for his poems has placed a copy in every house in the land, the taste for them has steadily increased, and the national pride in the writer's genius become a generous enthusiasm, which is ready to grant him an apotheosis while he lives."

We shall not attempt to criticise Mr. Bryant as a poet. An anonymous critic says, and justly, we think:

"His versification is preëminently fine. In rythmic melody and cadence, his lines have few equals, and no superiors. His diction is admirable, being pure, polished, and gemmed perpetually with picturesque and felicitously graphic epithets. In these respects he need not shrink from competition with the highest on the bardic roll of Anglo-Saxondom.

"As hitherto manifested, however, his poetic faculty (as I said before) is neither very fruitful, various, nor comprehensive. His forte would seem to be a most life-like portraiture of natural scenery, wherein is developed with impressive exactitude the moral significance of these works of the Creative Hand.

"Of his original poems, most are of this strain. And the same meditative temper, which signalizes this, his favorite class of effusions, follows him into whatever spheres else he may occasionally enter. Witness his 'Ages,' a lengthened and beautiful resume of man's historic evolution. Note also his 'Lines to a Waterfowl,' a gem of rarest water, with a fully corresponding setting, whose final stanza utters a moral alike transcendantly beautiful and religiously sublime."

A few stanzas from some of his finest poems, it may not be improper for us to quote—especially from those which give evidence of his warm sympathy for the poor and down-trodden. Of this latter class he has written many poems which are calmly, sadly beautiful.

One of his poems oft read and oft quoted, is entitled

THE AFRICAN CHIEF.

Chained in the market-place he stood,
  A man of giant frame,
Amid the gathering multitude
  That shrunk to hear his name.
All stern of look, and strong of limb,
  His dark eye on the ground,
And silently they gazed on him,
  As on a lion bound.

Vainly but well that chief had fought,
  He was a captive now;
Yet pride, that fortune humbles not,
  Was written on his brow.
The scars his dark, broad bosom wore,
  Showed warrior true and brave,
A prince among his tribe before,
  He could not be a slave!

Then to his conqueror he spake:—
  "My brother is a king;
Undo this necklace from my neck,
  And take this bracelet ring.
And send me where my brother reigns,
  And I will fill thy hands
With store of ivory from the plains,
  And gold-dust from the sands."

"Not for thy ivory nor thy gold
  Will I unbind thy chain;
That bloody hand shall never hold
  The battle-spear again.
A price thy nation never gave
  Shall yet be paid for thee;
For thou shalt be the Christian's slave,
  In lands beyond the sea."

Then wept the warrior chief, and bade
  To shred his locks away;
And, one by one, each heavy braid
  Before the victor lay.
Thick were the platted locks, and long,
  And closely hidden there
Shone many a wedge of gold among
  The dark and crisped hair.

"Look, feast thy greedy eye with gold,
  Long kept for sorest need;
Take it—thou askest sums untold,
  And say that I am freed.
Take it—my wife, the long, long day
  Weeps by the cocoa tree,
And my young children leave their play,
  And ask in vain for me."

"I take thy gold—but I have made
  Thy fetters fast and strong,
And ween that by the cocoa shade
  Thy wife will wait thee long."
Strong was the agony that shook
  The captive's frame to hear,
And the proud meaning of his look
  Was changed to mortal fear.

His heart was broken—crazed his brain
  At once his eye grew wild;
He struggled fiercely with his chain,
  Whispered, and wept, and smiled;
Yet wore not long those fatal bands,
  And once at shut of day,
They drew him forth upon the sands,
  The foul hyena's prey.

This poem is one of the most beautiful and pathetic ever written by an American bard. Its simplicity is striking, yet it is one of its beauties. The last verse is not often surpassed—especially this line:

"Whispered, and wept, and smiled."

In this little poem the poet preaches a more eloquent anti-slavery sermon, than was ever delivered from the pulpit—a more touching oration against human chattelism, than was ever pronounced from the platform.

There are so many exquisite passages in the poems of Bryant, that in quoting them one knows not when or where to stop. His great poems—Thanatopsis, The Prairies, etc., etc., are so well known, that we will not extract from them here, but will close the sketch with one of his most finished, perfect pieces. It is well known, but will bear reading again and again.

TO A WATERFOWL.

Whither midst falling dew,
While glow the heavens with the last steps of day,
Far, through their rosy depths, dost thou pursue
Thy solitary way?

Vainly the fowler's eye
Might mark thy distant flight to do thee wrong
As, darkly painted on the crimson sky,
Thy figure floats along.

Seek'st thou the plashy brink
Of weedy lake, or marge of river wide,
Or where the rocking billows rise and sink
On the chafed ocean side?

There is a Power whose care
Teaches thy way along that pathless coast,—
The desert and illimitable air,—
Lone wandering, but not lost.

All day thy wings have fanned,
At that far height, the cold, thin atmosphere,
Yet stoop not, weary, to the welcome land,
Though the dark night is near.

And soon that toil shall end;
Soon shall thou find a summer home, and rest,
And scream among thy fellows; reeds shall bend,
Soon o'er thy sheltered nest.

Thou'rt gone; the abyss of heaven
Hath swallowed up thy form; yet, on my heart
Deeply hath sunk the lesson thou hast given,
And shall not soon depart.

He who, from zone to zone,
Guides through the boundless sky thy certain flight,
In the long way that I must tread alone,
Will lead my steps aright.

LYMAN BEECHER, D. D.

We believe it was Theodore Parker who said that Dr. Beecher was "the father of more brains than any other man in America." The saying is a just one; and not only is Lyman Beecher the *father* of brains, but he is the *possessor*. If he were simply the father of such an illustrious set of children, it would not be out of place for us to sketch him here; but inasmuch as he is one of the pioneers of reform in this country, it would be improper not to say a few words about him.

Dr. Beecher is a thoroughly *original* character. He is unlike any one else,—unless it be his own children, upon whom he has impressed his own character. He is one of the most popular public men in the country, though he is one of the boldest thinkers and most earnest actors. His energy of character is greater than that of any other living American. He was born just as the fires of the revolution were kindling, and it would seem as if the energy, patriotism, and ardor of those days were stamped at an early age upon his character. The date of his birth is October 12, 1775; the place, a house still standing on the corner of George and College streets, New Haven. His ancestors were godly men, men of strong constitutions and iron frames. His father was a blacksmith; his mother was a woman of fine, joyous spirits, always full of hope. He was named after his mother's family—Lyman—and was brought up by his uncle, Lot Benton, of North Guilford, Connecticut. He was a feeble, seven months' child, his mother dying four days after his birth. His uncle Lot was an erratic, yet kind-hearted old man. He one day asked Lyman if he wanted to go to College, and upon his answering in the affirmative, without another word he sent him to a preparatory school, and, when he was fitted, to college. He entered Yale college in September, 1793, at the age of eighteen. Many stories are told of him while in college, illustrating his energy and eccentricity of character.

He was first settled, we believe, in East Hampton, L. I., where several of his children were born. He next removed to Litchfield, Connecticut, where Mrs. Stowe and Henry Ward Beecher were born. While in Litchfield he wrote and preached his famous "Six Sermons" on temperance. It required a vast deal of genuine courage at that day to preach total abstinence from the pulpit, but having become thoroughly convinced of his duty, the brave man did it, and left the consequences with his Maker.

From Litchfield the doctor went to an influential Presbyterian church in Boston; soon after, he went through with a trial for heresy, being guilty of believing in what are termed new school theological doctrines. He next accepted the presidency of Lane Seminary, and remained at that post, accomplishing a vast amount of good by his example and his instructions, until 1850. A thousand anecdotes are told of the good man, which exhibit his singular yet noble character. A few of them we will quote, as they show us the man better than mere description can. The following illustrates his comical nature:

"One dark night, as he was driving home with his wife and Mrs. Stowe in the carriage, the whole party were upset over a bank about fifteen feet high. They had no sooner extricated themselves from the wreck, than Mrs. Beecher and Mrs. Stowe, who were unhurt, returned thanks for their providential escape. 'Speak for yourselves,' said the doctor, who was feeling his bruises, 'I have got a good many hard bumps any how.'"

This one his liberality:

"One day his wife had given him from the common purse twenty-five or thirty dollars in bills, with particular instructions to buy a coat, of which he stood in need. He went down to the city to make the purchase, but stopping on the way at a meeting in behalf of foreign missions, the box was handed round, and in went his little roll of bills. He forgot his coat in his anxiety for the Sandwich Islanders."

The following is a college anecdote:

"One night Mr. Beecher was awakened by a sound at his window, as if some one were drawing a cloth through a broken pane of glass; springing up, he dimly saw his clothes disappearing through a broken window—a thief having taken a fancy to them. Waiting for no ceremonies of toilet, he dashed out through the door after him. The rascal dropped the clothes at once, and put himself to his best speed. But Lyman was not the man to be easily out-run, especially when thus stripped to the race. After dodging a few times, and turning several corners, the caitiff was seized and marched back by the eager student. He ushered him into his room, compelled him to lie down on the floor by the side of his bed, while he, more comfortably ensconced in his bed, lay the night long watching him;—the silence being broken only by an occasional "*Lie still, sir.*" In the morning the culprit was taken before a magistrate, who was evidently a lineal descendant of Justice Shallow. The magistrate, after hearing the particulars, asked Mr. Beecher, 'whether in turning the corners he lost sight of the man at all.' He replied, that he was out of sight but a second, for he was close upon him. 'Ah, well, if you lost sight of him *at all*, you cannot swear to his identity,' and so the man was discharged. Mr. B. met the fellow several times afterward, but could not catch his eye."

The anecdotes which follow, have floated singly or in pairs over the country for years. J. Ross Dix has gathered them together in his "Pulpit Portraits," and they are too good to be overlooked:

"In a trip along the coast of Connecticut in a small craft for his health, being detained by baffling winds, it was in the midst of church service, on a sabbath morning, that he landed at a village where only the clergyman knew him. His was in full sea rigging. His entrance to the audience room attracted no attention. But when, during the prayer, after sermon, he walked up the aisle, and began to ascend the pulpit steps, all eyes were on him. The young people tittered, and the *tithing men* began to look authoritative, as if business was on hand. The officiating clergyman, at the close of his prayer, cordially shook him by the hand, to the growing surprise of spectators—not lessened by the doctor's rising to make some 'additional remarks.' 'When I began,' we once heard the doctor say, 'I could see all the good and sober people looking rather grave at such an appearance, while all the young people winked at each other, as if they expected some sport. But it was not long before I saw the old folks begin to look up and smile, and the young folks to look sober.' If any one has heard Dr. Beecher in one of his best moods, in an extemporaneous outburst, they can well imagine with what power an application would come from him, and how the sudden transitions of feeling, and the strange contrasts between his weather-beaten appearance and seaman's garb, and his impassioned eloquence, would heighten the effect. When he concluded, he turned to the pastor and said, 'how could you have such a grand sermon without any application?' 'I wrote out the body of the sermon, meaning to extemporize the application, but after you came in it scared it out of my head.'

"He once received from several ladies of his church a sum

of money for his wife, to be used in the purchase of a carpet. It was put into his vest pocket, and of course forgotten. There was, about this time, an effort on foot to build an orthodox church in a neighboring village, in which the doctor took great interest. Meeting a gentleman engaged in the enterprise, the doctor expressed a wish to give something himself. Ransacking his pockets, he discovered this carpet money, and expressed great surprise at its unexpected presence. 'Why—when did I get this? I am sure I do not remember this money! Well, it is plain Providence provided it for this cause.' Accordingly it was given. Not many weeks after, the lady donors called, expecting to see a new carpet on their pastor's parlor. Nothing was known about it by the good wife. The doctor was summoned, and the case stated. 'There, that was it! I remember now. It must have been the money I gave for that church.'

"When he was sixty-eight or seventy years of age, he visited a son in the interior of Indiana. One of the young men in the village kindly volunteered to go out with the doctor to hunt. After some success, they took a little circuit each of his own. Hearing the doctor's gun, Mr. V. made toward him, and to his surprise, saw the doctor, boots and coat off, about twenty feet up a tree, and making his way nimbly. 'Doctor, what are you doing?' 'I shot a squirrel, and he ran into that hole, and I am determined to have him out.' It was only on the promise of his young friend that he would go up and eject him, that he consented to give over his perilous climbing.

"When about seventy-five years of age, he spent a fortnight in the eastern part of Maine. A party of gentlemen at Calais, went with him upon a little expedition into the Indian territories, spending several days there hunting and fishing. When about to embark upon a chain of lakes in birch canoes, the Indian guide, Etienne, rather objected to so old a man attempting the adventure, fearing that he would give out. He did not know his man. The doctor rowed with the best of the youngsters; caught more trout than all the party together, and returned each day from the various tramps, in the lead; eat his fish on a rock, with a sea-biscuit for a trencher, and fingers for knives and forks: slept on the ground, upon hemlock branches under a tent, and, at length, the Indian guide went from the extreme of depreciation to the highest expression of admiration in his power,—saying, 'Ah! old man all Indian?'

"While residing on Long Island, in early life, he was returning home just at evening from a visit to old Dr. Woolworth. Seeing what he thought, in the dark, to be a rabbit by the road-side, a little ahead, he reasoned with himself—'They are rather tender animals—if the fellow sits still till I come up, I think I could hit him with these books,' a goodly bundle of which he had in his handkerchief. Hit him he surely did; only it proved to be not a rabbit, but a skunk. The logical consequences followed, and he returned to his family in anything but the *odor* of sanctity. In after life, being asked why he did not reply to a scurrilous attack which had been made upon him, the doctor answered, 'I discharged a quarto once at a skunk, and I then made up my mind never to try it again.'

"During the prevalence of a revival in his church in Boston, the number of persons desiring religious conversation was so great, sometimes amounting to several hundred, that he was accustomed to employ younger clergymen to assist him. On one occasion, a young Andoverian was conversing with a person, who believed herself to be converted, within the doctor's hearing. The young man was probing the grounds of her evidence, and among other questions was overheard asking the lady if she 'thought that she was willing to be damned for the glory of God?' Instantly starting up, the doctor said to him, 'What was that you were asking?' I was asking her if she would be willing to be damned for the glory of God.' 'Well, sir, would *you* be willing?' 'Yes, sir, I humbly hope I should be.' 'Well, then, sir, you *ought* to be damned.' And, afterward, he took occasion to enlighten him to a better theology. His absorption in thought gave rise to absent-mindedness and to forgetfulness, frequently to ludicrous stories. On several occasions he entered his neighbors' houses in Boston, for his own, and was only awakened to the truth by the appearance of the kind mistress, who saluted him with 'Good morning, doctor; we are happy to see you here.' But, in one case, in another mansion, where the good woman had a sweet heart, but a sour tongue, the salutation was more piquant:— 'Doctor, if you can't find your own house, I wish you would hire a man to go and show you.' Well, it is not very comfortable to have a neighbor walk into your parlor, with two or three clergymen in train, appropriate your chairs, call for the servants, and even stand at the foot of the stairs, calling out, 'My dear—my dear! will you come down?' Hundreds of stories related of the doctor are mere fictions, or ascriptions to him of things belonging to other men. He once said, if I should write my own life, the first volume should contain the things which I did *not do* and did *not say*. Nevertheless, not a few are authentic."

Dr. Beecher, physically, is not a large man; indeed, is rather small, but he is firmly, strongly made. His head is large; the hair combed straight back from his forehead, giving him a bold and fearless look, which comports well with his character. His eyes are light blue, his nose is prominent, mouth large, and his complexion is florid. A stranger would hardly think, upon seeing Dr. Beecher in the pulpit, and not knowing him, that a great man was before him. Says a good critic of pulpit eloquence:

"Well do I remember the first time I heard him preach. It was seventeen years ago. From early childhood I had been taught to reverence the name of the great divine and orator, and I had long promised myself the pleasure of listening to him. My first Sunday morning in Cincinnati found me sitting with his congregation. The pastor was not as punctual as the flock. Several minutes had elapsed after the regular hour for beginning the service, when one of the doors opened, and I saw a hale looking old gentleman enter. As he pulled off his hat, half a dozen papers, covered with notes of sermons, fluttered down to the floor; the hat appeared to contain a good many more. Stooping down and picking them up deliberately, he came scuttling down the aisle, with a step so quick and resolute, as rather to alarm certain prejudices I had on the score of clerical solemnity. Had I met him on a parade ground, I should have singled him out as some general in undress, spite of the decided stoop contracted in study; the iron-gray hair brushed stiffly toward the back of the head; the keen, sagacious eyes, the firm, hard lines of the brown and wrinkled visage, and the passion and power latent about the mouth, with its long and scornful under lip, bespoke a character more likely to attack than to suffer. His manner did not change my first impression. The ceremonies preliminary to the sermon were dispatched in rather a summary way. A petition in the long prayer was expressed so pithily I have never forgotten it.

"I forget now what reprehensible intrigue our rulers were busy in at the time, but the doctor, after praying for their adoption of various useful measures, alluded to their conduct in the following terms: 'And, O Lord, grant we may not despise our rulers; and grant they may not act so, that we can't help it.' It may be doubted whether any English bishop has ever uttered a similar prayer for king and parliament. To deliver his sermon, the preacher stood bolt upright, stiff as a musket. At first, he twitched off and replaced his spectacles a dozen times in as many minutes, with a nervous motion, gesturing meanwhile with frequent pump-handle strokes of his right arm; but as he went on, his unaffected language began to glow with animation, his simple style became figurative and graphic, and flashes of irony lighted up the dark groundwork of his puritanical reasoning. Smiles and tears chased each other over the faces of many in the audience. His peroration was one of great beauty and power. I have heard him hundreds of times since, and he has never failed to justify his claim to the title of 'the old man eloquent.'

The "father of the Beechers" is worthy of everlasting remembrance, *because of his manliness.* We want *iron men* in these days, more than we want splendid preachers or passionate poets. Lyman Beecher has infused into the ministry a new spirit of reform. He is a living rebuke to all ministerial cowards. He has lived a life of incessant toil, yet has habituated himself to such manly recreations that he has not been obliged to waste one half his existence in recovering lost health. One hundred such men can revolutionize a nation, for they impress themselves ineffaceably upon their generation.

Engraved by J. C. Buttre.

HENRY WARD BEECHER.

Henry Ward Beecher is one of the most popular men in America, and at the same time he is one of our most radical reformers. He is the pulpit reformer—the man who thunders forth the most unpopular truths, every Sunday, from his pulpit, to an audience consisting not of independent country farmers, who have little temptation to do wrong, or young enthusiasts without prudence or position in society—but of sober, staid merchants, and their sons and daughters. No pulpit orator in this country is more fearless in his utterance of truth than Mr. Beecher; yet he is loved and admired by his church and congregation. The reason is, that while he always insists upon being independent, he is at the same time manly and honest. His denunciations of oppression and oppressors do not proceed from a soured mind, but from a profound sympathy with the oppressed. It is at once evident to his hearers that he is agonizing over the wrongs of the poor; and in that frame of mind, with his great heart, it is impossible for him not to pour forth with astonishing power his convictions of right—his hot censures upon those who deliberately and purposely tread the poor beneath their feet. To gain any just idea of Mr. Beecher's style of eloquence he must be seen in the pulpit. The moment that he arises to commence religious service the listener is struck with his manly, vigorous appearance. There is nothing soft or bland in his manners; he reads a hymn, or a chapter from the bible, in a clear, firm tone of voice, or utters a prayer, not as if he were studying to so modulate his sentences as to create an effect, but as if he were really wrestling with his Maker. We by no means would give the idea that he is harsh, coarse, and without a proper manner, for such is not the case. We have heard him pray when every word sounded like the moaning sob of a child upon the heart of its mother; so too we have heard him launch his electrical eloquence at the heads of notorious sinners in the most impassioned, declamatory manner. But we were saying, when he rises in the pulpit his *manliness* strikes first upon the attention of the stranger, and next his eager, almost terrible earnestness. He scarcely ever writes out his sermons, but comes into the pulpit with but a few rough notes before him. This allows him a command over his audience which he could not hold were he confined to written sermons. He seems to be talking directly to each individual hearer. There is no escape; he bends over the pulpit and looks you in the face; he intends that you shall not go home without appropriating a portion of the discourse to yourself. You come perhaps prejudiced against him. You have heard that he is harsh, impudent, and an unpleasant orator; but when you have heard his opening prayer, you feel inclined to give a candid hearing to what so sincere, so honest a man can say. To tell the truth, your prejudices have half melted before a word of the sermon is uttered. He does not open abruptly, but in a clear, straightforward manner lays the subject before his congregation. By and by he warms up with his subject. Is it upon intemperance or slavery? With what vigor does he expose the wickedness of the rum-traffic, or the traffic in human flesh! How clearly he unfolds the law of God! How plainly exhibits the loving humanity of Christ! He draws a picture of the poor hunted fugitive; he leads you among the cotton fields of the fair, sunny south, where the breezes are scented with orange blossoms; and there he asks you to listen to the heart-broken sighs of some miserable slave mother, parted from her children. His voice and manner are not vehement, though solemnly in earnest. His manly tones are modulated by feeling; there is a slight tremble in his words; his eyes overrun with tears! You are weeping yourself, for your sympathies are touched. He grows more impassioned—passes from the slave to *the master!* His voice changes; his manner grows more declamatory; his tears are dried. You leap along with him, and as he smites the oppressor with God's truth, you have no thought of rebuking him for vehemence; he expresses your own thoughts in better language than you could command. But before he is done he smites *you*; he charges those before him with indifference to this giant wrong; he tells them that the blood of the oppressed will be found on their skirts, for conniving at the servitude of three millions of their fellow-men.

It is the same with every subject; he is fearless yet tender, vehement yet gentle. He preaches few of what are called doctrinal sermons, but he dwells often and fully upon the wonderful love of God—upon the every day duties of men. He never preaches upon "the exceeding sinfulness of sin," but addresses himself to *sinners*. But though he is bold, he rarely offends any honest inquirer after truth. Such a mind likes his frankness—is charmed by his boldness—is moved to tears by his pathos.

There are some who charge Mr. Beecher with uttering irreverent, witty things in the pulpit. He *is* sometimes almost humorous in the pulpit, but it is because he cannot help it. It is as natural for him to speak his thoughts in an *original* manner, as it is for some clergymen to preach stupidities. Occasionally a sentence drops from his lips which starts the smile upon the faces of his audience. He intended no wit, but the odd comparison, or the sparkling sentence bursts forth involuntarily. To set down and snarl over this feature of his pulpit oratory, when there are others so rare and attractive, is the mark of a small intellect and a still smaller heart.

We have spoken of the contrasts presented in Mr. Beecher's sermons—they are *in the man*. His own character is full of contrasts—his writings are the same. No man has a more refined love of the beautiful. We cannot resist the temptation to copy one of his most exquisite sketches of a country scene, and when we have done that we will contrast it with one of his vehement, magnificent outbursts against despotism and wrong. The article which we quote is entitled—

TROUTING.

Where shall we go? Here is the More brook, the upper part running through bushy and wet meadows, but the lower part flowing transparently over the gravel, through the grass and pasture grounds near the edge of the village, where it curves and ties itself into bow knots. It is a charming brook in which to catch trout, when you catch them, but they are mostly caught.

"Well, there is the Caney brook. We will look at that. A man might walk through the meadows and not suspect its existence. The grass meets over the top of its upper section and quite hides it; and below, through that iron tinctured marsh land, it expands only a little, growing open-hearted by degrees, across a narrow field; and then it runs for the thickets—and he who takes fish among those alders will certainly earn them. Yet, for its length, it is not a bad brook. The trout are not numerous, nor large, nor especially fine; but every one you catch renews your surprise that you should catch *any* in such a ribbon of a brook. Still farther north is another stream, something larger, and much better or worse, according to your luck. It is easy of access, and quite unpretending. There is a bit of a pond some twenty feet in diameter, from which it flows, and in that there are five or six half-pound trout, who seem to have retired from active life, and given themselves to meditation in its liquid convent. They were very tempting, but quite untemptable. Standing afar off, we selected an irresistible fly, and with a long line we sent it pat into the very place. It fell like a snow-flake. No trout should have hesitated a moment. The morsel was delicious. The nimblest of them should have flashed through the water, broken the surface, and with a graceful but decisive curve plunged downward, carrying the insect with him. Then we should in our turn, very cheerfully have lent him a hand, relieved him of his prey, and admiring his beauty but pitying his untimely fate, buried him in the basket. But he wished no translation. We cast our fly again and again; we drew it hither and thither; we made it skip and wriggle; we let it fall splash, like a surprised miller; and our audience calmly beheld our feats.

"Next we tried ground bait, and sent our vermicular hook down to their very sides. With judicious gravity they parted, and slowly sailed toward the root of an old tree on the side of the pool. Again changing place, we will make an ambassador of a grasshopper. Laying down our rod, we prepare to catch the grasshopper; that is in itself no slight feat. The first step you take at least forty bolt out, and tumble headlong into the grass; some cling to the stumps, some are creeping under the leaves, and not one seems to be in reach. You step again; another flight takes place, and you eye them with a fierce penetration, as if you could catch some one with your eye. You cannot, though. You brush the ground with your foot again—another hundred snap out, and tumble about in every direction. At length you see a very nice young fellow climbing a steeple stem. You take a good aim and grab him. You catch the spire, but he has jumped a safe rod. Yonder is another, creeping among some delicate ferns. With broad palm you clutch him, and all the neighboring herbage too. Stealthily opening your little finger, you see his leg; the next finger reveals more of him; and opening the next you are just beginning to take him out with the other hand, when out he bounds and leaves you to renew your entomological pursuits. Twice you snatch handfuls of grass, and cautiously open your hand to find that you have only grass. It is very vexatious. There are thousands of them here and there, climbing and wriggling on that blade, leaping off from that stalk, twisting and kicking on that vertical spider's web, jumping and bouncing about under your very nose, hitting you in the face, creeping on your shoes, and yet not one do you get. If any tender-hearted person ever wondered how a humane man could bring himself to such cruelty as to impale an insect, let him hunt for a grasshopper in a hot day among tall grass, and when at length he secures one, the affixing him upon the hook will be done without a single scruple, as a mere matter of penal justice, and with judicial solemnity.

"Now then, the trout yonder. We swing our line to the air, and give it a gentle cast toward the desired spot, and a puff of south wind dexterously lodges it in the branch of the tree. You plainly see it strike, and whirl over and over, so that no gentle pull loosens it; you draw it a jerk up and a pull down; you give a series of nimble twitches; you coax it in this way and solicit it in that way in vain. Then you stop and look a moment, first at the trout and then at your line. Was there ever anything so vexatious? Would it be wrong to get angry? In fact, we feel very much like it. The very things you wanted to catch, the grasshopper and the trout, you could not; but a tree, that you did not want, you have caught fast at the first throw. You fear that the trout will be scared. You cautiously draw nigh and peep down. Yes, they are looking at you, and laughing as sure as trout ever laughed. They understand the whole thing. With a very decisive jerk you snap your line, regain the remnant of it, and sit down to repair it, to put on another hook, catch another grasshopper, and move on down stream to catch a trout.

"Meantime the sun is wheeling behind the mountain, for you are just at the eastern ridge of Mount Washington (not of the White Mountains, but in Massachusetts and Connecticut.) Already its broad shade begins to fall down upon the plain. The side of the mountain is solemn and sad. Its ridge stands sharp against a fire-bright horizon. Here and there a tree has escaped the ax of the charcoalers, and shaggily marks the sky. Here and there through the heavens are slowly sailing continents of magnificent fleece mountains—Alps and Andes of vapor. They, too, have their broad shadows. One you see cast upon yonder hill, far to the east, while the base is radiant with the sun. Another cloud-shadow is moving with stately grandeur along the valley of the Housatonic, and if you rise to a little eminence you may see the brilliant landscape growing dull in its sudden obscuration on its forward line, and growing suddenly bright upon its rear trace. How majestically that shadow travels up those steep and precipitous mountain sides! how it sweeps down the gorge and valley! how it moves along the plain!

"But now the mountain shadow is creeping down into the meadow. It has crossed the road where your horse stands hitched to the paling of a deserted little house. You forget your errand. You select a dry, tufty knoll, and lying down you gaze up into the sky. O, those depths! Something within you reaches out and yearns; you have a vague sense of infinity—of vastness—of the littleness of human life, and the sweetness and grandeur of divine life and of eternity. You people the vast ether. You stretch away through it and find that Celestial City beyond, and therein dwell O how many that are yours! Tears come unbidden. You begin to long for release. You pray. Was there ever a better closet? Under the shadow of the mountain, the heavens full of cloudy cohorts, of armies of horsemen and chariots, your soul loosened from the narrow judgments of human life, and touched with a full sense of immortality and the liberty of a spiritual state. An hour goes past. How full has it been of feelings struggling to be thoughts, and of thoughts deliquescing into feeling. Twilight is coming, you have miles to ride home. Not a trout in your basket! Never mind, you have fished in the heavens, and taken great store of prey. Let them laugh at your empty basket. Take their raillery good-naturedly; you have certainly had good luck.

"But we have not yet gone to the brook for which we started. That must be for another tramp. Perhaps one's experience of 'fancy tackle' and of fly-fishing might not be without some profit in moral analogies: perhaps a mountain stream and good luck in real trout may afford some easy side-thoughts not altogether unprofitable for a summer vacation. At any rate, it will make it plain that often the best part of trout fishing is not the fishing."

And now the same poet's hand that drew the above—the same heart which appreciated the tender and beautiful in nature—wrought that which follows. And why not? If we examine closely we shall find that it is the true poet who thunders loudest if needs be against tyrants; we shall see that the gentlest are after all the strongest, the profoundest. Who is gentler than a mother? Whose love is stronger than hers? Who can suffer as she often does for a loved, mayhap ruined, child?

The article from which we make extracts is one in which Mr. Beecher defends his right *in the pulpit* to speak of slavery. He had been attacked by the *Journal of Commerce* for carrying abolitionism into the church, and he thus replies:

"It is vain to tell us that hundreds of thousands of slaves are church members; does that save women from the lust of their owners? does it save their children from being sold? does it save parents from separation? In the shameless processions every week made from the Atlantic to the Gulf, are to be found slaves ordained to preach the gospel, members of churches, baptized children, Sunday-school scholars carefully catechized, full of gospel texts, fat and plump for market. What is religion worth to a slave, except as a consolation from despair, when the hand that breaks to him the bread of communion on Sunday takes the price of his blood and bones on Monday; and bids him God speed on his pilgrimage from old Virginia tobacco fields to the cotton plantations of Alabama?

"What is church fellowship, and church privilege, and church instruction worth, if the recipient is still as much a beast, just as little loved, just as ruthlessly desolated of his family, just as coolly sold, as if he were without God and without hope? What motive is there to the slave to strive for Christian graces, when, if they make him a real man, they are threshed out of him; or if they make him a more obedient and faithful man, raise his market price, and only make him a more merchantable disciple of Christ? It is the religious phase of slave-life that reveals the darkest features of that all-perverting system.

"These things are not new; nor out of the reach of the *Journal of Commerce;* yet when upon this state of facts the christianity of the north, too long unsensitive, lifts up its voice, the *Journal of Commerce* assails it as if it were a monster ravening for its prey! Three million men, against natural law, against every fundamental principle of our state and national government, are, by law, thrown over the pale of the race and denied to be men. This is not fit for the pulpit to mention; it is allowed, nevertheless, to preach about China and India! Every year thousands of children are snatched from their parents' bosoms, and remorselessly sold every whither. The pulpit is not the place for mentioning such things, though it *be* allowed to snatch children from the Ganges, and to mourn over infanticide in Polynesia! Every year husbands and wives are torn asunder, christian or no christian; and the *Journal of Commerce* browbeats that pulpit that utters a word about such politics, when it should rather be busy in expostulating with cannibals in Malaya, or snatching devotees from under the wheels of Juggernaut! Every year thousands of women are lashed for obstinate virtue; and tens of thousands robbed of what they have never been taught to prize; and the *Journal of Commerce* stands poised to cast its javelin at that meddlesome pulpit that dares to speak of such boundless licentiousness, and send it to its more appropriate work of evangelizing the courtesans of Paris, or the loose virtue of Italy; and it assures us that multitudes of clergymen are thanking it for such a noble stand. Some of those clergymen we know. The platforms of our benevolent societies resound with their voices urging christianity to go abroad: stimulating the church not to leave a corner of the globe unsearched, nor an evil unredressed. But when the speech ended, they steal in behind the *Journal of Commerce* to give it thanks for its noble stand against the right of the pulpit to say a word about home heathen—about their horrible ignorance, bottomless licentiousness, and about the mercenary inhumanity which every week is selling their own christian brethren, baptized as much as they, often preachers of the gospel like themselves, eating from the same table of the Lord, praying to the same Savior, listening to snatches of that same bible (whose letters they have never been permitted to learn) out of which these reverend endorsers of the *Journal of Commerce* preach!

"It requires *distance*, it seems, to make a topic right for the pulpit. Send it to Greenland, or to Nootka Sound, and you may then practice at the far-away target. And the reason of such discrimination seems to be, that preaching against foreign sins does not hurt the feelings nor disturb the quiet of your congregation; whereas, if the identical evils at home, which we deplore upon the Indus, or along the Burampootra, are preached about, the *Journal* says that it will risk the minister's place and bread and butter. * * * * * *

"Our laws scarcely recognize a crime against man save murder and violence akin to it, that is not legal under slave laws. There is not a sensual vice which we are taught to abhor, which slavery doth not monstrously engender. There is not a sin which religion condemns, that is not garnered and sown, reaped and sown again, by American slavery. Among freemen the road of honor lies *away* from animal passion, from sensation, toward conscience, hope, love, and spiritual faith. But slavery sharply turns the wretch downward, and teaches and compels him to evolve the task of life from such motives as are common to him with the ox, the ass, and the dog. The slave's pleasures are our appetites. His motives are, almost of necessity, those from which religion most earnestly dehorts us. To our children labor is honorable, because it is God's ordination of mercy; because it is an education; because it is the road alike to health and temperate pleasure; because it is the parent of wealth; because by it the cheerful laborer builds his house, rears his children, gives to them the means of knowledge. By labor the north has subdued nature, changed a parsimonious soil to fertility, built dwellings for almost her whole population, raised the school-house, established the church, encircled the globe with her ships, and made her books and her papers to be as blades of grass and as leaves of summer for number. But in the South, as if unredeemed from the primal curse, labor, a badge of shame, is the father of misery. The slave labors, but with no cheer—it is not the road to respectability—it will honor him with no citizen's trust—it brings no bread to his family—no grain to his garner—no leisure in after days—no books or papers to his children. It opens no school-house door, builds no church, rears for him no factory, lays no keel, fills no bank, earns no acres. With sweat, and toil, and ignorance, he consumes his life to pour the earnings into channels from which he does not drink—into hands that never honor him, but perpetually rob, and often torment.

"This vast abomination, which seethes and smokes in our midst, which is enervating and demoralizing the white by the oppression of the black—in which adultery, fornication and a concubinage so awful exist, that, in comparison with it a Turkish harem is a cradle of virgin purity—which every hour does violence to nature, to the sentiment of justice, and to the embodiment of that sentiment into national law—a system which makes a home impossible, and the word family as much a misnomer as it would be to a stable or a sheep-fold—which subsists only by keeping the subject ignorant—which is obliged to rank and treat the qualities which our community most esteems—independence, ambition, self-reliance, thirst for knowledge, self-respect, as most punishable crimes in the slave—a system whose practice requires what its laws recognize, that man must be subverted—that the slave must be intelligent only for work, and religious only to the extent of obedience—a system which, taking away all inducements to labor natural to man, is obliged to enforce it by suffering, or the fear of suffering; which, denying to the faculties of the soul a natural expression, forces the miserable wretch to cunning and craft, to lying and subterfuge—whose whole natural tendency it is to produce labor upon compulsion and laziness by choice, lying and thieving under a sense of justice, and truth and honesty with a feeling of their injustice—and which, at length, as its worst and most damnable result, so subverts that instinct of liberty which belongs to man the world over, that the slave agrees to his condition, grows fat, and laughs and sings, preferring slavery, with indulgence to eat and drink enough, to liberty, if he must pay the price of that liberty by sustained exertion;—this huge, infernal system for the destruction of men, soul and body, must not be mentioned in the pulpit, lest the Sabbath be desecrated and the peace of the congregation be disturbed.

"We now re-affirm our doctrine of the pulpit.

"The gospel is a system of truths designed to be this world's medicine. It has no intrinsic value as a system. Its end and value are in its power to stimulate the soul, to develop its faculties, to purify its emotions, to cleanse its evils, and to lead forth the whole man into a virtuous and holy life.

J

"The pulpit is therefore the dispensatory of society. The minister, a physician. Preaching, a prescription of medicinal truth for heart evils. There is not an evil which afflicts life, nor a temptation proceeding from any course of life, which the pulpit should not study. The sources of right conduct, the hindrances, the seductions of business, the lures of pleasure, the influences of public life, the maxims of society, its customs, its domestic, commercial and public institutions; in short, whatever directly or indirectly moulds the human character, is to be studied by the minister, and its benefit or its danger made known from the pulpit.

"In this work it is to deal first and most faithfully with the evils of its own age, its own country, its own city, its own congregation. Wherever men go, the pulpit is to follow them with its true light. Whatever invades its province—that province is Right, Humanity, Purity—be it Fashion, Commerce, Politics, they are fearlessly to be met, grasped and measured by the word of God. Not only *may* the pulpit thus explore Life, but it *must*, or else prove bankrupt to Fidelity. It is not to follow the camp; but in spiritual things to *lead* the people. It is not to wait till foes are slain before it raise its spear; nor go asking of political cabals what it may say, nor cringe to supercilious men of commerce; but occupy itself with only this twin thought, how best to please God and benefit man.

"Therefore, against every line of the Coward's Ethics of the *Journal of Commerce* we solemnly protest, and declare a minister made to its pattern fitter to be sent to the pyramids and tombs of Egypt, to preach to old-world mummies, than to be a living man of God among living men, loving them but never fearing them! God be thanked! that in every age hitherto, such pulpits have been found the ally of suffering virtue, the champion of the oppressed. And if in this day, after the notable examples of heroic men in heroic ages, when life itself often paid for fidelity, the pulpit is to be mined and sapped by insincere friends and insidious enemies, and learn to mix the sordid prudence of business with the sonorous and thrice heroic counsels of Christ, then, O my soul, be not thou found conspiring with this league of iniquity! that so, when in that august day of retribution, God shall deal punishment in flaming measure to all hireling and coward ministers, thou shalt not go down, under double-bolted thunders, lower than miscreant Sodom, or thrice-polluted Gomorrah!"

Here is one more sketch in Mr. Beecher's best humorous vein, which we cannot forbear to quote:

BOOK-AUCTIONS, BOOK-STORES, BOOKS.

We have examined the catalogue of books to be sold in ten days, beginning May 24th, by Bangs, Brothers & Co. We have also examined the books themselves, and with sore temptation. This is no ordinary sale. It is not the refuse stock of a bankrupt bookseller; nor a private library, drugged by large infusions of unsaleable books; nor a trade sale of staple books. It is a literary curiosity of itself. The catalogue is a book of no mean literary interest. Mr. Welford, long familiar with rare and curious books, spends many months in England, collecting with good taste, not merely standard editions of standard works, but literary treasures of every sort. Here are works which a man would not have an opportunity of purchasing once in his lifetime, in the ordinary course of affairs. The books are in excellent condition, and in fine bindings.

Nothing marks the growth of the public mind, and the increasing wealth of our times, more than the demand for books. Within ten years the sale of common books has increased probably two hundred per cent., and is daily increasing. But the sale of expensive works, and library editions in costly binding, is yet more noticeable. Ten years ago, and such a display of magnificent works as is to be found at the Appletons' would have been a precursor of bankruptcy. There was no demand for them. A few dozen, in one little show-case, was the prudent whole. Now, one whole side of an immense store is not only filled with most admirably bound library-books, but from some inexhaustible source the void continually made in the shelves is at once re-filled. A reserve of heroic books supply the places of those that fall. Alas! Where is human nature so weak as in a book-store! Speak of the appetite for drink; or a *bonvivant's* relish for dinner! What are these mere animal throes and ragings, to be compared with those fantasies of taste, of imagination, of intellect, which bewilder a student, in a great bookseller's temptation-hall?

How easily one may distinguish a genuine lover of books from the worldly man! With what subdued and yet glowing enthusiasm does he gaze upon the costly front of a thousand embattled volumes! How gently he draws down the volumes, as if they were little children; how tenderly he handles them! He peers at the title-page, at the text, or the notes, with the nicety of a bird examining a flower. He studies the binding: the leather,—Russia, English calf, morocco; the lettering, the gilding, the edging, the hinge of the cover! He opens it, and shuts it, he holds it off, and brings it nigh. It suffuses his whole body with book magnetism. He walks up and down, in a maze, at the mysterious allotments of Providence that gives so much money to men that spend it upon their appetites, and so little to men that would spend it in benevolence, or upon their refined tastes! It is astonishing, too, how one's necessities multiply in the presence of the supply. One never knows how many things it is impossible to do without, till he goes to Windle's or Smith's house-furnishing stores. One is surprised to perceive, at some bazaar, or fancy and variety store, how many *conveniences* he needs. He is satisfied that his life must have been utterly inconvenient aforetime. And thus, too, one is inwardly convicted at Appletons, of having lived for years without books, which he is now satisfied one cannot live without!

Then, too, the subtle process by which the man satisfies himself that he can afford to buy. Talk of Wall street and financiering! No subtle manager or broker ever saw through a maze of financial embarrassments half so quick as a poor book-buyer sees his way clear to pay for what he *must* have. Why, he will economize; he will dispense with this and that; he will retrench here and there; he will save by various expedients hitherto untried; he will put spurs on both heels of his industry; and then, besides all this, he will *somehow* get along when the time for payment comes! Ah! this SOMEHOW! That word is as big as a whole world, and is stuffed with all the vagaries and fantasies that fancy ever bred on hope. And yet, is there not some comfort in buying books, *to be* paid for? We have heard of a sot, who wished his neck as long as the worm of a still, that the draught might taste good so much longer. Thus, it is a prolonged excitement of purchase, if you feel for six months in a slight doubt whether the book is honestly your own or not. Had you paid down, that would have been the end of it. There would have been no affectionate and beseeching look of your books at you, every time you saw them, saying, as plain as a book's eyes can say, "Do not let me be taken from you."

Moreover, buying books before you can pay for them, promotes caution. You dont feel quite at liberty to take them home. You are married. Your wife keeps an account-book. She knows to a penny what you can and what you cannot afford. She has no "speculation" in her eyes. Plain figures make desperate work with airy "somehows." It is a matter of no small skill and and experience to get your books home, and in their places undiscovered. Perhaps the blundering express brings them to the door just at evening. "What is it, my dear?" she says to you. "Oh! nothing—a few books that I cannot do without." That smile! A true housewife, that loves her husband, can smile a whole arithmetic at him at one look! Of course she insists, in the kindest way, in sympathizing with you in your literary acquisition. She cuts the strings of the bundle, (and of your heart,) and out comes the whole story. You have bought a whole set of costly English books, full bound in calf, extra gilt, and admirably lettered.

Now, this must not happen frequently. The books must be smuggled home. Let them be sent to some near place. Then when your wife has a headache, or is out making a call, or has lain down, run the books across the frontier and threshold, hastily undo them, stop only for one loving glance as you put them away in the closet, or behind other books on the shelf, or on the topmost shelf. Clear away the twine and wrapping-paper, and every suspicious circumstance. Be very careful not to be too kind. That often brings on detection. Only the other day, we heard it said somewhere, "Why, how good you have been lately. I am really afraid you have been carrying on mischief secretly." Our heart smote us. It was a fact. That very day we had bought a few books which "we could not do without." After a while you can bring out one volume, accidentally, and leave it on the table. "Why, my dear, *what* a beautiful book! Where *did* you borrow it?" You glance over the newspaper, with the quietest tone you can command: "*That!* oh! that is *mine.* Have you not seen it before? It has been in the house this two months;" and you rush on with anecdote and incident, and point out the binding, and that peculiar trick of gilding, and everything else you can think of; but it all will not do; you cannot rub out that roguish arithmetical smile. People may talk about the equality of the sexes! They are not equal. The silent smile of a sensible, loving woman, will vanquish ten men. Of course you repent, and in time form a habit of repenting.

But we must not forget our errand, which was, to say that lovers of books who desire rare and curious works, should attend the sale of Mr. Welford's books; and they should remember with gratitude that he has removed all temptation from them to buy more than they have the money to pay for, by making the terms cash.

Of Mr. Beecher's personal history we have not much to say. He was born in Litchfield, Connecticut, was educated at Amherst college, Massachusetts, and spent a number of years in the west before accepting a call to preach in Brooklyn, where he is at the present time. When a boy, he was full of the Beecher spirit and independence. We have heard a friend of the family tell a story of young Henry, which illustrates not only the lad's full flow of animal spirits, but the subtle knowledge of human nature possessed by his father. For some cause or other, while pursuing his studies, Henry one day informed his parents that he was *going to sea.* If he could not obtain the consent of his parents, he gave them very distinctly to understand that he could run away—at any rate, he was not going to endure any opposition. To the boy's profound surprise, his father made no objection to his resolution, but the next day coolly informed him, that a tailor should fit him out with a suit of sea-clothes, and that he had written to a maritime friend to make arrangements for his reception on board his ship. He wound up by saying, that he *had* indulged the thought that he (Henry) would go on successfully in his studies until prepared to enter college, and that he would hereafter live a life of honor and usefulness; but that he had decided without advice to adopt a sailor's profession, and he should not be opposed. The more the boy-student thought of the matter, the more he felt. To tell the truth, he threatened to go to sea more to rouse the opposition of his father, than for any other purpose; and now, to be actually *helped off*—it was altogether too bad; and he one morning, with a burst of penitent tears, confessed that he would like to go on with his preparation for college!

At an early age Mr. Beecher was admitted into the ministry. He was overflowing with an enthusiastic desire to preach the truth to the people. He was willing to go anywhere to do this, and was ready to undergo any suffering or privations if only he could preach Christ. He went to the west, and carried light and peace to the lonely cabins of the farmers, and to the rough homes of the artisans. For years he lived among the grand prairies, and he left his impress there in many a home and heart. But a man of such powers of mind could not be allowed to waste himself in any humble place. Just such a man was needed in New York to speak the truth into the ears of the merchants and lawyers of our empire city. More than this: in New York (or rather Brooklyn) a man of his talents would be sure of attracting transient residents from all parts of the Union, and thus he would be felt all over the country. Such is the case. Scarce a merchant goes to New York to buy goods, whether from Maine, Wisconsin, or Ohio, who leaves the city without hearing Henry Ward Beecher preach.

Socially, Mr. Beecher is one of the most interesting men we ever met. He is brim full of anecdote and humour. No man can tell a story better than he—no man can set a circle into a roar quicker than he, nor is he surpassed in all that is affectionate and lovely. He has a big heart, which takes in all his friends. He is half worshipped in his family, and no one wonders at it who knows him.

In his person Mr. Beecher is not very remarkable. He is of medium height, has a firm, independent air, look, and gait, has dark hair, an intelligent eye, and a hearty voice. He dresses well—not finely. He is the exact opposite of a modern fop in dress and manners, for in everything he is *manly*.

Mr. Fowler, the phrenologist, speaking of the main points in his character says:

"The first is the soundness and vigor of his physical constitution. Every bodily organ is strong, and exceedingly active; his vital organs are large, and peculiarly healthy. Only his stomach is in the least degree affected, and that only partially and occasionally. His lungs are very large and very fine; he measures under the arms more than one in thousands, and his muscles are uncommonly dense, sprightly and vigorous. All his motions are quick and elastic, yet peculiarly firm and strong, tossing his body about as if it were as light as a foot-ball—a condition always characteristic of distinguished men; for no man can be talented without a first-rate muscular system. He fosters this condition by taking a great amount of physical exercise, and also of rest and recreation. When he does work, he works with his whole might, until his energies are nearly expended, and then gives up to sleep, relaxation, and cheerful conversation, perhaps for days together, until having again filled up the reservoir of life-power, he becomes capable of putting forth another vigorous effort.

* * * * * * * * *

"The second cardinal point in his character, is the unwonted size of his benevolence. In all my examinations of heads, I have rarely, if ever, found it surpassed, or even equaled. It towers above every other organ in his head, and is the great phrenological center of his brain. While most heads rise higher at firmness than at benevolence, his rises higher at benevolence. It is really enormous, and forms altogether the dominant motive of his life; and this constitutes the second grand instrumentality of his success.

* * * * * * * * *

"His social affections are also large, and working in conjunction with his supreme benevolence, mutually aid and strengthen it. Adhesiveness is very large. I rarely find it as large in men. Hence he makes friends of all, even those who oppose him in doctrine, and is personally attached to them; and this explains one of the instrumentalities by which he so powerfully wins all within range of his influence. They love the man, and therefore receive his doctrines. His philoprogenitiveness is also large; and hence his strong and almost paternal interest in the success of young men just starting in life; for this faculty, rightly directed, especially in public men, extends a helping hand not to physical children merely, but to those who are just starting in life, whatever may be their occupation; and he also preaches most effectually upon the education of children.

"His amativeness is fully developed, yet conjoined with his fine-grained temperament and exalted moral affections, it values woman mainly for her moral purity, and her maternal and other virtues, and seeks the elevation of the sex. Probably few men living place the family relations of parents and children, husbands and wives, upon higher grounds, either practically in his family, or in his public capacity, than Henry Ward Beecher. He is perfectly happy in his family, and his family in him; and this is one cause of his peculiarly bland, persuasive, and winning address.

"His third point of character is his force. This is consequent on his large combativeness and firmness, and his enthusiastic temperament. What he does, he does with all his might. He takes hold of great things as though they could and must be done. Every sentence is uttered with an energy which carries it home to the innermost souls of all who hear; yet his combativeness is never expended in personal defense, or in opposing his enemies, but simply in pushing forward his benevolent operations.

"His destructiveness is fair, but always subordinate.

"Acquisitiveness is almost entirely wanting. I rarely find it as small, and, unlike too many reverends, he never thinks whether this or that sermon or doctrine will increase or diminish his salary, but simply asks whether it is TRUE.

"His firmness is extraordinary, but, acting under his higher faculties, he never evinces obstinacy, but only determination and perseverance in doing good. Though cautiousness renders him careful in taking grounds, yet he is one of the most straightforward men we meet with."

E. H. CHAPIN.

Among the foremost of popular lecturers in America is Rev. E. H. Chapin. He is eminently a social philosopher; a man who does not look upon society merely in the aggregate, as a molten current of flowing humanity, but who views a collection of individuals, each possessing a character, an ambition, an aim exclusively his own. He has so accustomed himself to study out the character, the thoughts and feelings, the hopes and trials of each, that when the subject presents itself to the mind of the lecturer he has the whole picture vividly before his imagination; he paints it from life; he has seen it, has contemplated it in every varying shade in which it could be presented. In his convulsive grasp the miser, the mean man, the political demagogue, and the hypocrite, exhibit to the world all their hideous deformities; while the virtues of the good, the kind, the benevolent, and the noble are beautified by his touch with a perfection hardly native. If he turns his attention to the city, the broad field of humanity is all bare before his gaze. He walks abroad in the street; every man he meets affords him a theme for meditation, and every child a text for a sermon. Not a circumstance of his life seems to have passed but has furnished him the pith of some crammed apothegm, or the parallel for a striking simile. Not a cry of wo has reached his ear but has found the way to his heart, and will come forth again in pathetic beauty to deepen some sketch of human suffering; not a shout of laughter but will reëcho in some vivid sentence to brighten the shade of our humanity. It is this characteristic which has made Mr. Chapin eminently popular among the masses. His learning might have made him a profound rhetorician; his talent and beauty of expression a fine writer; his real native eloquence a splendid orator; but all these could not have made him the *man* that he is. Superadd to these his susceptible heart, his benevolent spirit, his gentle disposition, and christian refinement, and you have Chapin.

He is presented to our notice as a writer, a speaker, a poet—for he has written some beautiful lyrics—a preacher, and a reformer. The last distinction might once have been thought needless, but in the era of Lords—many, of Spragues, of Springs, *et cetera*, we think it essential.

There are few men living from whose writings more beautiful sentences can be taken than from Mr. Chapin's. Here is one upon the blessings of home:

"Oh! mother, mother; name for the earliest relationship, symbol of the divine tenderness; kindling a love that we never blush to confess, and a veneration that we cannot help rendering; how does your mystic influence, imparted from the soft pressure and the undying smile, weave itself through all the brightness, through all the darkness of our after life! * * * And when on this familiar hearth our own vital lamp burns low, and the golden bowl begins to shudder, and the silver cord to untwine, let our last look be upon the faces that we best love; let the gates that open into the celestial city be those well known doors—and thus may *we* also die at home!"

Here also is a fine glimpse of childhood snatched from nature; it is one of a perpetual supply of gems that are strung upon the thread of his discourse:

"And all of us, I trust, are thankful that God has created not merely men and women, crimped into artificial patterns, with selfish speculation in their eyes, with sadness, and weariness, and trouble about many things, carving the wrinkles and stealing away the bloom; but pours in upon us a fresh stream of being that overflows our rigid conventionalisms with the buoyancy of nature, plays into this dusty and angular life like the jets of a fountain, like floods of sunshine, upsets our miserable dignity, meets us with a love that contains no deceit, a frankness that rebukes our quibbling compliments, nourishes the poetry of the soul, and perpetually descending from the threshold of the Infinite, keeps open an archway of mystery and heaven."

In fact, the charm of Mr. Chapin's declamation consists mainly in the beauty and force of his expression. With some men it is the manner; with him the matter. When he would demolish a vice or praise a virtue he first paints the one in hideous truth, or the other with strange beauty, until you loathe the one or love the other. He does not employ his pen in systematizing sin, and shielding the individual behind the organization, or the party, or the association in which he acts, but brings the charge right home to the door of every guilty man's conscience, and if that door be not double barred from the force of truth, will batter down the barricade and lay the load of crime upon the hearthstone of the heart. And here permit a brief illustrating paragraph upon individual responsibility:

"God does not take account of parties; party names are not known in that court of divine judgment; but your name and mine are on the books there. If the party lies, then *you* are guilty of falsehood. If the party—as is very often the case—does a mean thing, then you do it. It is surely so, as far as you are one of the party, and go with it in its action. There is no such thing—and this is true, perhaps, in more senses than one—there is no such thing as a party conscience. It is individual conscience that is implicated. Party! party! Ah, my friends, here is the influence which, it is to be feared, balks and falsifies many of these glorious symbols. Men rally arouna musty epithets. They take up issues which have no more relation to the deep, vital, throbbing interest of the time than they have to the fashions of our grandfathers. * * * And surely it is a case for congratulation, when some great, exciting question breaks out and jars their conventional idols, and so sweeps and shatters their party organization and turns them topsy-turvy, that a man is shaken out of his harness, does not know exactly what party he does belong to, and begins to feel that he has a soul of his own."

This quotation hurries him into our view as a public speaker or lecturer, for we agree with a recent writer that Mr. Chapin is one of the most splendid of American orators. To the platform he brings a stout body, rather heavily proportioned for his height. He is very near-sighted, to palliate which defect he wears glasses, and keeps his eyes and face close to his notes. He generally writes out his address, though in the pulpit he occasionally extemporizes. He is possessed of many of those qualifications which draw full houses, and send them home well satisfied. He is always spirited, nervous, enthusiastic, and often rises into a vein of thrilling eloquence. To a rapid but distinct enunciation he unites a fervor and ardor which is sure to win the profound attention of his audience. His style of thought is quite original, his expression terse and powerful, and as he becomes warmed with his subject his excitement spreads as by a magic influence to the listeners. Where at first he only caught the attention by some eccentric description of a human animal, he now rivets it by a more gloomy picture. Where a moment since you were only interested, you are now watching intensely to devour his words with eager avidity as they fall. Gradually you forget that any one is in the room but yourself and the speaker. On he leads you and with you every soul in his audience to feed on new fruits of intellect, and dazzle with new diamonds from his brilliant imagination. Scarcely are your sympathies apoise and your eyes ready to pay the "draft on sight," when a pungent satire brings down the house with a tumult of applause. Then away his fancy flies in a new direction; all the beauties of heaven rise up in beatific vision to the enraptured gaze. Spread out before you are fields of living green, and streamlets from eternal mind, in every direction, through gardens of surpassing loveliness. From those ever blooming flowers celestial odors are wafted down to earth. Angelic choirs fill the great dome of heaven with music too enchanting for mortal ears, yet you seem to catch the faint echoes. Over all the scene a blaze of glory falls from "Him that liveth and sitteth upon the throne." All is still, for all are wrapt in the magnificent dream-mantle with which he has enveloped you; the climax is at length reached, and when in a clear, melodious voice he repeats the chorus, "Blessing and honor and glory be unto Him that sitteth upon the throne and to the Lamb for ever and ever," you can hardly restrain yourself from shouting "hallelujah," like a Methodist.

This strange fascination Mr. Chapin wields, alike over young and old. Most of the popular speakers of our day have a class which it is their peculiar forte to please. But Mr. Chapin pleases all. The high and low, the rich and poor, the cultivated intellect and the untutored mind of the laborer, the aristocrat and the democrat are alike charmed by the wonderful beauty of his eloquence. Without adulatory flattery, he compliments the virtues of the generous, and, without giving offense, chastises the defects of the parsimonious. With a keen knife he removes a vice as a skillful surgeon excises a tumor, having first made the patient see that it is absolutely necessry for his health. If he applies an acrid irritant, you are confident that the deep-seated disease could be removed in no other way, and are satisfied.

As a poet, the world only regrets that he has written so little. Who has not read and admired that sweet poem—"Oh bury me not in the deep blue sea?" Half of his prose is in measured periods, and all of it tinged with the rich blush of his splendid imagination.

We were to glance at his character as a minister of the gospel. It is well known that Mr. Chapin is an able champion of the doctrine of universal salvation. We have neither time nor inclination to inquire now what is the foundation of his belief. That he is sincere in it, probably few will dispute; and it makes him a better man and more like a christian, than many who profess a more orthodox faith. By his own congregation, at least, he is deemed an earnest laborer, and by others, a mistaken workman in the great harvest. By all it is admitted that he is extensively useful. His idea of religion is well given by himself, in the following passage:

"It must be understood that 'being religious' is not a work apart by itself, but a spirit of faith and righteousness, flowing out from the center of a regenerated heart, into all the employments and intercourse of the world. Not merely the preacher in the pulpit, and the saint on his knees, may do the work of religion, but the mechanic, who smites with the hammer and drives the wheel; the artist, seeking to realize his pure ideal of the beautiful; the mother, in the gentle offices of home; the statesman, in the forlorn hope of liberty and justice; and the philosopher, whose thoughts tread reverently among the splendid mysteries of the universe. * * * It is needed that men should feel that every lawful pursuit is sacred and not profane; that every position in life is close to the steps of the divine throne; and that the most beaten and familiar paths lie under the awful shadow of the Infinite; and they will go about their daily pursuits, and fill their common relationships, with hearts of worship, and pulses of unselfish love, instead of regarding religion as an isolated peculiarity for a corner of the closet and a fraction of the week, and leaving all the rest of time and space an unconsecrated waste, where lawless passions travel, and selfishness pitches its tents."

We leave the diversity of theories for those who take a deeper interest in metaphysical disquisition than we, and turn to the contemplation of his character as a reformer. If we have rightly estimated his talents and training, he is the man, of all others, who would be selected to lead the sympathies of a progressive age. His main efforts have been directed in two channels: one, the relief of the poor, the degraded, and the outcast about him; the other, to the cause of temperance generally. In pleading the cause of "humanity in the city," no one has labored more faithfully than Mr. Chapin. He seems acquainted with every phase of their wretched life. He enumerates the causes of their destitution, and points them to the remedy. Their miserable condition comes home to his philanthropic spirit, and spurs him to vigorous action. No matter how low-sunken may be the victim of appetite or lust, he reaches out the helping hand, with a dollar in it, and says, "Brother, take courage, you may yet be a man." The assurance inspires the wanderer with new life, and he forgets, for a time, that "no man cares for his soul," or his body either. He takes confidence, and goes on his way rejoicing.

For the young men of New York Mr. Chapin has always manifested a deep and lively interest. Many of his public lectures have been exclusively for their benefit. The cause of temperance has ever found in him one of its most ardent supporters. In his own city he fought the license law with all the force he could bring to bear upon it. He took the ground that it was a legalized system of crime. He maintained that if any shops should be licensed, they should be the low kennels, which could tempt only those who were already, comparatively speaking, past hope. He has also lectured much upon the subject in other places, and stands among the first of speakers upon the platform of temperance.

In Mr. Chapin's sermons we find frequent allusions to slavery, which evince hostility to the system, but he has not made that a special branch of his labor. We should be slow to believe that a man of his honesty and humanity would withhold his influence from the right side of the question.

As has been intimated, Mr. Chapin is now settled in New York. He labored for a number of years in Richmond, Virginia, and in Boston and Charlestown, Massachusetts. He is a little more than forty years of age, and is now hale and hearty, in the meridian of his usefulness.

JOHN GREENLEAF WHITTIER.

The poet Whittier was born in the year 1808, in Haverhill, Massachusetts. His home was upon the banks of the wild and beautiful Merrimack river. His ancestors for a number of generations had lived upon the same spot, and it is dear to him, not alone for its beauty of scenery, or from the fact that it was his birth-place, but because every nook and corner in it, or around it, is connected with him, through his ancestors. They were Quakers of the old George Fox stamp; men of iron endurance, christian integrity, and sublime simplicity, and consequently suffered severely at the hands of the Puritans. The father of the poet was a plain farmer, and Whittier either worked upon his father's farm, or attended a district school until he was eighteen years old. He then devoted a year to study in a Latin school, and this, we believe, comprises what is popularly called his education. He was a home-student, however, and probably at twenty possessed a better disciplined mind than one-half of the graduates of our colleges, and his store of valuable knowledge was by no means small.

In 1828 Mr. Whittier went to Boston to undertake the editorship of "*The American Manufacturer*," a journal principally devoted to the support of a protective tariff. At this time, and for some time after, he was an ardent admirer of Henry Clay and his political views. Before assuming the editorship of the "*Manufacturer*," he had contributed articles to journals published near his early home, and had now a favorable reputation as a writer, of both prose and poetry, in that vicinity. He conducted the "*Manufacturer*" with remarkable ability for one so young and inexperienced, but he shortly gave it up. In 1830 he went to the city of Hartford to edit the "*New England Weekly Review*," where he remained for two years. He exhibited marked talents in his management of the *Review*. A portion of the time he was warmly engaged in politics, and a part was devoted to literature. About this time he published his "Legends of New England," and wrote a memoir of his friend Brainard, the Connecticut poet. While he was connected with the *Review*, he contributed to it several poems of great beauty, which attracted attention throughout the country. In 1831 he left the *Review*. His nature was too gentle, too refined and sensitive for the heartless strife of journalism. He could not feel at ease tied to an editor's chair, compelled to write a great deal which was distasteful to him, and to read everything whether good or bad, issuing from the whole press of the country. Besides, his true, poet's heart sighed for the still and beautiful country. And so he went back to the banks of the Merrimack, and rested beneath the same trees which spread over him their cool shade when he was a boy. For five or six years he engaged in agricultural pursuits in Haverhill. In 1835, he was elected to the state legislature; in 1836, ditto, and in 1837, he declined a reëlection.

At an early period Mr. Whittier consecrated himself to the cause of freedom, and through the dark years of the anti-slavery agitation, when mob-law was triumphant even in New England, he sustained the courage of the "despised few," by his passionate songs of liberty. The fiery eloquence of his numbers roused their spirits to a degree of fearlessness which overlooked all personal dangers, transformed them into men willing, if it were necessary, to wear the crown of martyrdom. In 1836 he published his celebrated poem "Mogg Megone," and the same year he was elected one of the secretaries of the American Anti-slavery Society. Still later he separated from the Garrison party, and became an active member of the political anti-slavery organization known as the Liberty party. He at present acts with the free democratic party. It is unnecessary for us to record his literary or political history for the last few years, for it is well known to all intelligent persons. As corresponding editor of the *National Era*, he has written some of the best of his prose and poetic articles. He resides with his sister—a lady of uncommon talents—and mother in Amesbury, Massachusetts, upon a small farm, to which, we believe, he devotes a portion of his time, the rest being occupied with literary and plilanthropical pursuits. The personal appearance of Mr. Whittier is striking. He is tall and slender, with a classical head, delicate features, eyes of fiery black, and a quick, nervous manner. A smile generally rests upon his countenance, though his nervous organization is so exquisitely sensitive that he is often startled from his equilibrium in his contact with the world. He is exceedingly bashful in general society, and is not fond of it, though he is ardently attached to the "select few," who form his favorite circle of friends.

In our opinion, Mr. Whittier is surpassed in poetical genius by no living American. It is almost impossible, however, to compare him with many of our poets. He occupies a distinct position as a poet. He is the poet of freedom, and as such will go down to future generations gloriously. The free American of the future can never forget the poet who consecrated his lyre to the panting, discouraged friends of human liberty, when their cause was at its lowest ebb.

In Whittier, it seems as if we revived the old race

of poets, who sang their spirited songs in defense of their country's rights, and who were ready to use harp or sword, as the occasion demanded. We know that his lightning-tongued stanzas are familiar to all, but in this sketch we must repeat two or three as specimens of his style, or, in truth, his different styles. To us, one of his loftiest, grandest poems is, that written on the adoption of Pinckney's resolutions in the house of representatives, and the passage of Calhoun's "bill of abominations," in the senate. Some of the stanzas for strength and impassioned beauty are unsurpassed. They stir a man's blood like a trumpet-call to battle. We quote the poem entire:

"Now, by our fathers' ashes! where's the spirit
Of the true hearted and the unshackled gone?
Sons of old freemen, do we but inherit
Their names alone?

"Is the old Pilgrim spirit quenched within us?
Stoops the proud manhood of our souls so low,
That mammon's lure or party's will can win us
To silence now?

"No! when our land to ruin's brink is verging,
In God's name let us speak while there is time!
Now, when the padlock for our lips is forging,
Silence is crime!

"What! shall we henceforth humbly ask as favors
Rights all our own? In madness shall we barter
For treacherous peace the freedom nature gave us,
God and our charter?

"Here shall the statesman seek the free to fetter?
Here lynch law light its lurid fires on high?
And, in the church, their proud and skilled abettor,
Make truth a lie?

"Torture the pages of the hallowed bible,
To sanction crime, and robbery, and blood?
And, in oppression's hateful service, libel
Both man and God?

"Shall our New England stand erect no longer,
But stoop in chains upon her downward way,
Thicker to gather on her limbs and stronger,
Day after day?

"Oh, no; methinks from all her wild, green mountains—
From valleys where her slumbering fathers lie,
From her blue rivers, and her welling fountains,
And clear, cold sky—

"From her rough coast, and isles, which hungry ocean
Gnaws with his surges—from the fisher's skiff,
With white sail swaying to the billows' motion,
Round rock and cliff—

"From the free fireside of her unbought farmer—
From her free laborer at his loom and wheel—
From the brown smith-shop, where, beneath the hammer,
Rings the red steel—

"From each and all, if God hath not forsaken
Our land, and left us to an evil choice,
Loud as the summer thunderbolt shall waken
A people's voice!

"Startling and stern, the northern winds shall bear it
Over Potomac's to St. Mary's wave;
And buried freedom shall awake to hear it,
Within her grave.

"Oh, let that voice go forth! The bondman sighing
By Santee's wave, in Mississippi's cane,
Shall feel the hope within his bosom dying,
Revive again.

"Let it go forth! The millions who are gazing
Sadly upon us from afar, shall smile,
And unto God devout thanksgiving raising,
Bless us the while.

"Oh, for your ancient freedom, pure and holy,
For a deliverance of a groaning earth,
For the wronged captive, bleeding, crush'd, and lowly,
Let it go forth!

"Sons of the best of fathers! will ye falter
With all they left ye peril'd and at stake?
Ho! once again on freedom's holy altar
The fire awake!

"Prayer-strengthen'd for the trial come together,
Put on the harness for the moral fight,
And, with the blessing of your heavenly Father,
Maintain the right!"

Another of Whittier's grand poems is that written after a meeting had been held in Faneuil Hall, by certain citizens of Boston, *to suppress the freedom of speech.* We will quote it entire; but, before doing so, must relate an anecdote connected with this poem. A dear friend of ours, now, alas, beneath the sod, was a most passionate admirer of Whittier's poetry. To him there was no other American poet living, and there could be no other. Possessed of lofty enthusiasm, he revelled in some of Whittier's magnificent songs, and as his life was often cast far away from his native New England, he committed to memory all of Whittier's finest poems, so that he could repeat them at pleasure. It was his habit to do this often to others, or alone in a meditative mood to himself. Our paths chanced once to lie in one direction, across the Atlantic, and one starry night we sat late upon the quarter-deck listening to his recitation of his favorite poems. Appreciating every shade of the poet's thought, sharing his enthusiasm, by constant practice he had acquired the art of reading very finely, and it was a great treat to hear him. By thinking often of each poem, our friend, having a brisk imagination, had acquired the habit of prefacing each recitation with a story of the author, or the peculiar occasion which called the poem forth. We know not, as he pretended, they were all in every particular true, but we never shall forget the impression which the poem we quote below ("*Stanzas for the Times*,") made upon a small, English audience, after his prefatory story. As we copy the poem, we will venture also the anecdote, not vouching, however, for its exact truth. It was substantially as follows:

Whittier, at the time this poem was written, was a young, modest man, little used to city customs—in fact, fragrant of clover blossoms, unsophisticated, a pure, young, country Quaker. He had heard but little of the infamous conduct of the wealthy and respectable supporters of slavery, living as he did in a quiet, country town. One day his father sent him to Boston on business. He came into the city in his father's plain carriage, dressed in the sober, homely, Quaker garb, and put up at a "farmer's hotel." He went out into the streets, and very soon noticed that there was a great gathering of excited citizens. The faces of the multitude wore a demoniac expression; they seemed to be hungry for the blood of some person or persons. His thought was that some horrible murder had been perpetrated, and that the indignation of the people could not be restrained from summary justice; but if even that were the case, he was horror-struck at their eagerness for vindictive punishment. He hastily retraced his steps, and sought information from his landlord. The reply to his questions was, that the people were on the scent of an abolitionist—were trying to kill a citizen of Boston for asserting the simple rights of manhood. Was it indeed so? *Could* it be so? "Yes, verily so." The shock was lightning-like; his pure nature could not easily believe it, and when he did, he uttered no fiery words, but went sadly again into the street. When evening came, he went to that "cradle of liberty," old Faneuil Hall, having heard that the enemies of freedom would hold a meeting there that night. He was a silent, shocked spectator of that disgraceful attempt to padlock the lips of freemen; he listened with mute horror to the slavish sentiments uttered by sons of the old Pilgrims and children of the revolutionary heroes. He heard men counsel *the forcible suppression of the freedom of speech* upon the question of slavery—yes, even in old Massachusetts! They would *compel men to silence*, even in Boston, upon the great subject of human liberty! He walked slowly, sadly home to his hotel, and calling for a pen, ink, and paper, and a light, he went to his little room, where he wrote the following

STANZAS FOR THE TIMES.

Is this the land our fathers loved,
The freedom which they toiled to win?
Is this the soil whereon they moved?
Are these the graves they slumber in?
Are *we* the sons by whom are borne
The mantles which the dead have worn?

And shall we crouch above these graves,
With craven soul and fetter'd lip?
Yoke in with marked and branded SLAVES,
And tremble at the driver's whip?
Bend to the earth our pliant knees,
And speak—but as our masters please?

Shall outraged Nature cease to feel?
Shall mercy's tears no longer flow?
Shall ruffian threats of cord and steel—
The dungeon's gloom—the assassin's blow,
Turn back the spirit roused to save
The Truth—our Country—and the *Slave*?

K*

Of human skulls that shrine was made,
Round which the priests of Mexico
Before their loathsome idol prayed—
Is freedom's altar fashioned so?
And must we yield to Freedom's God,
As offering meet the negro's blood?

Shall tongues be mute, when deeds are wrought
Which well might shame extremest Hell?
Shall freemen lock the indignant thought?
Shall Pity's bosom cease to swell?
Shall honor bleed! Shall Truth succumb?
Shall pen, and press, and *soul* be dumb?

No—by each spot of haunted ground,
Where Freedom weeps her children's fall—
By Plymouth's rock, and Bunker's mound,
By Griswold s stained and shattered wall—
By Warren's ghost—by Langdon's shade—
By all the memories of our dead!

By their enlarging souls, which burst
The bands and fetters round them set—
By the FREE PILGRIM SPIRIT nursed
Within our inmost bosoms, yet,—
By all above, around, below,
Be ours the indignant answer—No!

No—guided by our country's laws,
For truth, and right, and suffering man,
Be ours to strive in Freedom's cause,
As christians *may* —as freemen *can!*
Still pouring on unwilling ears
That truth oppression only fears.

What! shall we guard our neighbor still,
While *woman* shrinks beneath his rod,
And while he tramples down at will
The image of a common God!

Shall watch and ward be round him set,
Of Northern nerve and bayonet?

And shall we know and share with him
The danger and the growing shame?
And see our Freedom's light grow dim,
Which should have filled the world with flame?
And, writhing, feel where'er we turn,
A world's reproach around us burn?

Is't not enough that this is borne?
And asks our haughty neighbor more?
Must fetters which his slaves have worn,
Clank round the Yankee farmer's door?
Must *he* be told beside his plow,
What he must speak, and *when* and *how*?

Must *he* be told his freedom stands
On Slavery's dark foundations strong—
On breaking hearts and fettered hands,
On robbery, and crime, and wrong?
That all his fathers taught is vain—
That Freedom's emblem is the chain?

Its life—its soul from *slavery* drawn?
False—foul—profane! Go—teach as well
Of holy Truth from Falsehood born!
Of Heaven refreshed by airs from Hell!
Of Virtue nursed by open Vice!
Of Demons planting Paradise!

Rail on, then, "brethren of the South"—
Ye shall not hear the truth the less—
No seal is on the Yankee's mouth,
No fetter on the Yankee's press!
From our Green Mountains to the Sea,
One voice shall thunder—WE ARE FREE!"

But if Whittier can rouse the stormy passions by his warlike songs, so can he moan the saddest plaints, so can he sing the gentlest songs. After reading one of his battle-hymns, the reader unacquainted with his poetry, would scarcely believe that the same author has written some of the most touching stanzas to be found in modern poetry; but such is the fact. One of his poems entitled "*The Farewell*," is one of the sweetest, saddest, most musical poems ever written. It is the farewell of a Virginian slave-mother to her children sold to the far south. We quote one verse:

"Gone, gone—sold and gone
To the rice-swamp dank and lone,
Where the slave-whip ceaseless swings,
Where the noisome insect stings,
Where the Fever Demon strews
Poison with the falling dews,
Where the sickly sunbeams glare
Through the hot and misty air,—
Gone, gone—sold and gone,
To the rice-swamp dank and lone.
From Virginia's hills and waters,—
Woe is me, my stolen daughters!"

But perhaps as fine a specimen of his poetry in this vein, is his poem upon the death of Oliver Torrey, who was Secretary of the Boston Anti-Slavery Society, a young man of lovely character:

LINES ON THE DEATH OF TORREY.

Gone before us, O our brother,
To the spirit-land!
Vainly look we for another
In thy place to stand.
Who shall offer youth and beauty
On the wasting shrine
Of a stern and lofty duty,
With a faith like thine?

Oh! thy gentle smile of greeting
Who again shall see?
Who amidst the solemn meeting
Gaze again on thee?—
Who, when peril gathers o'er us,
Wear so calm a brow?
Who, with evil men before us,
So serene as thou?

Early hath the spoiler found thee,
Brother of our love!
Autumn's faded earth around thee,
And its storms above!
Evermore that turf lie lightly
And, with future showers,
O'er thy slumbers fresh and brightly
Blow the summer flowers?

In the locks thy forehead gracing,
Not a silvery streak;
Not a line of sorrows's tracing
On thy fair young cheek;
Eyes of light and lips of roses,
Such as Hylas wore—
Over all that curtain closes,
Which shall rise no more.

Will the vigil Love is keeping
  Round that grave of thine,
Mournfully, like Jazar weeping
  Over Sibmah's vine—
Will the pleasant memories swelling
  Gentle hearts of thee,
In the spirit's distant dwelling
  All unheeded be?

If the spirit ever gazes,
  From his journeyings back;
If the immortal ever traces
  O'er its mortal track;
Wilt thou not, O brother, meet us
  Sometimes on our way,
And in hours of sadness greet us
  As a spirit may?

Peace be with thee, O our brother,
  In the spirit-land!
Vainly look we for another
  In thy place to stand.
Unto Truth and Freedom giving
  All thy early powers,
Be thy virtues with the living
  And thy spirit ours!

The selections we have made are connected, as are a majority of Whittier's poems, with the subject of slavery, and there are many quite equal, and some very possibly superior, to the ones we have quoted, upon the same subject. Some of his most beautiful poems, however, have nothing to do with reform. His songs of labor are very beautiful. No living poet loves more intensely the beauties of nature than he.

We should perhaps beg the pardon of our readers for copying so many examples of Whittier's poetry; but it is the very shortest road to an appreciation of his character. So little can be said of the man—he has always been so modest and retiring—that we cannot refrain from remarking upon some of his finest poems. His lines upon the death of the sister of Joseph Sturge are full of a solemn grandeur of style and thought. Joseph Sturge is one of the noblest reformers of Great Britain. He is a member of the Society of Friends, but has no bigotry, no repulsive fondness for form in dress, though he conforms to the usual customs of his sect. He is a lovable man—a man who is almost adored by the poor people of Birmingham, where he resides. He is wealthy; and constantly, unremittingly devotes a large share of his income to alleviate the sufferings of the poor about him. His sister, Sophia Sturge, was in her nature very much like her brother Joseph, only with a softer, woman's nature. She was benevolent, affectionate, and untiring in her devotion to the poor. Duty was always her master. No hardship could cause her to shrink one moment from it. She was not only a friend to the slave, but a consistent advocate of total abstinence from all intoxicating liquors. To hold such a position in English society, even among the Friends, costs much more self-denial than here. So severely rigorous was Sophia Sturge that she refused in her last sickness to take, at the order of her physician, one drop of the poisonous liquid, prescribed under the various names of brandy, wine, gin, etc., etc.

It was upon this noble woman that Whittier wrote the following lines:

TO MY FRIEND ON THE DEATH OF HIS SISTER.

Thine is a grief, the depth of which another
    May never know;
Yet, o'er the waters, O my stricken brother!
    To thee I go.

I lean my heart unto thee, sadly folding
    Thy hand in mine,
With even the weakness of my soul upholding
    The strength of thine.

I never knew, like thee, the dear departed;
    I stood not by
When, in calm trust, the pure and tranquil-hearted
    Lay down to die.

And on thy ears my words of weak condoling
    Must vainly fall:
The funeral bell which in thy heart is tolling,
    Sounds over all.

I will not mock thee with the poor world's common
    And heartless phrase,
Nor wrong the memory of a sainted woman
    With idle praise.

With silence only as their benediction,
God's angels come
Where, in the shadow of a great affliction,
The soul sits dumb!

Yet, would I say what thy own heart approveth:
Our Father's will,
Calling to him the dear one whom he loveth,
Is mercy still.

Not upon thee or thine the solemn angel
Hath evil wrought;
Her funeral anthem is a glad evangel—
The good die not!

God calls our loved ones, but we lose not wholly
What he hath given;
They live on earth, in thought and deed, as truly
As in his heaven.

And she is with thee; in thy path of trials
She walketh yet;
Still with the baptism of thy self-denial
Her locks are wet.

Up then, my brother! Lo, the fields of harvest
Lie white in view!
She lives and loves thee, and the God thou servest
To both is true.

Thrust in thy sickle! England's toil-worn peasants
Thy call abide;
And she thou mourn'st, a pure and holy presence
Shall glean beside!

Another of Whittier's sweetest poems is that entitled "Gone," and commencing as follows:

"Another hand is beckoning us,
Another call is given;
And glows once more with angel steps
The path which reaches heaven."

There is a subdued, softened pathos in it scarcely surpassed in the whole range of modern poetry. We will give the remaining stanzas:

"Our young and gentle friend, whose smile
Made brighter summer hours,
Amid the frosts of autumn time
Has left us, with the flowers.

"No paling of the cheek of bloom
Forewarned us of decay;
No shadow from the silent land
Fell round our sister's way.

"The light of her young life went down,
As sinks behind the hill
The glory of a setting star—
Clear, suddenly, and still.

"As pure and sweet her fair brow seemed,
Eternal as the sky;
And like the brook's low song, her voice—
A sound which could not die.

"And half we deemed she needed not
The changing of her sphere,
To give to heaven a shining one,
Who walked an angel here.

"The blessing of her quiet life
Fell on us like the dew;
And good thoughts, where her footsteps press'd
Like fairy blossoms grew.

"Sweet promptings unto kindest deeds
Were in her very look;
We read her face, as one who reads
A true and holy book.

"The measure of a blessed hymn,
To which our hearts could move;
The breathing of an inward psalm;
A canticle of love.

"We miss her in the place of prayer,
And by the hearth-fire's light;
We pause beside her door to hear
Once more her sweet 'Good night!'

"There seems a shadow on the day,
Her smile no longer cheers;
A dimness on the stars of night,
Like eyes that look through tears.

"Alone unto our Father's will
One thought hath reconciled;
That He whose love exceedeth ours
Hath taken home His child.

"Fold her, oh Father! in thine arms,
And let her henceforth be
A messenger of love between
Our human hearts and Thee.

"Still let her mild rebuking stand
Between us and the wrong,
And her dear memory serve to make
Our faith in goodness strong.

"And, grant that she who, trembling, here,
Distrusted all her powers,
May welcome to her holier home
The well-beloved of ours."

The last poem we shall quote is one of the latest productions of Mr. Whittier, and to us it seems one of the very best of his gentle poems. The contrast between it and one of his warlike pieces is great. The poem is entitled

MAUD MULLER.

Maud Muller, on a summer's day,
Raked the meadow sweet with hay.

Beneath her torn hat glowed the wealth
Of simple beauty and rustic health.

Singing, she wrought, and her merry glee
The mock-bird reëchoed from every tree.

But when she glanced to the far-off town,
White from its hill-slope looking down,

The sweet song died, and a vague unrest
And a nameless longing filled her breast—

A wish, that she hardly dared to own,
For something better than she had known.

The Judge rode slowly down the lane,
Smoothing his horse's chestnut mane.

He drew his bridle in the shade
Of the apple-trees, to greet the maid,

And ask a draught from the spring that flowed
Through the meadow, across the road.

She stooped where the cool spring bubbled up,
And filled for him her small tin cup,

And blushed as she gave it, looking down
On her feet so bare, and her tattered gown.

"Thanks!" said the Judge, "a sweeter draught
From fairer hand was never quaffed."

He spoke of the grass, and flowers, and trees,
Of the singing birds and humming bees;

Then talked of the haying, and wondered whether
The cloud in the west would bring foul weather.

And Maud forgot her brier-torn gown,
And her graceful ankles bare and brown;

And listened, while a pleased surprise
Looked from her long-lashed hazel eyes.

At last, like one who for delay
Seeks a vain excuse, he rode away.

Maud Muller looked and sighed: "Ah me!
That I the Judge's bride might be!

"He would dress me up in silks so fine,
And praise and toast me at his wine.

"My father should wear a broadcloth coat;
My brother should sail a painted boat.

"I'd dress my mother so grand and gay
And the baby should have a new toy each day.

"And I'd feed the hungry and clothe the poor,
And all should bless me who left our door."

The Judge looked back as he climbed the hill,
And saw Maud Muller standing still.

"A form more fair, a face more sweet,
Ne'er hath it been my lot to meet.

"And her modest answer and graceful air
Show her wise and good as she is fair.

"Would she were mine, and I to-day,
Like her, a harvester of hay;

"No doubtful balance of rights and wrongs,
Nor weary lawyers with endless tongues,

"But the low of cattle and song of birds,
And health and quiet and loving words."

But he thought of his sister, proud and cold,
And his mother, vain of her rank and gold.

So, closing his heart, the Judge rode on,
And Maud was left in the field alone.

But the lawyers smiled that afternoon,
When he hummed in court an old love-tune;

And the young girl mused beside the well,
Till the rain on the unraked clover fell.

He wedded a wife of richest dower,
Who lived for fashion as he for power.

Yet oft, in his marble hearth's bright glow,
He watched a picture come and go;

And sweet Maud Muller's hazel eyes
Looked out in their innocent surprise.

Oft, when the wine in his glass was red,
He longed for the way-side well instead;

And closed his eyes on his garnished rooms,
To dream of meadows and clover blooms.

And the proud man sighed with a secret pain
"Ah, that I were free again!

"Free as when I rode that day,
Where the barefoot maiden raked the hay!"

She wedded a man unlearned and poor,
And many children played round her door.

But care and sorrow, and child-birth pain,
Left their traces on heart and brain.

And oft, when the summer sun shone hot
On the new-mown hay in the meadow lot,

And she heard the little spring-brook fall
Over the road-side, through the wall,

In the shade of the apple-tree again
She saw a rider draw his rein,

And, gazing down with a timid grace,
She felt his pleased eyes read her face.

Sometimes her narrow kitchen walls
Stretched away into stately halls;

The weary wheel to a spinnet turned,
The tallow candle an astral burned,

And for him who sat by the chimney-lug
Dozing and grumbling o'er pipe and mug,

A manly form at her side she saw,
And joy was duty and love and law.

Then she took up the burden of life again,
Saying only, "It might have been."

Alas for maiden, alas for Judge,
For rich repiner and household drudge!

God pity them both! and pity us all,
Who vainly the dreams of youth recall.

For of all sad words of tongue and pen,
The saddest are these: "It might have been!"

Ah! we'll for us all, some sweet hope lies
Deeply buried from human eyes;

And, in the hereafter, angels may
Roll the stone from its grave away.

The clear, bright morning, the burning noon, the still, calm evening, the rocky mountains of New England, the broad prairies of the west, and the gorgeous scenery of the south, have each and all been the theme of his song. There is a quiet beauty, a half-sad gentleness in many of his poems, which contrasts strangely with the fiery eloquence which characterizes others. No American poet has, in our opinion, equaled Whittier in all that is intensely passionate, impetuous and warlike, and there are few that equal him in the pathetic and the beautiful. His sarcasm is terribly keen—as a sample of this, we refer the reader to his poem upon the publisher of a popular magazine, who took such exceeding pains to let the south know that he employed no anti-slavery writers upon his namby-pamby monthly. One of the most memorable of his poems, is that upon Daniel Webster. It is like the wildly solemn wind in late autumn, moaning through the pines over the desolateness of Nature. No ordinary poet could write a poem, meet even for the fall of such a great man as Webster—but "Ichabod" is a poem which, in grandeur, is fit to commemorate the downfall of such a collossal man! But we will not attempt a criticism upon Whittier—we have intended only to point out what are to us some of his most striking characteristics, illustrating these by a few specimens of his reform-poetry. We know of no man more worthy of the name Agitator than he, and few there are living in the world, more sure to live in the hearts of future generations.

L

HORACE BUSHNELL, D. D.

It is our intention in these sketches of modern agitators, not to be confined to one class of reformers. We shall endeavor to draw the portraits of agitators in church as well as in state; of some of those noble men who have battled manfully the slavery of intemperance, as well as of the agitators against negro slavery. But we have been struck with surprise to find that the modern agitator is usually an advocate of *all* the just reforms of the day. It is very difficult to find a man of original and reformatory ideas in the church, who is an opponent of the cause of temperance, or who withholds his sympathy from the friends of freedom. The leading enemies of rum are generally friendly to the cause of the slave, and the anti-slavery men of the land are almost unanimously devoted temperance advocates.

The reader will perhaps naturally suppose that when we placed Dr. Bushnell's name at the head of this article, we had in mind the theological agitation caused throughout the country, and especially in Connecticut, by his somewhat celebrated volume, entitled, "*God in Christ.*" Such was not the case. As to the merits of that controversy, which is not yet settled, we have here nothing to say, either in approval or condemnation of Dr. Bushnell. We make no pretensions to theological acquirements, and are not competent to discuss, much less decide, the points in dispute. But we look upon Dr. Bushnell as one of the most profound agitators of the age. We think in reference to theological matters, that *the spirit of the age* is in him. The drift of his published writings is continually toward a liberal, unsectarian, and practical christianity. He makes deadly war upon mere creeds, and urges most earnestly upon the christian world a better practice. "Deeds, not words," is the essence of the religion he preaches. It seems to us that the reader must be obtuse who reading Bushnell sees only his peculiar views of the trinity and the sufferings of Christ. His opinions upon these points may be accepted or rejected, and the time may be coming when they will be forgotten, but *he* will be remembered; and the books which contain his peculiar views may live, but they will not detract from the author's reputation. As an early, eloquent, and intellectually powerful advocate of a more generous christianity than that born of creeds, as a great defender of the important truths of the gospel upon philosophical principles, he will live in future generations. In this skeptical age, such a man is precious to the cause of pure religion, for he meets the skeptic with sound argument, instead of denunciation, with a profound love for Christ, instead of a burning hatred of those who unfortunately have lost, or never found, the path which leads to Him. It is this catholic, charitable tendency in all Dr. Bushnell's writings which awakens agitation wherever they are read, and which excites the bitter opposition of conservatives in the church. He has been accused by men actively engaged in important reforms of withholding his aid from them, and of being so absorbed in convincing men of the importance of more religion in the life, as to overlook the miserable drunkard in the streets, and the panting fugitive at his door—in fact, to neglect to practice what he preaches. But it must be remembered, that, to some men, it is given to enunciate great principles which underlie the foundations of society, or which *should* underlie society, and of such men little more can be asked. A slave-holder cannot live upon the food which Dr. Bushnell offers to him; the rumseller would choke upon it. And though the doctor does not often preach anti-slavery or temperance sermons (perhaps not so often as he should,) yet when he does, he speaks boldly for the right. Years ago, on the eve of an exciting election, he came out in his pulpit one Sabbath day with a sermon upon the duties of christian voters, which was like a bomb-shell thrown into a peaceful town. It was unexpected; the people were not prepared for it; but it was a bold enunciation of God's truth, and his hearers sat still, and listened somewhat as children do to God's thunder. He has also condemned in the strongest language the fugitive slave act, so that his views upon this part of the great compromise are everywhere known. But he deals usually in great general principles, rather than every-day applications of such principles. Perhaps he errs in this; we have thought it would be a greater service to the world if he would dwell more upon the sins which are eating into its very heart; but we cannot ignore the fact, that all his productions and performances tend toward reform in church and state.

Horace Bushnell is a native of the town of Litchfield, Connecticut, and is about fifty years of age. His father was a clothier, a man of sterling character and intellect. His mother was one of the gentlest and most affectionate of women. When Horace was two years old, his father moved into the town of New Preston, where we believe he continued to reside for a number of years. The little that we know of Dr. Bushnell's early life can quickly be written. He entered Yale College, and graduated in the year 1827. Two years afterward he was appointed a tutor in the same institution, which office he filled for two years. He next removed to the city of New York, where for a time he edited a newspaper. He at length entered upon a theological course, to prepare himself for the ministry. He was ordained over the North church, in Hartford, May 22, 1833, and has continued to preach with great acceptance to the same church until the present day. He was married when young, to Miss Mary Apthorpe, of New Haven, by whom he has had five children, three of whom are living.

In Dr. Bushnell's discourse, delivered at the centennial celebration of Litchfield county, he has given us a picture or two of his boyish days, which are sufficiently graphic and beautiful to excuse us for quoting them here. He says:

"But the schools — we must not pass by these if we are to form a truthful and sufficient picture of the home-spun days. The schoolmaster did not exactly go round the district to fit out the children's minds with learning, as the shoe-maker often did to fit their feet with shoes, or the tailors to measure and cut for their bodies; but, to come as near it as possible, he boarded round, (a custom not yet gone by,) and the wood for the common fire was supplied in a way equally primitive, viz: by a contribution of loads from the several families, according to their several quantities of childhood. * * * * There was no complaint in those days of the want of ventilation; for the large open fire-place held a considerable fraction of a cord of wood, and the windows took in just enough air to supply the combustion. Besides, the bigger lads were occasionally ventilated by being sent out to cut wood enough to keep the fire in action. The seats were made of the outer slabs from the saw-mill, supported by slant legs driven into and a proper distance through auger holes, and planed smooth on the top by the rather tardy process of friction. But the spelling went on bravely, and we ciphered away again and again, always till we got through "loss and gain." The more advanced of us, too, made light work of Lindley Murray, and went on to the parsing, finally, of extracts from Shakspeare and Milton, till some of us began to think we had mastered their tough sentences in a more consequential sense than was exactly true. O, I remember (about the remotest thing I can remember) that low seat, too high, nevertheless, to allow the feet to touch the floor, and that friendly teacher who had the address to start a fresh feeling of enthusiasm and awaken the first sense of power. He is living still, and whenever I think of him, he rises up to me in the far background of memory, as bright as if he had worn the seven stars in his hair."

Still farther on, he says:

"I remember being despatched, when a lad, one Saturday afternoon, in the winter, to bring home a few bushels of apples engaged of a farmer a mile distant; but the careful, exact man looked first at the clock, then out the window at the sun, and turning to me said, 'I cannot measure out the apples in time for you to get home before sundown, you must come again Monday;' then how I went home venting my boyish impatience in words not exactly respectful, assisted by the sunlight playing still upon the eastern hills, and got for my comfort a very unaccountably small amount of specially silent sympathy."

In 1833 Dr. Bushnell, we have said, was ordained over the North church, in Hartford. Twenty years afterward—last May—he preached a "commemorative discourse," in which he alluded, in the following language, to his first visit to said church:

"I received a letter in February, 1833, inviting me to come and preach, for a time, to this congregation, of which I knew nothing save that you had recently parted with your pastor. I arrived here late in the afternoon, in a furious snow storm, after floundering all day in the heavy drifts the storm was raising among the hills between here and Litchfield. I went, as invited, directly to the house of the chairman of the committee; but I had scarcely warmed me, and not at all relieved the hunger of my fast, when he came in and told me that arrangements had been made for me with one of the fathers of the church, and immediately sent me off with my baggage to the quarters assigned. Of course I had no complaint to make, though the fire seemed very inviting and the house attractive; but when I came to know the hospitality of my friend, as I had abundant opportunity of knowing it afterward, it became somewhat of a mystery to me that I should have been despatched in this rather summary fashion. But it came out three or four years after, that as there were two parties strongly marked in the church, an old and new school party, as related to the New Haven controversy, the committee had made up their mind, very prudently, that it would not do for me to stay even for an hour with the new school brother of the committee; and for this reason they had made interest with the elder brother referred to, because he was a man of the school simply of Jesus Christ. And here, under cover of his good hospitality, which I hope he has never found reason to regret—extended by him and received by me in equal simplicity—I was put in hospital and kept away from the infected districts, preparatory to a settlement in the North church, of Hartford. I mention this fact to show the very delicate condition prepared for the young pastor, who is to be thus daintily inserted between an acid and an alkali, having it for his task both to keep them apart and to save himself from being bitten of one or devoured by the other."

No pastor was ever more loved and respected than is Dr. Bushnell by his church and congregation. For twenty years he has occupied the pulpit of the old North church, and not a whisper of his dismission ever yet was heard. We do not mean that he has never raised a storm in the church by his faithful preaching, but his hearers have loved him so well that they could not remain angry with him. When he came out so fearlessly in condemnation of the corrupt politics of the time, an angry agitation for a little while surrounded him, but it soon passed away. In his "Discourse," preached May, 1853, he speaks thus pithily of it:

"I preached a fast-day sermon, showing that "politics are under the law of God." Wise or unwise in the manner, it was greatly offensive to some, but the offense was soon forgiven; in consideration, I suppose, of the fact that, apart from the manner, the doctrine was abundantly wanted, and even sol emnly true."

We will not attempt to sketch the history of the late agitation in reference to his "*God in Christ*," for it is too near the present, even had we the space, to justify such a history. Dr. Bushnell first preached a sermon before the *Concio ad Clerum*, at New Haven. He was selected by the district association for that purpose, and the general association, as is its usual custom, selected his subject. The sermon thus preached constitutes the first part of "*God in Christ*." He was next invited to deliver an address before some society at Cambridge, which he accepted, and that sermon constitutes the second part of his celebrated book. He next delivered an address before the theological students at Andover, at their request, and that constitutes the third and last part of his book. These three parts, together with an introductory essay upon language, make up the book, which has created such an agitation among the churches, and which has been republished and sold extensively in England. He was charged with heresy, and the association to which he belonged instituted an inquiry into the truth of the charge, and after examination voted seventeen to three, that while his peculiar views were not accepted by that body, yet they saw no such heresy as would warrant further proceedings. It is claimed by his accusers, that he tramples upon the orthodox doctrines in reference to the trinity, the person of Christ, and the atonement. In the sermon from which we have made quotations, he says:

"It is very true that I have presented some explanations of three important doctrines, the trinity, the person of Christ, and atonement, which differ in their shade from the explanations given by my brethren. Are we therefore to exclude each other? Still we can preach a trinity, Father, Son, and Holy Ghost, three persons, in a hearty love of trinity itself, and regarding it as a conception of God without which he were a being practically distant from us. And if we should happen to preach three persons meaning something a little different by the word *person*, just as all the wisest teachers of the ages before us have consented in the right to do, might we not have good cause to say that in effect we agree?

"As regards the divinity of Christ, we have happily no appearance of controversy. And if we do not conceive the philosophy of his person just alike, let it be enough that we can preach him as a person, Son of God and Son of Man, tempted in all points as we are, without sin, one with us in the line of Adam, born into the race, the child of a virgin, conceived by the Holy Ghost, grown up to be a perfect, the only perfect man, God manifest in the flesh.

"As regards the work or sacrifice of Christ, we can agree in showing that he lives a suffering life, dies a suffering death; that by his life and death he so compensates the dishonored law and fortifies the divine justice that pardon is dispensed, not in mere paternal clemency, but in a way of justification; consequently that we are justified by faith without the deeds of tne law, and so that Christ is made unto us wisdom, righteousness, sanctification and redemption."

The Presbyterian Quarterly says:

"His (Dr. Bushnell's) mind is one of no common force or compass. Original, imaginative, shrewd, cultivated, comprehensive, naturally, at least, ambitious, it is not strange that he should make an impression upon the American Church. His is one of the most active, versatile, outlooking natures which the atmosphere of an age, especially such an atmosphere as that of ours, would reach soonest. We do not know when we have been so much struck with anything as with an oration of Dr. Bushnell's, delivered to the Phi Beta Kappa, at Cambridge, and which we have seen for the first time among his publications, in a recent collection we made of them, for careful study. He declines giving any name for his theme, but it appears to be "Work and Play."

"It is quite obvious, we think, that Dr. Bushnell had conceived the idea of converting the Unitarians, by fusing their views and those of the Orthodox together, in the crucible of a profounder philosophy, by dissolving scriptural truth, so to speak, in an oriental atmosphere. * * * It were a great feat of spiritual ambition, not to speak of nobler motives, to bring in, on the deep current of Platonism, a compromise that, melting New Haven and Cambridge together, might reünite all the Congregational churches, and present the finest essence of New England mind and character, blended in religion, upon the profoundest grounds of philosophy. Thus, one of the discourses in the book, called "God in Christ," was delivered at Cambridge, to the Divinity School. It is upon the Atonement, and is a kind of ultimate in the way of compromise, a method of doctrinal torture of a most transcendant kind, intended to show Harvard how a man may hold a Calvinistic Atonement so as to be almost an æsthetic Unitarian."

N. P. Willis, in his *Journal*, quotes him, and remarks:

"But the evangelical world will be interested to know that this sermon of Dr. Bushnell is not a new one. He preached it seventeen years ago, and to us individually—or at least, a ser mon turning precisely on the same convergent and reciproco frictionizing philosophy. The reader will presently see how we have had a daily mnemonic, since, to remind us to practice what it taught.

"Seniors and classmates at Yale, in 1827, we occupied the 'third story, back, north college, north entry'—Bushnell in the north-west corner. As a student, our classmate and neighbor was a black-haired, earnest-eyed, sturdy, carelessly-dressed, athletic and independent good fellow—popular in spite of being both blunt and exemplary. We have seen him but once since those days, and then we chanced to meet him on a steamer on the Rhine—in the year 1845, we think—both of us, (overworked in our respective parishes,) voyagers for health. But to our story.

"The chapel bell was ringing us to prayers one summer's morning; and Bushnell, on his punctual way, chanced to look in at the opposite door, where we were—with the longitudinal straight come and go which we thought the philosophy of it—strapping our razor. (The beard was then a new customer of ours.) The pending shave, of course, was not to release us in time for more than the tutor's amen; but that was not the text of our classmate's sermon. 'Why, man!' said he, rushing in and seizing the instrument without ceremony, 'is that the way you strap a razor?' He grasped the strop in his other hand, and we have remembered his tone and manner almost three hundred and sixty-five times a year ever since, as he threw out his two elbows and showed us how it should be done. 'By drawing it from heel to point, both ways,' said he, 'thus, and thus; you make the two cross frictions correct each other.' And dropping the razor, with this brief lesson, he started on an overtaking trot to the chapel, the bell having stopped ringing as he scanned the improved edge with his equally sharp black eye. Now, will any one deny that these brief but excellent directions, for making the roughness of opposite sides contribute to a mutual fine edge, seem to have been 'the tune' of the doctor's sermon to the Unitarians? Our first hearing of the discourse was precisely as we have narrated it, and we thank the doctor for most edifying comfort out of the doctrine, as we trust his later hearers will, after as many years."

Dr. Bushnell possesses few of the graces of a pulpit orator. He lacks in forcible gesture, is scarcely ever impassioned in his manner, and has a disagreeable nasal utterance. But the matter richly compensates for the want of manner. He has always crowded houses, and silent, eager auditors. We have heard him when a sigh could be heard throughout the house, so enrapt was every person present, with his calm, majestic eloquence. He possesses great logical acumen, but is also a great poet, though he does not write rhymes. We could quote passages from some of his sermons which, in magnificent conception and splendid imagery, are surpassed by the writings of few living men, be they poets or orators. He is not declamatory, is not passionate, but is nevertheless at times exceedingly powerful. One is amazed at the profoundness of his intellect, and at the impression which he makes upon the hearer with it, without the usually considered necessary oratorical accompaniments.

In his person, Dr. Bushnell is slim, and of the average height. His features appear small but his head is of large size. His eyes are small and piercing, his forehead is expansive, his hair is dark gray, and he is graceful in his conversation and manners.

Feeling confident that whatever judgment the world may pronounce upon Dr. Bushnell's views of the trinity, Christ and the atonement, it will in due time recognize in him, not only a powerful intellect, but a great Christian reformer—the advocate of principles which, carried out, will produce a nobler Christianity than that which has characterized many of the leaders in the church—principles which will overthrow injustice, robbery and oppression, because they teach that the *practical* is of more importance than the theoretical, we have penned this feeble portrait of him, as one of the important agitators of the time.

William H. Seward

WILLIAM H. SEWARD.

We do not attempt a pen-portrait of Mr. Seward because he is a man of splendid intellect and acquirements; it is not because he is in the fullest sense of the word a statesman; nor yet because he has throughout the whole of his career thus far, shown himself to be possessed of humane and christian principles. We can say with truth that he is one of the first agitators of the age. It may be without design upon his part, but it is no less a fact. The higher law agitation was begotten by him. For he, in the United States senate, opposed the enactment of the abominable fugitive slave law — God's "higher law."

Daniel Webster, that giant intellect which held New England in thrall for a quarter of a century, is known throughout this country, and perhaps the world, as the defender of the constitution, but long after Seward the advocate, or Seward the politician, shall have been forgotten, the memory of Seward the defender of the higher law will be fresh in the hearts of a nation of freemen. That was a sublime scene, when he, surrounded by men of eminent abilities, but abilities devoted to the perpetration of injustice, ventured almost alone, and certainly with a mighty array of both talent and power against him, to thunder in the ears of listening senators the sentiment that there is a law *higher* than any they could make—higher than even the constitution itself — the law written upon the hearts of men by the finger of God.

The agitation which this simple, gospel truth created, in a country professedly christian, is truly astonishing, and we think it astonished no one more than Mr. Seward. He certainly could not have anticipated that not only politicians, but the professed expounders of God's word, would join the chorus against him, and against one of the profoundest and most self-evident truths contained in holy writ.

William H. Seward was born in Florida, N. Y., May 16th, 1801, and is consequently nearly fifty-four years old. His ancestors were of Welsh extraction upon his father's side, and Irish upon the side of his mother. His father was a physician in the state of New-York, of good character and respectable abilities, while his mother was a woman of clear intellect and warm heart. The inhabitants of the little town of Florida were principally emigrants from Connecticut and other New England states, and the tone of society was puritanic—using the word in its noblest sense. It was a quiet village, and the influences which surrounded the boy were excellent. He was noted for a studious turn of mind, a precocious development of his intellect, and a frank and gentle disposition. When nine years old he was sent to school at an academy in Goshen. At fifteen years of age the pale, thin, studious lad entered Union College, where he soon distinguished himself by his severe studies, his brilliant talents, and a manly and generous character. His favorite studies were rhetoric, moral philosophy, and the ancient classics. He rose at four in the morning and sat up late. It was in college, perhaps, that he acquired those habits of continuous mental toil which distinguish him now.

He graduated with distinguished honors. Among his fellow-graduates were William Kent, Dr. Hickok, and Professor Lewis. Mr. Seward shortly after entered the law-office of John Anthon, of the city of New York, where his thorough devotion to his studies, as before while in college, attracted the attention of his teachers. He completed his legal studies with Judge Duer and Ogden Hoffman, in Goshen, and was admitted to the bar of the supreme court at Utica, in 1822. The year following he took up his residence in the beautiful village of Auburn, which contains his "household gods" at the present day. He became the law partner of Judge Miller, of Auburn, and in 1824 married his youngest daughter, Frances Adeline Miller. The fruits of this union were five children, one of whom died young; one is in the United States army; another follows the profession of his father, while the remaining two are quite young.

Mr. Seward's personal appearance can scarcely be said to be prepossessing. At least we never knew a person who had, through the medium of the journals, become acquainted with his master-pieces of eloquence, afterward *see* him without an expression of disappointment. And yet there are many noble points in his personal appearance. He is scarcely average-sized, is modest in his ways, and often wears upon his face a sleepy look, which gives no indication of the powerful intellect behind that dreamy front. The first time we saw him he was at home among the charming scenery of Auburn, and beneath the roof of a mutual friend. His face struck us at first unpleasantly; it seemed too expressionless for so great a man; but in a moment the dreamy cloud furled off, and the eyes grew bright, and we felt the fascination of his voice, look, manner, and brilliant conversation—a fascination which thousands of others have experienced who have met him in conversation, or have listened to his speeches. His whole appearance seemed to have suddenly changed. The compact brow expressed power, the eyes genius, the lips force, the whole body grace mingled with stateliness, unassuming as it really was. An air of pleasant frankness pervaded his conversation and manners, and the listener forgot *the man*, his achievements, and position, in the topic of conversation. He has no affected dignity, but is simple and natural in all his ways and habits. There are distinguished politicians, so-called great men, in this country, whose greatness consists principally in a pompous dignity of manners and rhetoric. The chronic dullness of such men passes with the multitude for profundity of intellect. We hear a great deal of the look of *latent* power which such men wear, and indeed if they possess power it must be latent, for they never give the world any *evidence* of their godlike proportions of mind. Mr. Seward has not achieved the brilliant position which he occupies by any such method; he has *earned* it by a life of severe labor, and the fruits of his earnest toil remain an imperishable monument to his memory.

He has long been a resident of Auburn—one of the most beautiful cities in the state of New York—and early became distinguished in his profession. His social position is a happy one; his wealth is sufficient for his wants, and he is universally beloved by his townsmen. Though wealthy, his habits are simple, and he is as much the friend of the poor man when at home, as of the wealthy and influential. He is not merely theoretical, therefore, in his professions of democracy. For several years he has been a member of the Episcopal church, at Auburn, and has always conducted himself like a christian gentleman.

The father of Mr. Seward was a Jeffersonian democrat, and the son accepted the politics of his father; but in a short time after he had begun the practice of law, he left the democratic ranks for those of the great opposing party. When the Missouri compromise agitation swept over the country, he at once sided, instinctively, with the friends of freedom, and made several public speeches against any compromise with slavery. In 1830 he was elected to the state senate on anti-masonic grounds. In 1833 he made the tour of Europe. One year later he was nominated for governor by the whig party of his native state, and was defeated. In 1838 he was again nominated to that office, and was elected by ten thousand majority. When his term of office expired he was reëlected by a handsome, though not quite so great, a majority. While occupying the executive chair he used his influence for the repeal of all state laws which in any manner countenanced the institution of negro slavery. The law which permitted a southern slave-owner to retain possession of his slave, while traveling through the state, was repealed. A law was also passed which allowed a fugitive the benefit of a jury trial. An act was also passed prohibiting state officers from assisting in the recovery of fugitives, and denying the use of the jails for the confinement of fugitive slaves under arrest. Afterward, these laws were very unjustly pronounced unconstitutional by the United States supreme court. Another law was passed, chiefly through his influence, for the recovery of kidnapped colored citizens of New York. Under the operation of this humane enactment, Solomon Northup, who for twelve years, had been forced to toil upon southern soil, was rescued, to the great joy of his family and friends. The history of the wrongs perpetrated upon him have since been published in a book form, and have met with an extraordinary sale. To crown his official acts, just before retiring from office, Mr. Seward recommended the abolition of that law which demanded a freehold qualification of negro voters. He saw the bitter injustice of the law, and recommended that negroes be admitted to the exercise of the same rights accorded to white men. The manly courage which he displayed in this recommendation can never be forgotten, so long as humane and generous hearts beat upon American soil. One of the noblest of his official acts, however, we have yet to relate. The governor of Virginia made a requisition upon him for the surrender of men accused of assisting certain slaves to escape from their owners. He refused to comply with the demand, upon the ground that the article in the constitution authorizing a demand of fugitives from justice, contemplated only crimes which were such by the universal laws of the states, and by the general opinion of the civilized world. Aiding a slave to escape from oppression was an act of humanity, and as the laws of New York did not acknowledge it to be a crime, he did not feel authorized to surrender the accused. A long controversy was the result of this righteous decision, and retaliatory measures were tried by Virginia, but Governor Seward remained firm to the end.

In 1847, Mr. Seward defended John Van Zandt, who was accused of aiding the escape of slaves from their master, at the bar of the Supreme Court of the United States. His argument made on that occasion, is one of the most eloquent ever delivered at Washington. He would accept no compensation for his services. Still later, in the famous Van Nest murder case, Mr. Seward proved the depth of his philanthropy and the loftiness of his courage.

While riding once upon the banks of the beautiful Owasco Lake, the friend who was with us pointed out a pleasant farm-house as the scene a few years ago of a terrible murder, and not far distant in a lonely churchyard, we saw the graves of the victims. A negro by the name of William Freeman, at the age of sixteen, was sent to the state prison for five years for alleged horse stealing. He declared his innocence of the charge, and it has since been admitted by those who tried him, that he was undoubtedly innocent of the crime; but through the perjury of the real thief he was sent to prison. The injustice of his punishment, coupled with barbarous treatment while confined in prison, resulted in an insanity which bordered upon idiocy, and when at last his term expired, he went forth into the world demented, with only this one idea in his brain—that the world had deeply wronged him. One night, without any provocation, this lunatic negro entered the house of a Mr. Van Nest, and murdered him, his wife, a child, and the mother of Mr. Van Nest, a woman of seventy. He was arrested the next day, and such was the terrible indignation of the people of Auburn, that it was with great difficulty that they were prevented from hanging him upon the spot. Freeman, like an idiot, as he was, confessed, and laughed at the murder. This only the more enraged the populace. They clamored for his blood. Mr. Seward had acquired a great reputation for defending successfully accused criminals, and it at once was feared that he would be employed in the defense of the crazy negro. Such was the excitement against him—he was absent at the south—that his law partners were obliged publicly to promise that he would not defend the accused. Upon his return, his family expected the populace would outrage his person. He saw the feeling was intense upon the subject—that it was predetermined that the negro should be hung. He made the necessary examinations, and became thoroughly convinced that Freeman was insane when he committed the awful deed, but hoping that other counsel would appear for the wretched man, he did not offer his services. The day of trial came, and the people boasted that no lawyer *dared* to defend the murderer. The district attorney read the indictment against the man, and asked if he plead guilty or not guilty. His only reply was "ha!" He was asked if he was ready for trial; he "did'nt know"—if he had counsel; he "didn't know." The poor idiot had no conception of what was transpiring. His life was being taken from him, and he knew it not. Mr. Seward was present, and the sight of the poor, friendless, hated, idiot negro, so wrought upon his heart, that he burst into tears, but shortly recovering his calmness he arose and said, "May it please the Court: *I shall remain counsel for the prisoner until his death.*" And for two weeks, amid the most depleting weather, did he, without any compensation, give himself up body and soul for the defense of the poor negro. He was insulted by his townsmen, he became instantly unpopular—he who a few days before was the pride of Auburn; yet he flinched not a hair from his duty, but worked on bravely and nobly to the end. The well known John Van Buren was the opposing counsel, and with the predetermination of the jury, it was not difficult for him to win a verdict. In Mr. Seward's argument, which will ever be one of the brightest of his laurels, both as an advocate and a philanthropist, he, in allusion to the fact that he had lost his popularity in Auburn, and indeed throughout the state, for his defense of Freeman, said most eloquently:

"In due time, gentlemen of the Jury, when I shall have paid the debt of nature, my remains will rest here in your midst, with those of my kindred and neighbors. It is very possible they may be unhonored, neglected, spurned! But perhaps years hence, when the passion and excitement which now agitate this community shall have passed away—some wandering stranger—some lone exile—some *Indian*, some *Negro* may erect over them an humble stone, and thereon this epitaph, 'HE WAS FAITHFUL.'

Freeman was convicted of murder, but an appellate court granted a new trial. But before it came on the prisoner died. A *post mortem* examination was made by the most distinguished physicians in the state, who reported *that the brain of the negro was one mass of disease, and indeed nearly destroyed.* Thus it was proved incontestibly, that Mr. Seward had from the beginning been right, and that he was entitled to the warmest thanks of all humane men for the courageous and noble course which he had pursued. The people of Auburn restored him to his former place in their affections, and he was, if possible, more popular throughout the state, than he was before the trial. He had *proved* that he was not a demagogue, for he had given up reputation, friends, everything, to save a despised negro. In his argument he fearlessly rebuked the inhuman spirit of caste which shuts out the free black man from the sympathies of white people, though conscious that the expression of such sentiments must identify him with that unpopular class of men called "abolitionists."

As a writer, Mr. Seward occupies a high position. He writes clearly, comprehensively, and convincingly. If he does not ornament his style luxuriantly, it is the more impressive from its simplicity. It has directness and force, and his diction is always copious. Fit language is always at his command. He exhausts a subject. He does not indeed like some dissect in its every part—he disdains generally to employ much of his time over mere trifles—but he passes over a subject as an eagle flies over a province, not stopping to alight at every rocky height, not peering in at every farm-house window, but sailing majestically over all, *viewing everything*, scanning keenly river and height, village and city, the sheep browsing in the quiet pasture—the gathering tempest far away in the horizon.

Mr. Seward has paid, we believe, comparatively little attention to merely polite literature. That is, his earnest attention has been directed to politics and statesmanship. Yet in the volume of his life (published by Redfield) and in other places may be found brilliant proofs of his abilities as an author. His description of his European travels are exceedingly well written. We will give a specimen of his style, by extracting two short pieces of his—one upon the death of Adams, the other upon the death of Napoleon. The contrast is finely drawn.

DEATH OF J. Q. ADAMS.

The thirtieth congress assembled in this conjuncture, and the debates are solemn, earnest, and bewildering. Steam and lightning, which have become docile messengers, make the American people listeners to this high debate, and anxiety and interest, intense and universal, absorb them all. Suddenly the council is dissolved. Silence is in the capitol, and sorrow has thrown its pall over the land. What new event is this? Has some Cromwell closed the legislative chambers? or has some Cæsar, returning from his distant conquests, passed the Rubicon, seized the purple, and fallen in the senate, beneath the swords of self-appointed executioners of his country's vengeance? No! Nothing of all this. What means, then, this abrupt and fearful silence? What unlooked-for calamity has quelled the debates of the senate, and calmed the excitement of the people? An old man, whose tongue once indeed was eloquent, but now through age had well nigh lost its cunning, has fallen into the swoon of death. He was not an actor in the drama of conquest—nor had his feeble voice yet mingled in the lofty argument—

'A gray-haired sire, whose eye intent,
Was on the visioned future bent.'

In the very act of rising to debate, he fell into the arms of conscript fathers of the republic. A long lethargy supervened and oppressed his senses. Nature rallied the wasting powers, on the very verge of the grave, for a very brief space. The rekindled eye showed that the re-collected mind was clear, calm and vigorous. His weeping family and his sorrowing compeers were there. He surveyed the scene, and knew at once its fatal import. He had left no duty unperformed; he had no wish unsatisfied, no ambition unattained; no regret, no sorrow, no fear, no remorse. He could not shake off the dews of death that gathered on his brow. He could not pierce the thick shades that rose up before him. But he knew that eternity lay close by the shores of time. He knew that his Redeemer lived. Eloquence, even in that hour, inspired him with his ancient sublimity of utterance. "THIS," said the dying man, "THIS IS. THE END OF EARTH." He paused for moment, and then added, "I AM CONTENT." Angels might well draw aside the curtain of the skies to look down on such a scene—a scene that approximated even to that scene of unapproachable sublimity, not to be recalled without reverence, when in mortal agony, ONE who spake as never man spake, said, "IT IS FINISHED."

DEATH OF NAPOLEON.

He was an emperor. But he saw around him a mother, brothers and sisters, not ennobled; whose humble state reminded him and the world, that he was born a plebeian; and he had no heir to wait for the imperial crown. He scourged the earth again, and again fortune smiled on him even in his wild extravagance. He bestowed kingdoms and principalities upon his kindred—put away the devoted wife of his youthful days, and another, a daughter of Hapsburgh's imperial house, joyfully accepted his proud alliance. Offspring gladdened his anxious sight; a diadem was placed on its infant brow, and it received the homage of princes even in its cradle. Now he was indeed a monarch—a legitimate monarch—a monarch by divine appointment—the first of an endless succession of monarchs. But there were other monarchs who held sway in the earth. He was not content; he would reign with his kindred alone. He gathered new and greater armies from his own land—from subjugated lands. He called forth the young and brave—one from every household—from the Pyrenees to the Zuyder-Zee—from Jura to the ocean. He marshaled them into long and majestic columns, and went forth to seize that universal dominion, which seemed almost within his grasp. But ambition had tempted fortune too far. The nations of the earth resisted, repelled, subdued, surrounded him. The pageant was ended. The crown fell from his presumptuous head. The wife who had wedded him in his pride, forsook him when the hour of fear came upon him. His child was ravished from his sight. His kinsmen were degraded to their first estate, and he was no longer emperor, nor consul, nor general, nor even a citizen, but an exile and a prisoner on a lonely island, in the midst of the wild Atlantic. Discontent attended him here. The wayward man fretted out few long years of his yet unbroken manhood, looking off at the earliest dawn and in the evening's latest twilight, toward that distant world that had only just eluded his grasp. His heart corroded. Death came, not unlooked for, though it came even then unwelcome. He was stretched on his bed within the fort which constituted his prison. A few fast and faithful friends stood around, with the guards who rejoiced that the hour of relief from long and wearisome watching was at hand. As his strength wasted away, delirium stirred up the brain from its long and inglorious inactivity. The pageant of ambition returned. He was again a lieutenant, a general, a consul, an emperor of France. He filled again the throne of Charlemagne. His kindred pressed around him, again invested with the pompous pageantry of royalty. The daughter of the long line of kings again stood proudly by his side, and the sunny face of his child shone out from beneath the diadem that encircled its flowing locks. The marshals of Europe awaited his commands. The legions of the old guard were in the field, their scarred faces rejuvenated, and their ranks, thinned in many battles, replenished. Russia, Prussia, Denmark, and England, gathered their mighty hosts to give him battle. Once more he mounted his impatient charger, and rushed forth to conquest. He waved his sword aloft and cried, "TETE DE'ARME!" The feverish vision broke—the mockery was ended. The silver cord was loosened, and the warrior fell back upon his bed a lifeless corpse. THIS WAS THE END OF EARTH. THE CORSICAN WAS NOT CONTENT.

As a political writer, Mr. Seward ranks high. As an orator, he will by no means compare with such men as Phillips, Soulé, and other of the most brilliant of our native orators. We mean, of course, in the *mere graces of oratory*. In lofty eloquence he has few equals among the great men of America, if he has any; but his *manner* of speaking is too dry and passive.

"His rapid idealization, his oriental affluence, though not vagueness, of expression, and the Ciceronian flow of his language, proceeding not 'from the heat of youth, or the vapors of wine,' but from the exceedingly fertility of his imagination, combine to render him an interesting speaker. Yet his enunciation is neither clear nor distinct, and the tones of his voice often grate harshly upon the ear. He is not devoid of grace, however; he is calm and dignified, but earnest.

"His style is elegant, rather than neat; elaborate, rather than finished. It possesses a sparkling vivacity, but is somewhat deficient in energetic brevity. It is not always easy, for there is more labor than art; but if the wine has an agreeable *bouquet*, the connoisseur delights to have it linger. Like young D'Israeli, whose political position in some respects resembles his own, he has occasionally a tendency to verbose declamation, a natural predilection, perhaps, for Milesian floridness and hyperbole, and, like Napoleon, a love for gorgeous paradoxes. But, in general, his words are well chosen, and are frequently more eloquent than the ideas. His sentences are constructed with taste; they have often the brilliancy of Mirabeau, and the glowing fervor of Fox."

We must finally speak of Mr. Seward as a statesman. He is thought by many to be the first of living American statesmen. We are not disposed either to admit or deny this. He is certainly *among* the very first not only in America, but the world. He has the breadth, the calmness, the comprehensiveness of a great statesman. He is not inclined to radicalism. He is naturally, we think, a conservative. He does not strike out boldly into new paths. He clings to old truths, wages warfare against those who would forget the ancient faith. He never flies before an enemy however powerful. He holds to his principles on all occasions. Whatever he has been he is to-day, but he is slow to see the practicability of a new system of tactics. He has never in the senate, however strong the temptation, spoken a word against his old anti-slavery principles. Yet when thousands of his whig friends saw the necessity of sinking mere whig issues, and joining in a great and new party of freedom, Mr. Seward clung to the dead garments of the ancient organization, and ran imminent risk of terrible ruin. Was this an indication of foresight? of political sagacity? We think not.

Mr. Seward opposed the Mexican war, eloquently and earnestly—and when it was declared, wished it prosecuted vigorously. If this was wise statesmanship, it was not good morality. If it was a *wicked* war, it should not have been declared, nor carried on after declared.

In 1849 Mr. Seward was chosen to represent the state of New York in the United States senate. In the great compromise struggle, Mr. Seward remained true to freedom and the north, when so many great men proved traitors. His conduct through that terrible struggle will, in the pages of history be described, that unborn generations may admire. One of his noblest speeches in the senate upon this question, was delivered March 11, 1850. He said:

"But it is insisted that the admission of California shall be attended by a *compromise* of questions which have arisen out of *slavery!*

"*I am opposed to any such compromise in any and all the forms in which it has been proposed.* Because, while admitting the purity and the patriotism of all from whom it is my misfortune to differ, I think all legislative compromises radically wrong, and essentially vicious. They involve the surrender of the exercise of judgment and the conscience on distinct and separate questions, at distinct and separate times, with the indispensable advantages it affords for ascertaining the truth. They involve a relinquishment of the right to reconsider in future the docision of the present, on questions prematurely anticipated. And they are a usurpation as to future questions of the province of future legislators.

"Sir, it seems to me as if slavery had laid its paralyzing

hand upon myself, and the blood were coursing less freely than its wont through my veins, when I endeavor to suppose that such a compromise has been effected, and my utterance forever is arrested upon all the great questions, social, moral, and political, arising out of a subject so important, and yet so incomprehensible. What am I receive in this compromise? Freedom in California. It is well; it is a noble acquisition; it is worth a sacrifice. But what am I to give as an equivalent? A recognition of a claim to perpetuate slavery in the District of Columbia; forbearance towards more stringent laws concerning the arrest of persons suspected of being slaves found in the free states; forbearance from the *proviso* of freedom in the charters of new territories. None of the plans of compromise offered demand less than two, and most of them insist on all these conditions. The equivalent then is, some portion of liberty, some portion of human rights in one region for liberty in another."

In this speech occurred Mr. Seward's famous enunciation of the HIGHER LAW doctrine. We will give the extract:

"It is true indeed that the national domain is ours. It is true it was acquired by the valor and with the wealth of the whole nation. But we hold, nevertheless, no arbitrary power over it. We hold no arbitrary power over anything, whether acquired by law or seized by usurpation. The constitution regulates our stewardship; the constitution devotes the domain to union, to justice, to defense, to welfare and to liberty. BUT THERE IS A HIGHER LAW THAN THE CONSTITUTION, WHICH

REGULATES OUR AUTHORITY OVER THE DOMAIN, AND DEVOTES IT TO THE SAME NOBLE PURPOSES. The territory is a part, no inconsiderable part, of the common heritage of mankind, bestowed upon them by the Creator of the universe. We are his stewards, and must so discharge our trust, as to secure in the highest attainable degree their happiness. This is a state, and we are deliberating for it, just as our fathers deliberated in establishing the institutions we enjoy. Whatever superiority there is in our condition and hopes over those of any other 'kingdom' or 'estate,' is due to the fortunate circumstance that our ancestors did not leave things to 'take their chance,' but that they 'added amplitude and greatness' to our commonwealth 'by introducing such ordinances, constitutions, and customs as were wise.' We in our turn have succeeded to the same responsibilities, and we cannot approach the duty before us wisely or justly, except we raise ourselves to the great consideration of how we can most certainly 'sow greatness to our posterity and successors.'

"And now the simple, bold, and even awful question which presents itself to us is this: Shall we, who are founding institutions, social and political, for countless millions; shall we, who know by experience the wise and the just, and are free to choose them, and to reject the erroneous and unjust; shall we establish human bondage, or permit it by our sufferance to be established? Sir, our forefathers would not have hesitated an hour. They found slavery existing here, and they left it only because they could not remove it. There is not only no free state which would now establish it, but there is no slave state which, if it had had the free alternative, as we now have, would have founded slavery. Indeed, our revolutionary predecessors had precisely the same question before them in establishing an organic law, under which the states of Ohio, Michigan, Illinois, Wisconsin, and Iowa have since come into the Union, and they solemnly repudiated and excluded slavery from those states forever."

In a speech made in the senate, July 2, 1850, occurs the following eloquent passage:

"Still it is replied that the slavery question must be settled. That question cannot be settled by this bill. Slavery and freedom are conflicting systems, brought together by the union of the states, not neutralized, nor even harmonized. Their antagonism is radical, and therefore perpetual. Compromise continues conflict, and the conflict involves unavoidably all questions of national interest—questions of revenue, of internal improvement, of industry, of commerce, of political rivalry, and even all questions of peace and of war. In entering the career of conquest you have kindled to a fierce heat the fires you seek to extinguish, because you have thrown into them the fuel of propagandism. We have the propagandism of slavery to enlarge the slave market, and to increase slave representation in congress, and in the electoral colleges—for the bramble ever seeks power, though the olive, the fig, and the vine, refuse it; and we have the propagandism of freedom to counteract those purposes. Nor can this propagandism be arrested on either side. The sea is full of exiles, and they swarm over our land. Emigration from Europe and from Asia, from Polynesia even, from the free states, and from the slave states, goes on, and will go on, IN OBEDIENCE TO LAWS WHICH I SHOULD SAY WERE HIGHER THAN THE CONSTITUTION, IF ANY SUCH LAWS WERE ACKNOWLEDGED HERE. And I may be allowed here to refer those who have been scandalized by the allusion to such laws to a single passage by an author whose opinions did not err on the side of superstition or of tyranny: 'If it be said that every nation ought in this to follow their own constitutions, we are at an end of our controversies; for they ought not to be followed unless they are rightly made; they cannot be rightly made if they are contrary to the universal law of God and nature.' (Discourses on Government, by Algernon Sydney, chap. 1, p. 48.) I spoke of emigrants; and wherever those emigrants go—whether they go from necessity or of choice—they form continuous, unbroken, streaming processions of colonists, founders of states, builders of nations. And when colonies are planted, states are founded, or nations built, labor is there the first and indispensable element, and it begins and prosecutes to the end its strife for freedom and power. While the sovereignty of the territories remains here, the strife will come up here to be composed. You may slay the Wilmot proviso in the senate-chamber, and bury it beneath the capitol to-day; the dead corse, in complete steel, will haunt your legislative halls to-morrow. When the strife is ended in the territories you now possess, it will be renewed on new fields, north as well as south, to fortify advantages gained, or to retrieve losses incurred, for both of the parties well know that there is 'Yet in that word Hereafter.'

"Senators have referred us to the promise of peace heralded in the Missouri compromise. Sir, that prophecy is but half its journey yet. The annexation of Texas, the invasion of Mexico, this prolonged struggle over California, this desperate contest for the sands and snows of New Mexico and Deseret, are all within the scope and limits of the prediction; and so are the strifes yet to come over ice-bound regions beyond the St. Lawrence and sun-burnt plains beneath the tropics.

"But while this compromise will fail of all its purposes, it will work out serious and lasting evils. All such compromises are changes of the constitution made in derogation of the constitution. They render it uncertain in its meaning, and impair its vigor as well as its sanctions. This compromise finds the senate in wide divergence from the house of representatives by reason of the undue multiplication of feeble, consumptive states, effected by former compromises of the same sort. * * *

"Sir, the agitations which alarm us are not signs of evils to come, but mild efforts of the commonwealth for relief from mischiefs past.

"There is a way, and one way only, to put them at rest. Let us go back to the ground where our forefathers stood. While we leave slavery to the care of the states where it exists, let us inflexibly direct the policy of the federal government to circumscribe its limits and favor its ultimate extinguishment. Let those who have this misfortune entailed upon them instead of contriving how to maintain an equilibrium that never had existence, consider carefully how, at some time—it may be ten, or twenty, or even fifty years hence—by some means, by means all their own, and without our aid, without sudden change or violent action, they may bring about the emancipation of labor, and its restoration to its just dignity and power in the state. Let them take hope to themselves, give hope to the free states, awaken hope throughout the world. They will thus anticipate only what must happen at some time, and what they themselves must desire, if it can come safely, and as soon as it can come without danger. Let them do only this, and every cause of disagreement will cease immediately and forever. We shall then not merely endure each other, but we shall be reconciled together and shall realize once more the concord which results from mutual league, united councils, and equal hopes and hazards in the most sublime and beneficent enterprise the earth has witnessed. The fingers of the powers above would tune the harmony of such a peace."

As a senator, Mr. Seward's uniform urbanity, his self-possession and tact as a debater—the many able, clear, and elaborate arguments, which he has made upon great public questions, have deepened to enthusiasm the attachment of his friends, and correspondingly excited the opposition and the fears of his political foes. On a recent occasion—February 6, 1855—on the question of his reëlection to the United States senate, this feeling was especially manifest; but his election, on that occasion, by a large majority, is at once a flattering endorsement of his course in the national councils, and an evidence of the deep and ardent devotion of his political friends.

It is perhaps useless to speculate upon the future; but we sometimes imagine that Mr. Seward will yet take a postion before the American people immeasurably superior to any which he has yet filled. The spirit of slavery is aggressive. Each day is a witness to its hungry cry for blood, and each day is witness to its triumphs. So far, the north has succumbed, not without ado, but she has invariably in the end succumbed. But it will not be so always. A profound reaction will by-and-by take place—perhaps next year, perhaps ten years hence—*but it will surely come, and a great man will be needed for such a crisis.* No compromiser, but a statesman of the first order; calm, generous, but sternly resolved upon the divorce of the federal government from all connection with negro slavery. We cannot tell if Mr. Seward is great enough for such a crisis, but we have sometimes thought that such would be his destiny.

JAMES RUSSELL LOWELL.

We have nothing biographical to say respecting Mr. Lowell; we know not that his history presents any striking facts. He is the son of a distinguished Boston divine; he graduated at Harvard, and with high honors, and he wrote excellent poetry at an early age.

But Lowell is a remarkable man and poet. He lacks the fire of Whittier; he is *possibly* inferior to many American poets in important respects, but that he is one of the first poets of this age no man will deny. He is sincerely a reformer; his sympathies are entirely with the oppressed and down-trodden; he has always been true to the cause of the negro slave, and many of his poems prove it. Some of his poems are exceedingly beautiful, while others are full of grand thoughts, which strike upon the ear and heart, like the booming cannon-shot, which tells that an ardently desired conflict has commenced. This class of poems are less fiery than Whittier's reform poetry, but a very few of them are, we have sometimes thought, characterized by more grandeur than any of Whittier's upon the same subject. One of the most beautiful of Lowell's poems is that entitled "*The Forlorn.*" It betrays the nature of his religion and philosophy; at least, it proves that his sympathies are with the poor and friendless. To us, it seems that this poem can never die—that some of its stanzas are unsurpassed by any modern poetry.

THE FORLORN.

THE night is dark, the stinging sleet,
  Swept by the bitter gusts of air,
Drives whistling down the lonely street,
  And stiffens on the pavement bare.

The street-lamps flare and struggle dim
  Through the white sleet-clouds as they pass,
Or, governed by a boisterous whim,
  Drop down and rattle on the glass.

One poor, heart-broken, out-cast girl
  Faces the east wind's searching flaws,
And, as about her heart they whirl,
  Her tattered cloak more tightly draws.

The flat brick walls look cold and bleak,
  Her bare feet to the side-walk freeze;
Yet dares she yet a shelter seek,
  Though faint with hunger and disease.

The sharp storm cuts her forehead bare,
  And, piercing through her garments thin,
Beats on her shrunken breast, and there
  Makes colder the cold heart within.

She lingers where a ruddy glow
  Streams outward through an open shutter,
Giving more bitterness to woe,
  More loneliness to desertion utter.

One half the cold she had not felt
  Until she saw this gush of light
Spread warmly forth, and seemed to melt
  Its slow way through the dead'ning night.

She hears a woman's voice within,
  Singing sweet words her childhood knew,
And years of misery and sin
  Furl off and leave her heaven blue.

Her freezing heart, like one who sinks
  Out-wearied in the drifting snow,
Drowses to deadly sleep, and thinks
  No longer of its hopeless woe:

Old fields, and clear blue summer days,
  Old meadows, green with grass and trees,
That shimmer through the trembling bare,
  And whiten in the western breeze;

Old faces—all the friendly past
  Rises within her heart again,
And sunshine from her childhood cast
  Makes summer of the icy rain.

Enhaloed by a mild, warm glow,
  From all humanity apart,
She hears old footsteps wandering slow
  Through the lone chambers of her heart.

Outside the porch below the door,
  Her cheek upon the cold, hard stone,
She lies, no longer foul and poor,
  No longer dreary and alone.

Next morning, something heavily
  Against the opening door did weigh,
And there, from sin and sorrow free,
  A woman on the threshold lay.

A smile upon the wan lips told
  That she had found a calm release,
And that, from out the want and cold,
  The song had borne her soul in peace;

For, whom the heart of man shuts out,
  Straightway the heart of God takes in,
And fences them all round about
  With silence mid the world's loud din;

And one of his great charities
  Is music, and it doth not scorn
To close the lids upon the eyes
  Of the polluted and forlorn.

Far was she from her childhood's home,
  Farther in guilt had wandered thence,
Yet thither it had bid her come
  To die in maiden innocence.

Mr. Lowell has shown that he is a wit and humorist in the publication of his "*Biglow Papers.*" He is the only American who has attempted to *laugh down* the oppressors of the slave—the propagandists of slavery. Some of the Biglow poems are capital specimens of Yankee wit and humor. They are of course written purposely in the rough, exaggerated, Yankee style. Hosea gives his ideas of war as follows:

"Ez for war, I call it murder,—
There you hev it plain an' flat;
I don't want to go no furder
Than my testyment for that;

"God haz sed so plump and fairly,
It's ez long ez it is broad,
An' you've gut to git up airly
Ef you want to take in God."

Occasionally in the midst of fun, a fine, grand verse occurs, which puts away all laughter from the face. For instance, the following verse from the same poem, from which the foregoing was extracted:

"Massachusetts, God forgive her,
She's a kneelin' with the rest,
She that ough' to ha' clung forever
In her grand, old eagle nest;
She that ough' to stand so fearless
While the wracks are round her hurled,
Holdin' up a beacon peerless
To the oppressed of all the world!"

One of the most popular of Lowell's Biglow poems, is that upon John P. Robinson. In it General Cushing gets the following hit:

"Gineral C. is a dreffle smart man:
He's been on all sides that give places or pelf;
But consistency still woz a part of his plan,—
He's been true to *one* party—an' that is himself;—
So John P.
Robinson he
Sez he shall vote for Gineral C.

"Gineral C. he goes in fer the war,
He don't vally principle more'n an old cud;
Wut did God make us raytonal creeters fer,
But glory an' gunpowder, plunder an' blood?
So John P.
Robinson he
Sez he shall vote for Gineral C.

* * * * * * *

"Parson Wilbur sez *he* never heerd in his life
Thet the Apostles rigged out in their swaller-tail coats,
An' marched round in front of drum an' a fife,
To git some on 'em office, an' some on 'em votes;
But John P.
Robinson he
Sez they don't know everything down in Judee."

Here is a capital hit at a certain class of men:

"I'm willin' a man should go tollable strong
Agin wrong in the abstract, fer thet kind of wrong
Is ollers unpoplar an' never gets pitied,
Because its a crime no one ever committed;
But he mustn't be hard on partickler sins,
Coz then he'll be kickin' the people's own shins."

"The debate in the Sennit," is a humorous poem, one or two stanzas of which we will copy:

"'Here we stan' on the Constitution, by thunder
Its a fact o' which there's bushels o' proofs;
Fer how could we trample on't so, I wonder,
Eft wornt that it's ollers under our hoofs?'
Sez John C. Calhoun, sez he;—
'Human rights haint no more
Right to come on this floor.
No mor'n the man in the moon,' sez he.

"'The North haint no kind o' bisness with nothin',
An' you've no idee how much bother it saves;
We aint none riled by their frettin' and frothin,'
We're *used* to layin' the string on our slaves'
Sez John C. Calhoun, sez he;—
Sez Mister Foote
'I should like to shoot
The holl gang, by the gret horn spoon,' sez he.

* * * * * *

"'The masses ough' to labor an' we lay on soffies,
Thet's the reason I want to spread Freedom's aree;
It puts all the cunninest on us in office,
And reelises our Maker's orig'nal idee,'
Sez John C. Calhoun, sez he;—
'That's ez plain,' sez Cass
'Ez that some one's an ass,
It's as clear as the sun is at noon,' sez he.

"'Slavery's a thing thet depends on complexion,
It's God's law that fetters on black skins don't chafe;
Ef brains woz to settle it (horrid reflection!)
Wich of our honnable body 'd be safe?'
Sez John C. Calhoun, sez he;—
Sez Mister Hannegan
Afore he began agin,
'Thet exception is quite oppertoon,' sez he.

"'Gen'le Cass, Sir, you needn't be twitchin' your collar,
Your merit's quite clear by the dut on your knees,
At the North we don't make no distinctions of color;
You can all take a lick at our shoes w'n you please,'
Sez John C. Calhoun, sez he;—
Sez Mister Jarnagin
'They wont hev to larn agin,
They all on 'em know the old toon,' sez he.

N

"'The slavery question aint no ways bewilderin'
North and South hev one int'rest, its plain to a glance;
Northern men, like us patriarchs, dont sell their childrin,
But they *du* sell themselves, ef they git a good chance.'
Sez John C. Calhoun, sez he;—
Sez Atherton here
'This is gittin severe
I wish I could dive like a loon,' sez he."

But we can give the reader no fair idea of the peculiar merit of the "Biglow Papers" in our brief extracts. Nor have we pretended to quote the best of Lowell's reform poetry; to gain a just idea of his talents and position, the reader must—if he has not already—read his books, a luxury such as one rarely enjoys. We have attempted no sketch of Lowell—no criticism—but have rather penned a few desultory thoughts upon him and his poetry, wishing at the same time to preserve among these papers one of the most touching and beautiful poems which sympathy for the poor and outcast has brought into being.

Engraved by J. C. Buttre

Horace Greeley

HORACE GREELEY.*

LAUGHED at by the pomatumed and conceited fops on Broadway; hissed at by the devotees of cotton in Wall-street; hated intensely by all demagogues and workers of iniquity, and disliked by mouldy conservatives, whether in church or state, Horace Greeley is nevertheless one of the greatest men in America. He possesses an intellect acute and powerful; a conscience which is not seared; a great heart, and a generous hand. We know of no living American who can at all compare with him as a writer of vigorous English, in that particular department of literature which he long ago made his own. He has all of Cobbett's graphic power without his brutality—he has all of the earnest sympathy for the unfortunate of every race, clime, and color which characterizes some of the most popular of transatlantic authors, without their sentimentalism. Some of his editorials, dashed off with his heart on fire, will compare favorably with some of the best of the modern thunderer, the *London Times*. The leaders of the *Times* are more polished perhaps, are certainly more classi-

*We are indebted to Parton's admirable *Life of Horace Greeley* for many of the facts in this sketch.

cal, but in tremendous power of expression, they cannot surpass some of the best of the editorials of Horace Greeley. With a shrewd, clear intellect, an astonishingly vigorous style, and a heart easily wrought up to that degree of passion necessary to the production of the best kind of writing, he fears not the quill of any man living. Bennett may iterate and reiterate his senseless gibberish in reference to Greeley's "*isms*," his "shocking bad hat," and the "old gray surtout"—he may affect to laugh at "the philosopher," but he fears and hates him as Milton's devils feared and hated their heavenly combatants. So it is everywhere. The enemies of Horace Greeley—and he has many and bitter ones—know and feel his power, though they often affect the contrary. Let him be careless, or even slovenly in his costume, say that he does ride a vast number of "hobbies," not one of his enemies dare meet him in fair combat in reference to those "hobbies." We by no means swallow everything which is pronounced good by Horace Greeley, but we are at the same time perfectly aware that among that large class of demagogues and unprincipled editors who make it a point to libel and ridicule him upon every possible occasion, there is not a man who could hold an hour's argument with him upon the most untenable of all his "isms," without securing to himself a severe defeat.

Although Mr. Greeley has long had the reputation

of being a shrewd politician, we think that his *forte* does not lie in that direction. He writes best as a philanthropist and reformer, and it is as such that he will be known hereafter. When pleading the cause of the poor, degraded inebriate, or the chained and scourged bondman, he rises into his true manhood, and becomes most graphic and eloquent in his language. His terse and fiery sentences fall like lightning upon the head of the rumseller or stealer of men, and when picturing the squalor and wretchedness of the drunkard's home, the misery of his wife and little ones, or the agony of the slave-mother from whose arms her child has been torn, he pours forth a genuine pathos which gives to him instantly the hearts of thousands.

We have said that Mr. Greeley has bitter enemies; it is true, but no man has warmer or more devoted friends. There are men who have the blood of ancient and renowned families in their veins, men of immense wealth, men of high station, of great intellect, who count it an honor to be intimate with that carelessly-attired, bald-headed editor. There are men who pride themselves upon their gentility who would walk down Broadway arm in arm with Greeley, feeling honored and being honored by the temporary intimacy, though his boots were cowhide, and his hat a half-dozen winters old. But the best, the heartiest friends of the great editor are *the workers* of this country, the men who have made America what she is. It is the intelligent farmers, the clear-headed mechanics, the teachers, the liberal and earnest clergymen, the reformers everywhere, who love and appreciate him best. To them he is a tower of strength, a city of refuge. Many a reformer, when ready to faint, has been cheered by the thought that the most powerful editor in the country, day after day writes his most vigorous articles for the drunkard and the slave. However much these men may in the past have disliked his political writings, or his political conduct, his philanthropic writings have won their warm esteem for the author.

From these general remarks we turn to trace his early history. It is a remarkable one; for the position which he has reached, as one of the first editors of the country, he has struggled for inch by inch. His birth and parentage gave him none of those advantages for intellectual improvement that are now afforded almost universally to every farmer's boy. The district school, from which he obtained his first knowledge of books, was taught during the three or four winter months by some young person who could barely "pass examination" before the village minister and one or two functionaries, of perhaps much less practical and rudimental education.

Mr. Greeley's maternal ancestors were Scotch-Irish, who migrated to this country in 1718, and settled in various parts of New England. They were a bold, enthusiastic, hardy set, and in them we find many of those traits of character which, bequeathed to Horace as his only legacy, have made him what he is. From the same source sprang Stark of revolutionary memory, and in the battle of Bennington perished two of Mr. Greeley's great uncles. His paternal ancestors were from Nottingham, England. They were early noted for an obstinacy of purpose, which, as it descended through successive generations to Zaccheus Greeley, the father of Horace, may be said to have softened to a tenacity hard to overcome. This is noticed not only in their will, but in every mental and physical development. Their memory was wonderful; they held on to life itself with a vigor which is surprising. Honest and courageous, though generally poor, they left to posterity better than a prince's patrimony—it was a character, an example worthy of imitation.

Zaccheus Greeley and Mary Woodburn were married in 1807. They lived upon a small farm, the fruits of their own industry, in Amherst, New Hampshire. Under circumstances rather inauspicious, in February, 1811, Horace, the subject of our sketch, was ushered into existence. Of seven children he was the third, and, according to all accounts, he was the most unlikely of the whole; his frame was light, and his constitution fragile; but both were to be toughened and invigorated by the hard work and the fresh, mountain air, that can hardly be found except among the hills and valleys of New England. The population of Amherst were, and are still, dependent for the means of subsistence upon a soil sterile, stony and forbidding, except to the gaze of those hardy men who, from year to year, follow the plow over its surface. These villages seem to be produced from some stereotype plate of nature, and once planted, are as unchangeable as the very hills upon which they are located. There will be found a "meeting-house," (Congregational,) a "church," (Episcopal,) and a store, where is sold everything in general and nothing in particular. Upon the open area, where two or more roads meet, the school-house is located; is in fact seemingly "turned out doors;" the people have indeed got to regard it as so much a nuisance, that, even now, when a new one is contemplated, the land requisite for a site can hardly be bought for any price. From this center the farm-houses are placed in every direction, at first thickly, or at neighborly distances; but as you recede from the church they grow less frequent, until you are alone in the forest or pasture lands. Such was the situation of Horace Greeley's birth-place, and such the scene of his early childhood; it was a place where destitution and wealth are alike unknown, though every one has for a contented mind an abundance; it was a community of honest, common-sense men—practical farmers.

Horace, from his own earliest recollections, as well as from the account of those who watched his infancy, seems to have had a great predilection for books. He says, in a letter to a friend, "I think I am indebted for my first impulse toward intellectual acquirement and exertion to my mother's grandmother, who came out from Ireland among the first settlers of Londonderry. She must have been well versed in Irish and Scotch traditions, pretty well informed and strong minded; and my mother being left motherless when quite young, her grandmother exerted great influence over her mental development. I was a third child, the two preceding having died young, and I presume my mother was more attached to me on that ground, and the extreme feebleness of my constitution. My mind was early filled by her with the traditions, ballads, and snatches of history she had learned from her grandmother, which, though conveying very distorted and incorrect ideas of history, yet served to awaken in me a thirst for knowledge, and a lively interest for learning and history."

In more than the common and trite sense was he a remarkable child. We think it exceedingly interesting and instructive to linger a little here, and examine facts, to see, if possible, what were the elements of a constitution which, under such circumstances, could develop so remarkable a man. His mother was a stout, muscular woman, who esteemed it no disgrace to hoe in the garden, or pitch and rake hay, and it is asserted that she could cradle with equal facility in the house and in the fields. She could do more farm work in a day than a man, and then tell stories all the evening. To the ladies of our day these would hardly be considered recommendations, but *then* they were considered a prodigious feat. She was also quick at the spinning-wheel, and to its hum her tongue kept a continual harmony, for the amusement and benefit of her children. With eager avidity Horace listened to the anecdotes which fell from her lips, and here he first felt that intense yearning for knowledge which afterward made him so indefatigable a student. At two years of age he pored over the pages of the bible with great interest, and newspapers thrown upon the floor furnished him great amusement; at three he could read any of the ordinary books designed for children; at four could read anywhere, and with his book sidewise, upside down, or in any position. When only three years old he commenced attending the district school, and so eager was he to be present, that if the snow was piled in drifts, he prevailed upon his aunt to carry him to the school-house. The great ambition of those days seems to have been to become the best speller in the school, and to this eminence our hero early aspired;

once gained, he always maintained it. For this attainment he was admired by his mates, but seems not to have been envied. He cared little for the ordinary sports which so much amuse children at this age, but, as early as his fifth or sixth year, preferred to steal away with a book to some secluded place, and devour its contents. In other respects he was quite singular; he never would fight a boy whatever might be the provocation; if another was disposed to quarrel with him, he quietly stood and bore the infliction, which soon became more tiresome to the author than to the recipient. He is described at this time as a delicate, flaxen-haired child, of a gentle and retiring disposition, remarkable mainly for his attachment to books. This grew with his mind, till it became the all absorbing passion of his life. As he grew older, he ransacked all the libraries in the neighborhood to satisfy his intellectual appetite; but so far were they from satiating it, they seemed only to act as stimulants. He borrowed from the minister, from the village collection, from every source in his reach, till he became a walking encyclopedia. It was a peculiarity of his manner of reading that he became so absorbed in his book as to lose all apparent consciousness of what was going on about him. Thus he stored his mind with that knowledge which was to be so invaluable to him in after life. It was the only education that nature offered him, and he gladly availed himself of it; so that when time came for reflection, he possessed a perfect mine of information, whose treasures were as exhaustless in extent as they were difficult in acquisition.

There is hardly a boy in New England so small but that upon the farm some work can be found simple enough for his capacities. From the time that spring opens, each season brings to the juvenile his proportion of light labor. The corn is to be dropped; the team to be driven for the plow; the stock to be fed; the horse to be ridden between the rows of corn and potatoes, previous to hoeing; the gathering of apples, and the various autumnal crops, afford work for all sizes and all ages. Horace never evaded these for his book, but by diligence in accomplishing his apportioned job, managed to save time for his favorite indulgence, without interfering with the requirements of the farm. Among sports he was fond only of fishing, and his "luck" always excelled that of his companions, "because that while they fished for fun, he fished for fish."

When only ten years old his father became involved in debt, by signing the obligations of some of his neighbors, was unable to meet the pecuniary demands upon him, and, as a consequence, his little farm, house, and all that in the childhood of Horace went to make up home, was swept away by creditors. His father, a ruined bankrupt, was forced to flee the state to avoid arrest, and left his family behind him. After thirty years Horace discharged the last of these obligations with honor. The family, with the little wreck of their household furniture, followed the father to Westhaven, Vermont, where he had hired a small house, and here they survived the first winter in extreme indigence. In this new region the book of Nature afforded more various beauties than at Amherst, and it was of all others the delight of the boy's contemplation. Lake Champlain, with its grand and beautiful environs, lay within three miles of the cottage and here and there among those hills, little streams, like threads of silver, wound about, with an occasional lake in their course, like a string of beads about the neck of a child. The hills lifted their summits to the clouds, and their sloping sides, covered with verdure, extended as far as the eye could reach. The whole extent of country became a grand cradle for Greeley's imagination. The circumstances in which the family were now placed compelled the utmost economy in every habit; the usual dress of Horace was a hat, cotton shirt, and a pair of pants, whose counterpart cannot be found, perhaps, upon the poorest wayfarer of modern times. It is stated that during his residence in Westhaven, his clothing did not average a cost of three dollars a year, and that until he was twenty-one probably not fifty dollars were expended upon his dress. Economy was the study of the family, and their teacher stern necessity. The habits which he was here forced to learn will perhaps account for some of the apparent eccentricities of his subsequent life. The family *did* save something by their frugality, and it became a ruling principle of Horace never to incur the slightest unnecessary expense while there remained a debt unpaid. To his store of intellectual knowledge Horace added but little in Westhaven. The schools were much the same as in Amherst, certainly no better; and though for a while he attended regularly, he could oftener inform the teacher than learn from him. The text books also being much the same, his mind found a respite and recreation in assisting boys older than himself, and three times as large, to master difficulties which he had solved long ago. At length he became to the teachers somewhat of an annoyance, by his inquisitiveness, which they were unable to satisfy, and as a final result he was kept at home. Here he assisted the other children in their studies, and continued his reading. At the age of fifteen he had thoroughly perused Robinson Crusoe, the Arabian Nights, Shakspeare, Robertson's and Goldsmith's histories, and as many romances and works of fiction as he could lay hold of.

Horace had always cherished the idea of becoming a printer. His father gave him but little encouragement, but at eleven permitted him to walk to Whitehall, where a news paper was published, to talk with the proprietor. That individual informed him that he was too young to think of it, so he had nothing to do but to return, work, and wait. With impatience he did so for four years longer, when occurred a circumstance which caused an epoch in his history. In the *Northern Spectator*, published at East Poultney, Vermont, he saw an advertisement for an apprentice, and determined to apply for the place.

In the spring of 1826, the gentlemanly editor of that paper was hoeing potatoes in his garden one morning, when in walked a boy, rudely clad, to inquire after the situation. How little thought the editor of that journal, that the uncouth lad—the "devil" —would one day not merely control a journal like his own, but edit and manage the first journal in America! Mr. Bliss thought he had indeed an unpromising look, but upon asking him a few questions, discovered that there was something more than ordinary about him. In the language of that gentleman, "On entering into conversation, and a partial examination of the qualification of my new applicant, it required but little time to discover that he possessed a mind of no common order, and an acquired intelligence far beyond his years. He had had but little opportunity at the common school, but he said 'he had read some,' and what he had read he well understood and remembered. In addition to the ripe intelligence manifested by one so young, and whose instruction had been so limited, there was a single-mindedness, a truthfulness and common sense in what he said, that at once commanded my regard." Terms were subsequently arranged, and Horace bade farewell to the farm, as a means of subsistence, forever. Shortly afterward, his father removed with his family to Erie county, Pennsylvania, and Horace, at the age of fifteen, was left to depend entirely upon his own resources for a living.

Horace felt that now was the time for him to gather up his energies, and improve them to the best advantage. The long anticipated hour had arrived, and to his new avocation he eagerly applied himself. The older apprentices utterly failed in their attempts to divert him from his business, and again we have revealed the secret of his success; it was his untiring application. During the intervals of work, he employed his leisure in reading the exchanges, and was thus unconsciously obtaining political information, which should hereafter be the substance of many a brilliant editorial. He here joined a debating society, where he became noted for his accurate knowledge of political transactions, and it was soon discovered that in debate he was a powerful ally and dangerous opponent. Against all opposition, single handed and alone, he would maintain his point with an energy almost prophetic. Thus early was it noticed that when he was convinced of the truth of a position, all attempts to dislodge him, without showing his error, were vain; he could not be "taken by storm."

His person presented much the same appearance as when upon the farm. He never dressed for the debating meetings, for the very simple reason that he had no better dress to put on. All that he could save from the meager remuneration of fifty dollars per year was sent to his father, who was struggling with poverty in the western wilds of Pennsylvania. Twice during his residence at East Poultney he visited the family, making the passages on foot and by canal. On one of these trips he passed through Saratoga, and at a subsequent period he writes this half humorous notice of his impressions of that watering place.

"Saratoga! bright city of the present! thou ever-during one-and-twenty of existence! a wanderer by thy stately palaces and gushing fountains salutes thee! Years, yet not many, have elapsed since, a weary roamer from a distant land, he first sought thy health-giving waters. November's sky was over earth and him, and more than all, over thee; and its chilling blasts made mournful melody amid the waving branches of thy ever verdant pines. Then, as now, thou wert a city of tombs, deserted by the gay throng whose light laughter reëchoes so joyously through thy summer-robed arbors. But to him, thou wert ever a fairy land, and he wished to quaff of thy Hygeian treasures as of the nectar of the poet's fables.

One long and earnest draught ere its sickening disrelish came over him, and he flung down the cup in the bitterness of disappointment and disgust, and sadly addressed him again to his pedestrian journey. Is it ever thus with thy castles, Imagination? thy pictures, Fancy? thy dreams, O Hope? Perish the unbidden thought! A health in sparkling congress to the rainbow of life! even though its promise prove as shadowy as the baseless fabric of a vision. Better even the dear delusion of Hope—if delusion it must be—than the rugged reality of listless despair. (I think I could do this better in rhyme, if I had not trespassed in that line already. However, the cabin conversation of a canal packet is not remarkably favorable to poetry.) In plain prose, there is a great deal of mismanagement about this same village of Saratoga. The season gives up the ghost too easily."

In the office of the *Northern Spectator* he continued for more than four years, aiding in the printing, and also considerably in the editing. In the commencement of the fifth year of his apprenticeship, the establishment was broken up, and he was left again to shift for himself. Nothing daunted, he tied up his clothes in a handkerchief, slung the bundle across his back, and after thankfully receiving the present of an old overcoat from his host, started for his father's farm in Pennsylvania. He arrives there in June, 1830, at which place he recruited his health and strength by a few day's respite, and then obtained work for a time at Jamestown. Five day's stay satisfied him that it was no place for him, and he obtained a situation temporarily at Lodi. This also proved a concern which wished to suspend payment indefinitely, and having worked six weeks for promises, he again returned to the farm.

He now determined to try that city of peanut-war and women-mob notoriety, yclept Erie. With pack and stick as before, he started for the office of the *Erie Gazette*. Judge Sterrett, then and now the editor of that paper, thus mentions him:

"I was not in the printing office when he arrived. I came in soon after, and saw him sitting at the table, reading the newspapers, and so absorbed in them that he paid no attention to my entrance. My first feeling was one of astonishment, that a fellow so singularly green in his appearance should be *reading*, and above all, reading so intently. I looked at him for a few moments, and then finding that he made no movement toward acquainting me with his business, I took my composing stick and went to work. He continued to read for twenty minutes or more, when he got up, and coming close to my case, asked, in a peculiar whining voice, 'Do you want any help in the printing business?' 'Why,' said I, running my eye involuntarily up and down the extraordinary figure, 'Did *you* ever work at the trade?' 'Yes,' was the reply, 'and I should be willing to work under instructions if you could find me a job.'"

Upon hearing this, the Judge immediately suspected the poor fellow of being a runaway, and told him that he had no need of help. Horace felt badly enough, and returned home. It happened soon after, that the Judge fell in with a farmer, who recommended Horace so highly that he was sent for to fill the vacancy. Once more at his old place, he was not long working himself into the favor of the proprietor, and he paid him the usual journeyman's price of twelve dollars per month and board. His leisure, as usual, was occupied with reading, and he became noted for his accurate knowledge of political transactions, both past and present. Here he remained seven months, when the workman, whose place he was supplying, recovered from his sickness, and Horace was again out of employment. Of his wages he had, during these months, used six dollars for a suit of clothes, and the balance was due him. Fifteen dollars of the remainder was paid down to him, and a note for the balance he gave to his father.

In Erie fortune gave him her last ugly scowl, and, full of hope, he resolved to push for New York. It certainly was not his fault that he had succeeded no better, for he had done all that the most faithful man could do, and all was in vain. He knew that, in New York, if he should not succeed it must be his own fault, and he felt willing to risk an adventure. Slinging his pack upon his back again, he traveled on foot and by canal, until, on the 18th of August, 1831, he landed in New York. His articles of dress were still the same that he had purchased at Erie; his cash in pocket was ten dollars; yet these were not his capital, and he valued them as minor affairs. He felt sure that if he could once get a foothold in that city of competition, he should not only get a living but make himself heard and felt.

He took board with an Irishman at two and a half dollars per week, and then, for once, he did attempt to remedy the looks of the outer man, by purchasing a suit of clothes. The next thing was to see if he could find employment. He went from one office to another; among others to the *Journal of Commerce*, where David Hale informed him that he thought him a runaway apprentice, who could do no better than to return to his employer; but it was not advice that he was just then seeking, but employment. For this he sought diligently, through Friday and Saturday, yet the evening of the last day in the week found him tired of walking the city, and more weary of his miserable success. In the course of the Sabbath, he heard, from a fellow boarder, that they were in want of hands at West's, No. 85 Chatham street. Accordingly, at half past five on Monday morning, he was seated on the door-step of McElrath & Bangs' bookstore, the second loft of which building was used by Mr. West, as their printer. He was not aware that at that hour New Yorkers were enjoying the best part of their night's rest, and of course he had some time to wait. Did Mr. McElrath, as he passed in that morning, realize that the seedy looking individual upon his steps was destined to be in a few years his partner in one of the most flourishing of the New York dailies? Unlikely as it seemed, yet so it was to be. A journeyman of West's passing in, a Vermonter, heard his story and took him up stairs. He was set at a very difficult job of work, upon a Polyglot Testament. After a short time West came in, and asked his foreman, "Did you hire that d——n fool?" The foreman replied, that, in the urgent want of help, he had set him at work. "Well," said the master, "Do for God's sake pay him off to-night, and let him go about his business." When Horace presented his day's work of proof to the printer, at night, the question of letting him go was quickly settled; his day's work excelled any that had been previously done upon the job. Horace for the next six months earned six dollars per week, upon the Polyglot. Of the company then in the office, two have since been members of congress, three influential editors, one has made a fortune and is now a leading member in a firm which manufactures annually over a million of artificial teeth, and nearly all of the remainder have reached stations of wealth and influence. In order to make respectable wages, Horace was obliged to work hard, early and late. In the busiest moments, however, he could sustain a vigorous conversation upon politics, religion, or any of the subjects likely to be discussed among men of considerable intelligence. He rose immediately in the estimation of his shopmates, and for his obliging disposition, as well as for his industry and intellectual ability, he became "the *lion* of the shop." Though exceedingly careful in his own personal expenses, he was generous enough if any of the journeymen wanted money; he was never behindhand in lending them. He retained his slouched hat, his cotton shirt, his linen jacket and short trowsers, that he might have something left to help those whom he had left away in Pennsylvania.

He remained in this office fourteen months, when its business declining, he found employment with Colonel Porter in conducting a new paper—the "*Spirit of the Times*"—for which he wrote a world of articles of various character and length. The following humorous epistle was thought exceedingly funny at the time; it was written in May, 1832:

"Messrs. Editors:—Hear me you shall, pity me you must, while I proceed to give a short account of the dread calamities which this vile habit of turning the city upside down, 'tother side out, and wrong side before, on the first of May, has brought down on my devoted head.

"You must know, that having resided but a few months in your city, I was totally ignorant of the existence of said custom. So, on the morning of the eventful, and to me disastrous day, I arose, according to immemorial usage, at the dying away of the last echo of the breakfast bell, and soon found myself seated over my coffee, and my good landlady exercising her powers of volubility (no weak ones) apparently in my behalf; but so deep was the reverie in which my half-awakened brain was then engaged, that I did not catch a single idea from the whole of her discourse. I smiled, and said 'Yes ma'am,' 'certainly, ma'am,' at each pause; and having speedily despatched my breakfast, sallied immediately out, and proceeded to attend to the business which engrossed my mind. Dinner time came, but no time for dinner; and it was late before I was at liberty to wend my way over wheelbarrows, barrels, and all manner of obstructions, toward my boarding house. All here was still; but by the help of my night-keys, I soon introduced myself to my chamber, dreaming of nothing but sweet repose; when, horrible to relate! my ears were instantaneously saluted with a most piercing female shriek, proceeding exactly from my own bed, or at least from the place where it should have been; and scarcely had sufficient time elapsed for my hair to bristle on my head, before the shriek was answered by the loud vociferations of a surly mastiff in the kitchen beneath, and reëchoed by the outcries of half a dozen inmates of the house, and these again were succeeded by the rattle of the watchman; and the next moment, there was a round dozen of them (besides the dog) at my throat, and commanding me to tell them instantly what the devil all this meant.

"'You do well to ask that,' said I, as soon as I could speak, 'after falling upon me in this fashion in my own chamber.'

"'O take him off,' said the one who assumed to be the master of the house, 'perhaps he is not a thief after all; but being too tipsy for starlight, he has made a mistake in trying to find his lodgings;'—and in spite of all my remonstrances, I was forthwith marched off to the watch-house, to pass the remainder of the night. In the morning I narrowly escaped commitment on the charge of 'burglary, with intent to steal, (I verily believe it would have gone hard with me, if the witnesses could have been got there at that unseasonable hour,) and I was finally discharged, with a solemn admonition to guard, *for the future*, against intoxication. (Think of that, sir, for a member of the cold water society!)

"I spent the next day in unraveling the mystery; and found that my landlord had removed his goods and chattels to another part of the city, on the established day, supposing me to be previously acquainted and satisfied with his intention of so doing, and another family had immediately taken his place; of which changes my absence of mind and absence from my dinner had kept me ignorant; and thus had I been led blindfold into a 'Comedy (or rather tragedy) of Errors.'

"Your unfortunate, TIMOTHY WIGGINS."

In November, 1832, he went to work for Mr. Redfield, who then was engaged in the stereotyping business. Mr. R. remarked in him the same untiring activity that has made so prominent a feature in his character. "He earned more," said Mr. Redfield, "than any other man in the office, notwithstanding which he could talk all the time." At this time there were no *cheap* daily papers published in New York, or in the United States. Almost the *only* one, in fact, was a heavy, dull thing, taken by merchants at ten dollars a year; it was about this period that Dr. Sheppard conceived the idea of starting a cheap daily, and the project seemed as ridiculous to the printers of New York, as did the idea of using steam as a means of locomotion, or lightning as an agent for running errands for all mankind. The originator of the penny paper project got little encouragement, and finally determined to start it himself. He persuaded Mr. Story—the foreman of the "*Spirit of the Times*"—and Horace Greeley to associate with him in its publication and editorial management. Mr. Greeley was not very sanguine in regard to its success, for he thought that a daily could not sustain itself at a less price than two cents. However, the new firm of Greeley & Story, with the limited capital of one hundred and fifty dollars, issued, on the first of January, 1833, the *Morning Post*. That paper lived about two and a half weeks, long enough, however, to convince Mr. Greeley that his first impression was correct, viz: that with a fair capital a first rate daily would be sustained at two cents. Although the paper was discontinued, the firm held together, doing printing and job work, and among the rest a great deal of lottery advertising. Their business increased, till by an unfortunate casualty Mr. Story lost his life, and the name of the firm was changed to Greeley & Co., Jonas Winchester having taken the place of the deceased partner. In 1834 the firm included also a third partner, Mr. E. Libbett, and was considered worth three thousand dollars. They resolved to commence a weekly paper, and, as the result of their deliberations, appeared the *New Yorker*. An interesting circumstance mentioned by Mr. Greeley is, that at about this date James Gordon Bennett applied to him to start a daily paper, in company with him, but for some reason Mr. Greeley declined, and Bennett, with another partner, commenced the issue of the *Herald*.

It was with the *New Yorker* that Mr. Greeley's career as an editor really commenced. It may not be amiss here to review and notice the origin of those political and religious opinions which have formed so prominent characteristics of the man, and which justly or unjustly have associated his name with nearly all the "isms" of the last twenty years. His parents were neither of them church-members, though they were considered as belonging to the orthodox faith; they were moral, went to church with their children when they lived near enough, and were strict in their observance of the Sabbath. While at Westhaven, Vermont, Horace begun to reflect upon the diversity of creeds; at the age of twelve he wavered in opinion in regard to the justice of eternal punishment; and at fourteen had a preference for the doctrine of universal salvation. Having read the history of Demetrius Poliocrates, prince of Athens, he was overcome with admiration at his benevolence in the treatment of the Athenians, for the vilest ingratitude, and he involuntarily asked himself, "If a mortal prince can be thus generous and forgiving for the greatest possible sins, shall not the infinite God pardon the transgressions of his frail and erring creatures? Can he see them exposed to endless punishment?" From that hour his confidence in these theories decreased, and he has never yet seen sufficient evidence in their favor to induce him to accept them as his creed. Such were some of the influences that made him a Universalist.

The theory of protection to American manufactures was the great burden of President Monroe's message in 1821. Horace was then in Westhaven, and in the exciting debates upon the subject he took a deep and unusual interest. Many and brilliant were the events then occurring throughout the world, to engross the attention of the young politician. The South American republics were recognized as indedependent governments. In our country, Lafayette was the great theme of attention. Clay, Adams, and Jackson were making their most splendid efforts in congress. Horace became an ardent admirer of the brilliant talents of Henry Clay, and learned to distrust the pretensions of the so-called "democratic party." In the presidential campaign of 1824, he acknowledges, in a later editorial, a deep interest. He says, "We were but thirteen when this took place, but we looked on very earnestly, without prejudice, and tried to look beyond the mere names by which the contending parties were called. Could we doubt that democracy was on one side and the democratic party on the other?" From this time forward he had a great desire to become well versed in politics. Political papers, political articles and leaders were his delight. He used to get copies of the old *Richmond Enquirer*, and devour, with the greatest avidity, its laborious political editorials and communications. He acquired the habit of putting his thoughts in type without the immediate use of ink and paper, and in this manner also acquired the invaluable art of writing good articles quickly. While at work upon the Jackson paper at Lodi, he was thinking of and hoping for the success of the antagonistic party. He says, in a letter to a friend, "You are aware that an important election is close at hand in this state, and of course a great deal of interest is felt in the result. The regular Jacksonians think they will elect Throop by twenty thousand majority; but having obtained all the information I can, I give it as my decided opinion that if none of the candidates decline, we shall elect Francis Granger governor. I need not inform you that such a result will be highly satisfactory to your humble servant." Such were some of the influences that made him a whig.

While in New York, and soon after the death of Mr. Francis Story, Mr. Greeley attended the lectures of Dr. Graham. His doctrines were at that time making considerable noise in New York and through the country. Every one is informed of his peculiar theory and its probable correctness; suffice it to say that his doctrines struck Mr. Greeley as being sound, and he embraced them, practically as well as in theory. It is true that he had never been addicted to the use of stimulants; that he had always cherished a hearty disgust for tobacco and alcohol; that he was a *natural* teetotaler; but he now discarded the over nutritious diet, and in its stead substituted the plain fare of Dr. Graham.

While describing his boyhood we alluded to his distaste for the usual amusements so much relished by children. As he grew older the aversion grew stronger, and we do not find that he ever cared for any games but checkers and whist. At the first, where there is a chance for much display of skill, he was a fine player; at the second, he now and then took a hand with his fellow-apprentices, but never seems to have lost much time with it. Through all his early life we find no mention made of any particular devotion to the fair sex. He never was foppish enough to suit their tastes, or dutiful enough to mind their whims. He never felt that he had much time or money to bestow upon them gratuitously, and unless a young man has considerable of both, he will not be much of a favorite with them. He was fond of poetry, and occasionally published a poem over his initials. Under date of May 31st, 1834, we discover the only one which indicates any breathings of the tender passion. It is interesting, in that it betrays the consciousness he seems to have had of his eccentricities, and of the estimate which the world placed upon him, and, if there be any truth in poetry, also reveals somewhat the reciprocal esteem which he cherished toward the world. It is entitled—

FANTASIES.

They deem me cold, the thoughtless and light-hearted,
  In that I worship not at beauty's shrine;
They deem me cold, that through the years departed,
  I ne'er have bowed me to some form divine.
They deem me proud, that, where the world hath flattered,
  I ne'er have knelt to languish or adore;
They think not that the homage idly scattered,
  Leaves the heart bankrupt ere its spring is o'er.

No! in my soul there glows but one bright vision,
  And o'er my heart there rules but one fond spell,
Bright'ning my hours of sleep with dreams elysian
  Of one unseen, yet loved, aye cherished well;
Unseen? ah! no; her presence round me lingers,
  Chasing each wayward thought that tempts to rove;
Weaving affection's web with fairy fingers,
  And waking thoughts of purity and love.

Star of my heaven! * * * * *
* * * * * * * * *

He bids a final farewell to the muse in a poem which appeared in the *Literary Messenger*, in 1840. Here is the last verse:

"Yet mourn not I—a stern, high duty
Now nerves my heart and fires my brain
Perish the dream of shapes of beauty,
So that *this* strife be not in vain;
To war on fraud entrenched with power—
On smooth pretense and specious wrong—
This task be mine, though fortune lower;
For this be banished sky and song."

After this digression, which we have made in order to trace in a connected manner his early religious, political, poetical, and social or unsocial tendencies, we return to where we left our hero on the eve of commencing the publication of the *New Yorker*. This was in the spring of the year 1834. The first number was issued on the 22d of March. He had fifteen pledged subscribers, and the first number sold one hundred copies. In the address to the public, contained in the first issue, we find the following passage, which we take the liberty to quote, because it shows the principles with which Horace Greeley started his career as an editor—principles to which almost alone he has faithfully adhered:

"There is one disadvantage attending our *debut*, which is seldom encountered in the outset of periodicals aspiring to general popularity and patronage. Ours is not blazoned through the land as 'The cheapest periodical in the world,' 'The largest paper ever published,' or any of the captivating clap-traps wherewith enterprising gentlemen, possessed of a convenient stock of assurance, are wont to usher in their successive experiments on the gullibility of the public. No likenesses of eminent and favorite authors will embellish our title, while they disdain to write for our columns. No 'distinguished literary and fashionable characters' have been dragged in to bolster up a rigmarole of preposterous and charlatan pretensions. And, indeed, so serious is the deficiency that the first (we may say the only) objection which has been started by our most judicious friends, in the discussion of our plans and prospects, has invariably been this: 'You do not indulge sufficiently in high-sounding pretensions. You cannot succeed without *humbug*.' Our answer has constantly been—'*we shall try;*' and, in the spirit of this determination, we respectfully solicit of our fellow-citizens the extension of that share of patronage which they shall deem warranted by our performances rather than our promises."

The average gain of the *New Yorker* was more than one hundred a week. In less than five months it had a circulation of two thousand five hundred. The second volume commenced with four thousand five hundred subscribers. This was Horace Greeley's first success, and from this time forward he became known and appreciated among the literary ranks, as a spicy and successful editor.

The *New Yorker* gradually became a political paper, and its statistical information was always to be relied upon. Mr. Greeley has always been exceedingly exact in his reports, never allowing his hopes to take the place of facts in his paper. It is the remark of a proof-reader — "If there is anything that will make Horace furious, it is to have a name spelled wrong, or a mistake in election returns." Mr. Greeley was at this time a supporter of the colonization scheme, and leaned to the opinion that, in existing disputes between the north and south, the north was the aggressor. He maintained this ground with great vigor in the numerous editorials of that day.

The firm of Greeley & Co. continued on with apparently increasing success, until, in October, 1837, its financial affairs were in rather a tottering condition. Mr. Greeley labored with most indefatigable energy to keep it afloat, although in five years, seven copartners had entered and left the concern. A single paragraph from Mr. Greeley's pen reveals the reason of his ill success:

"Probably we lack the elements of that very desirable kind of success. There have been errors, mismanagements, and losses in the conduct of our business. We mean that we lack, or do not take kindly to, the arts which contribute to a newspaper sensation. When our journal first appeared, a hundred copies marked the extent to which the public curiosity claimed its perusal. Others establish newspapers even without literary reputation, as we were, and five or ten thousand copies are taken at once—just to see what the new thing is. And thence they career onward on the crest of a towering wave. * * * * 'You don't humbug enough,' has been the complaint of more than one of our retiring associates; 'you ought to make more noise, and vaunt your own merits; the world will never believe you print a good paper unless you tell them so.' Our course has not been changed by these representations."

One great defect, however, in the paper was that the business department wanted an able manager, and Mr. Greeley was too confiding, honest, and generous to be that man. However delinquent his subscribers might be, he always paid roundly and promptly for every piece of work done for him. If he hired an article written, and the author did not charge as much as Greeley thought it worth, he would make up the amount gratuitously. Such generosity may be noble, but not successful, in a world like this. Toward the close of his connection with the *New Yorker*, he was for months on the verge of bankruptcy, and was terribly harassed by pecuniary difficulties. When just ready to abandon the paper, Mr. D. S. Gregory offered him assistance, and Greeley survived another year, to battle with hard times and delinquent subscribers. Park Benjamin, who contributed to his literary department at this time, paid Mr. Greeley the following tribute of esteem, upon leaving it:

Grateful to my feelings has been my intercourse with the readers of the *New Yorker*, and with its principal editor and proprietor. By the former I hope my humble efforts will not be unremembered; by the latter, I am happy to believe that the sincere friendship which I entertain for him is reciprocated. I still insist upon my editorial right so far as to say, in opposition to any veto which my coadjutor may interpose, that I cannot leave the association which has been so agreeable to me, without paying to sterling worth, unbending integrity, high moral principle, and ready kindness, their just due. These qualities exist in the character of the man with whom now I part; and by all to whom such qualities may appear admirable, must such a character be esteemed."

Henry J. Raymond, now the editor of the *New York Daily Times*, commenced his literary career at eight dollars per week, under Horace Greeley. He was a fine, rapid writer, and was destined for a more prominent position than sub-editor of any paper. He was then a recent graduate from college.

The weekly labors of Mr. Greeley included, besides the work upon the *New Yorker*, the editing of the *Jeffersonian*, a weekly paper, published in Albany, through the campaign of 1838. Either of these was enough for a man of ordinary writing abilities, but Mr. Greeley attempted and succeeded tolerably well with both. It was, however, only by the greatest exertions, for the traveling of that day was not what it is at present.

Horace Greeley was one of the principal leading working spirits, by whose incessant efforts the election of General Harrison, in 1840, was accomplished. In May he commenced the issue of the *Log Cabin*, the first edition of which sold twenty thousand copies, as soon as they were struck off. Another edition was printed, and another, until fifty thousand copies had been disposed of. It was a remarkable hit. Seven hundred subscribers were added daily, until the weekly issue was over ninety thousand. Such success was as little anticipated as prepared for, and it caused so much extra work and expense, for so short a time, that but little money was made from it. Subscribers, who had sent in their names in the excitement preceding the election, were exceedingly tardy about paying up. As a final result, it was continued in a weekly form, until it and the *New Yorker* were merged in the *Tribune*.

Mr. Greeley was now utterly absorbed in politics. It is related of him that he became frequently so engrossed in argument as to lose all consciousness of events transpiring immediately about him. It even happened that he could not tell whether or not he had been to dinner, and had to ascertain the fact by inquiring of the hands in the office. A good anecdote and true, is told of his being invited to take tea at the house of a friend, when some political subject being introduced as the theme of conversation, he defended one side with great warmth. While perfectly absorbed in the discussion, the lady of the house repeatedly invited him to tea, but he heard no more of the invitation than if it had been whispered in the street. She finally brought in a basket of "crullers," or "doughnuts," as they are called in some sections, and offered him one. All unconsciously he took the basket into his lap, and went on with his remarks. Gradually his hand wandered to the basket, took up a cake mechanically, and conveyed it to his mouth; bit by bit it disappeared, and then another, till the last was gone! The lady of the house was now thoroughly alarmed, and having heard that cheese was an excellent antidote in such a case, she passed him a plate that he might eat a piece. Still busily engaged in the merits of the question, he took the plate into his hand, and piece by piece, by the same abstracted process, the cheese followed the cakes! No ill consequences ensued, nor was Mr. Greeley conscious of having taken any food.

For his service in this campaign, Mr. Greeley received nothing but the splendid reputation he obtained as a fast and forcible writer. He had now on his hands the *Log Cabin* and the *New Yorker;* these he resolved to merge into one paper, and concentrate upon its editorial department all the intellectual ability he could command. He had saved as yet but little money, but he had the credit of an honest man, and the repute of a very able one. With these, and a thousand dollars from Mr. Gregory, whom we have before alluded to, he resolved to start anew, and the result was the *New York Tribune.* He made an arrangement with Mr. McElrath, a lawyer, who was capitally fitted to manage the business department of a news journal. The amount of work which Mr. Greeley accomplished was astonishingly great. His energy was almost superhuman. He applied himself closely every day from fifteen to eighteen hours—and oftener the latter than the former. Under the editorship of such an indefatigable man the *Tribune* could but thrive. It rose in circulation, and in the estimation of the people rapidly. Men who bitterly opposed its politics conceded its eminent ability. It was the leading journal of the whig party. It also advocated various beneficent reforms. We by no means defend the political course of that journal, while it was a party organ. While the *Tribune* was a whig journal, it was probably hated more intensely by its enemies than any other American journal. The eminent abilities of Mr. Greeley could not be vigorously used for party purposes, without drawing down upon him the hatred of thousands. Few men have been more abused than he; few more execrated than he by opposing politicians. It is easy enough to see why. He writes nervously, graphically, intensely. He has no soft words for an enemy, but blurts out what he conceives to be the truth, as an Indian tomahawks a white man. His vast energy, combined with his splendid writing talent, disposes him to annihilate an opposer. He has withal a capability, we think, for unjust prejudices against an enemy. This was the case when he was younger, but of late they seem to have died out of his heart. But, though as a writer Mr. Greeley is always impetuous, he is by nature cautious—almost cunning. Thus some of his political movements seem to his political enemies to have been prompted by cunning. We think, however, notwithstanding all the suspicious political moves which he has made in the past, that few honester men ever sat in the chair-editorial. He is one of the most earnest men of the age. There is nothing stagnant in his nature. He is decided, fixed, in his opinions.

The opposition which the *Tribune* received from the *New York Sun* was bitter and lasting. Every means that could be used, fair or unfair, were tried to prevent the *Tribune* from supplanting that paper. In it appeared the most scurrilous articles, with the manifest intention of "crushing out" the *Tribune;* farther even than this, the attempt was made to hinder the sale by direct violence. Fights were prompted between the newsboys, by the emissaries of Beach, and nothing that promised success was too mean for him to attempt. But, as when a strong, well managed ship is sailing against the wind, she moves fastest when it blows hardest, so with the *Tribune*, the greater the opposition the more rapid its progress. The public became interested in the affair, and justice was awarded to Mr. Greeley in the increasing demand for his paper. For the first number there were six hundred subscribers, and the editor remarks that,—"We had some difficulty in giving away the first edition." It steadily gained, however, in friends and patronage, and during the struggle with the *Sun* subscribers poured in at the rate of three hundred per day. The fourth week showed a circulation of six thousand, the seventh, eleven thousand, while the advertising business increased in proportion, although the price was raised from four to six cents a line. The news department of the *Tribune* was more accurate and prompt than that of its adversary. In a certain day the *Sun* informed the public that "*it is doubtful whether the land bill can pass the house*;" the *Tribune* of the same day announced the passage of the bill! The assistance of Mr. McElrath in the business department of the paper was invaluable, since it allowed to Mr. Greeley his whole time upon the writing and editorial management. His usual day's work at this period was three columns, equal to fifteen pages of foolscap, besides the arranging, clipping, &c.

Upon the subject of protection to American industry Mr. Greeley wrote repeatedly, and with great energy. After reading his able articles upon that subject, one can hardly fail to be convinced of the justness of his views. He advocated the subject, not solely because it was a *whig* measure, but because it seemed to him correct and best for the interests of the country at large. Nevertheless, he was, at this period, a zealous, earnest, almost bigoted supporter of the whig policy and whig administration. He hated and fought the doctrine of repudiation with telling energy. He supported John Tyler till he perceived that Tyler was selling himself and the whig party to locofocoism, and then he opposed him with all his might.

The history of the *Tribune* hereafter was the history of Mr. Greeley. It began its second year with a circulation of twelve thousand subscribers, and an average daily support of thirteen columns of advertisements. In writing the subsequent history of its editor, we shall most conveniently, almost necessarily, follow the track of the *Tribune* down to the present time, and, advancing, glance at the doctrines it sustained, and the theories it supported. The first to be noticed is Fourierism. At the time when this subject became a theme of discussion in this country,

Horace Greeley was a young man of twenty-six, who, from poverty, had struggled up to a competence only by the most arduous exertion. He knew by bitter experience what it was to be miserably poor; he had gone through a long course of training in the school of adversity, and was in every way qualified to sympathize with his schoolmates under the iron discipline of that stern tutor. It was not in Greeley to look upon destitution and misery without commiseration, nor was he willing that his sympathy should end until the means of relief were discovered and applied. New York was a vast theater for the display of humanity and kindness, and never more so than during the winter of 1837–8. Food and provisions were high, fuel scarce, the cold weather unusually protracted and severe. Business of all kinds was at a stand-still, laborers were thrown out of employment by thousands, and crowds of hungry men, women, and children went famishing through the streets. The picture was a most melancholy one, well calculated to inspire the energies of a humane disposition. What could be done to relieve the distress of these perishing thousands? There was wealth enough; there was enough in New York, and Greeley knew it; *their's* was the want, *there* the supply. Could not some plan be devised by which they could be brought together? In this emergency, Albert Brisbane, a liberally educated young man, the son of wealthy parents, returned from Paris, where the doctrines of Fourier was the theme of universal discussion. Brisbane was fascinated by the great beauty and apparent feasibility of these doctrines, and attributed the want of success in Europe to the form of government, and the utter ignorance and degradation of the masses. He thought that if transplanted to free, progressive America, they would operate like a charm. Full of his new enthusiasm, he returned to New York, and commenced lecturing on the subject. Greeley heard him; the remedy seemed adapted to the want; he espoused the cause, and in the *Tribune* earnestly advocated the adoption of the experiment. A very brief glance at the leading principles of these social reformers is given in a *Tribune* of November, 1841. He says:

"We have written something, and shall yet write much more, in illustration and advocacy of the great social revolution which our age is destined to commence, in rendering all useful labor at once attractive and honorable, and banishing want and all consequent degradation from the globe. The germ of this revolution is developed in the writings of Charles Fourier, a philanthropic and observing Frenchman, who died in 1837, after devoting thirty years of a studious and unobtrusive life to inquiries, at once patient and profound, into the causes of the great mass of social evils which overwhelm humanity, and the true means of removing them. These means he proves to be a system of industrial and household association, on the principle of joint stock investment, whereby labor will be ennobled and rendered attractive and universal, capital be afforded a secure and lucrative investment, and talent and industry find appropriate, constant employment and adequate reward, while plenty, comfort, and the best means of intellectual and moral improvement is guaranteed to all, regardless of former acquirements or conditions."

An association of gentlemen was formed, which obtained the use of a column of the *Daily Tribune* upon the subject. Much attention was attracted to the consideration of these measures throughout the United States. It met with all kinds of opposition, was declared a dangerous innovation, an unchristian scheme, and met universally with great hostility. It is always thus with reforms, whether social, religious, or political, and the only true test must be actual experiment. With a single exception the "associations" were failures, and many worthy men suffered severely with their everthrow. Odium was cast upon the originators of a scheme which, had it been successful, would have made them heroes; so great is the effect of success! Mr. Greeley's part in the drama wound up with a discussion between himself and Henry J. Raymond, who, at the solicitation of Colonel Webb, had joined the *Courier and Enquirer*. The dispute was prolonged through successive numbers, and both sides of the argument were published in both papers. Since then, the same sentiments have always formed a prominent feature in Mr. Greeley's opinions, but he seldom advances them in his paper, unless to repel attacks which originate from the attempt to vamp them up for party capital. The world is at present too ungenial, and its soil too uncultivated to ripen so delicate a fruit; it must be deferred for full realization to "the good time coming."

From a penny paper the *Tribune* raised its price to two cents, and at this the second volume commenced with a list of twelve thousand. For interfering in a local dispute in regard to election returns, it was at this early period threatened with an execution of mob law, and had it been carried out, the assailants would have met a *warm* reception. The office was put in a state of defense, and workmen, compositors, proof-readers, and all employed in the office, except Mr. Greeley, were ready to meet the assault; he remarked that he thought no violence would be attempted, and there was none.

In the summer of 1842, Mr. Greeley sought a temporary respite from the harrassing cares of editorial life in traveling. He visited Washington, Mount Vernon, Niagara, and his old home in Vermont. His style as a correspondent is sometimes racy, sometimes subdued, and always exceedingly interesting. We copy the following from the account of his visit to the burial place of Washington:

"Slowly, pensively, we turned our faces from the rest of the mighty dead, to the turmoil of the restless living—from the solemn, sublime repose of Mount Vernon, to the ceaseless intrigues, the petty strifes, the ant-hill bustle of the Federal City. Each has its own atmosphere; London and Mecca are not so unlike as they. The silent, enshrouding woods, the gleaming, majestic river, the bright, benignant sky—it is fitly here, amid the scenes he loved and hallowed, that the man who redeemed patriotism and liberty from the reproach which centuries of designing knavery and hollow profession had cast upon them, now calmly awaits the trump of the archangel. Who does not rejoice that the original design of removing his ashes to the city has never been consummated—that they lie where the pilgrim may reverently approach them, unvexed by the light laugh of the time-killing worldling, unannoyed by the vain or vile scribblings of the thoughtless or the base? Thus may they repose forever! that the heart of the patriot may be invigorated, the hopes of the philanthropist strengthened and his aims exalted, the pulse of the American quickened and his aspirations purified by a visit to Mount Vernon!"

In reply to an assault by Major Noah, who seems to have indulged quite a disposition to provoke him, and had published a nonsensical paragraph charging Mr. Greeley with the crime of eating with colored persons, the editor of the *Tribune* wrote the following cutting retort:

"We have never associated with blacks; never eaten with them; and yet it is quite probable that if we *had* seen two cleanly, decent colored persons sitting down at a second table in another room just as we were finishing our breakfast, we might have gone away without thinking or caring about the matter. We choose our own company in all things, and that of our own race, but cherish little of that spirit which for eighteen centuries has held the kindred of M. M. Noah accursed of God and man, outlawed and outcast, and unfit to be the associates of Christians, Mussulmen, or even self-respecting Pagans. Where there are thousands who would not eat with a negro, there are (or lately were) tens of thousands who would not eat with a Jew. We leave to such renegades as the Judge of Israel the stirring up of prejudices and the prating of the 'usages of society,' which over half the world make him an abhorrence, as they not long since would have done here. We treat all men according to what they are, and not whence they spring. That he is a knave, we think much to his discredit; that he is a Jew, nothing, however unfortunate it may be to that luckless people."

The famous libel suits of J. F. Cooper against the *Tribune* furnish us with the most amusing incidents in the history of that paper. Mr. Cooper was attempting to sustain his waning reputation as a novelist, and revive the depreciated state of his funds, by a series of exceedingly *novel* prosecutions. One of them was against Mr. Weed, the editor of the *Albany Evening Journal.* In a letter to the *Tribune* respecting that trial, occurs the following passage which is supposed to furnish the foundation for the charge: "The value of Mr. Cooper's character, therefore, has been judicially ascertained. It is worth exactly four hundred dollars."

Upon the issue of the letter from which this clause is taken, Fenimore Cooper determined to commence a suit against Horace Greeley. He did so, and for the description of the trial, &c., we shall refer to the *Tribune* containing Mr. Greeley's humorous account of it, premising that Mr. Greeley defended his case in person. In this account of it he says:

"We had, to the declaration against us, pleaded the general issue—that is not guilty of libeling Mr. Cooper, at the same time fully admitting that we had published all that he *called* our libels on him, and desiring to put in issue only the fact of their being or not being libels, and have the verdict turn on that issue. But Mr. Cooper told the jury (and we found to our cost that this was New York supreme and circuit court law) that *by pleading not guilty we had legally admitted ourselves to be guilty*—that all that was necessary for the plaintiff, under that plea, was to put in our admission of publication, and then the jury had nothing to do but to assess the plaintiff's damages under the direction of the court. In short, we were made to understand that there was no way under heaven—we beg pardon;

under New York supreme court law—in which the editor of a newspaper could plead to an action for libel that the matter charged upon him as libelous was not in its nature or intent a libel, but simply a statement, according to the best of his knowledge and belief, of some notorious and every way public transaction, or his own honest comments thereon, and ask the jury to decide whether the plaintiff's averments or his answers thereto be the truth!"

His closing address to the jury contained so much of manly eloquence and has so important a bearing on the freedom of the press, that our readers cannot fail to admire it; he continues:

"But, gentlemen, you are bound to consider—you cannot refuse to consider—that if you condemn me to pay any sum whatever for the expression of my opinion upon his conduct, you thereby seal your own lips, with those of your neighbors and countrymen, against any such expression in this or any other case; you will no longer have a right to censure the rich man who harasses his poor neighbor with vexatious lawsuits, merely to oppress and ruin him, but will be liable, by your own verdict, to prosecution and damages whenever you shall feel constrained to condemn what appears to you injustice, oppression, or littleness, no matter how flagrant the case may be.

"Gentlemen of the jury, my character, my reputation are in your hands. I think I may say that I commit them to your keeping untarnished; I will not doubt that you will return them to me unsullied. I ask of you no mercy, but justice. I have not sought this issue; but neither have I feared nor shunned it. Should you render the verdict against me, I shall deplore, far more than any pecuniary consequence, the stigma of libeler which your verdict would tend to cast upon me—an imputation which I was never, till now, called to repel before a jury of my countrymen. But, gentlemen, feeling no consciousness of *deserving* such a stigma—feeling, at this moment, as ever, a profound conviction that I *do not* deserve it, I shall yet be consoled by the reflection, that many nobler and worthier than I have suffered far more than any judgment here could inflict on me, for the rights of free speech and opinion—the right of rebuking oppression and meanness in the language of manly sincerity and honest feeling. By their example, may I still be upheld and strengthened. Gentlemen, I fearlessly await your decision!"

Mr. J. F. Cooper in person proceeded to sum up the cause for the prosecution, after which follow some general comments by Mr. Greeley, which are racy:

"Knowing what we did and do of the severe illness of the wife of Mr. Weed, and the dangerous state of his eldest daughter at the time of the Fonda trials in question—regarding them as we do—the jokes attempted to be cut by Fenimore over their condition—his talk of the story growing up from one girl to the mother and three or four daughters—his fun about their probably having the Asiatic cholera among them, or some other contagious disease, &c., &c., however it may have sounded to others, did seem to us rather inhu——hallo there! we had liked to have put our foot right into it again, after all our tuition. We mean to say considering that, just the day before, Mr. Weed had been choked by his counsel into surrendering at discretion to Fenimore, being assured (correctly) by said counsel that, as the law is now expounded and administered by the supreme court, he had no earthly choice but to bow his neck to the yoke, pay all that might be claimed of him, and publish whatever humiliations should be required, or else prepare to be immediately ruined by the suits which Fenimore and Richard had already commenced or were getting ready for him—considering all this, and how much Mr. Weed has paid and must pay towards his subsistence—how keenly W. has had to smart for his speaking his mind of him—we did not think that Fenimore's talk at this time and place of Weed's family, and of Weed himself, as a man so paltry that he would pretend to sickness in his family as an excuse to keep away from court, and resort to trick after trick to put off his case for a day or two—it seemed to us, considering the present relations of the parties, most ungen——there we go again! We mean to say that the whole of this part of Mr. Cooper's speech grated upon our feelings rather harshly. We believe *that* isn't a libel. (This talking with a gag in the mouth is rather awkward, at first, but we'll get the hang of it in time. Have patience with us, Fenimore on one side and the public on the other, till we nick it.) * * * * * Fenimore closed very effectively with an appeal for his character, and a picture of the sufferings of his wife and family—his grown up daughters often suffused in tears by these attacks on their father. Some said this was mawkish, but we consider it good, and think it told. We have a different theory as to what the girls were crying for, but we wont state it, lest another dose of supreme court law be administered to us. (Not any more at present, I thank ye!) * * * * * The jury retired, and the rest of us went to dinner. The jury were hungry, too, and did not stay out long. On comparing notes, there were *seven* of them for a verdict of one hundred, *two* for two hundred, and *three* for five hundred dollars. They added these sums up—total twenty-six hundred—divided by twelve, and the dividend was a little over two hundred; so they called it two hundred dollars damages and six cents costs, which of course carries full costs against us. We went back from dinner, took the verdict in all meekness, took a sleigh, and struck a bee-line for New York."

Upon the harmless jokes cracked by Mr. Greeley in this report, such as "inhu——," "ungen——," &c., Cooper commenced another action, but his better judgment returning before he had quite made a fool of himself, he abandoned it. Before we leave the subject we *must* find room for Greeley's closing piece of pleasantry; we call it rich:

"Our friend Fenimore Cooper, it will be remembered, chivalrously declared, in his summing up at Ballston, that if we were to sue him for a libel in asserting our personal uncomeliness, he should not plead the *general issue*, but *justify*. To a plain man, this would seem an easy and safe course. But let us try it: Fenimore has the audacity to say we are not handsome; we employ Richard (Fenimore's counsel)—we presume he has no aversion to a good fee, even if made of the editorial 'sixpences' Fenimore dilated on—and commence our action, laying the venue in St. Lawrence, Alleghany, or some other county where our personal appearance is not notorious; and if the judge should be a friend of ours, so much the better. Well; Fenimore boldly pleads justification, thinking it as easy as not. But how is he to establish it? We of course should not be so green as to attend the trial in person in such an issue—no man is obliged to make out his adversary's case—but would leave it all to Richard, and the help the judge might properly give him. So the case is on, and Fenimore undertakes the justification, which, of course, admits and aggravates the libel; so our side is all made out. But let us see how *he* gets along. Of course, he will not think of offering witnesses to swear point-blank that we are homely—that, if he did not know it, the judge would soon tell him would be a simple *opinion*, which would not do to go to a jury; he must present *facts*.

"*Fenimore.*—'Well, then, your honor, I offer to prove by this witness that the plaintiff is tow-headed, and half bald at that; he is long-legged, gaunt, and most cadaverous of visage—*ergo*, homely.'

"*Judge.*—'How does that follow? Light hair and fair face bespeak a purely Saxon ancestry, and were honorable in the good old days; *I* rule that they are comely. Thin locks bring out the phrenological developments, you see, and give dignity and massiveness to the aspect; and as to slenderness, what do our dandies lace for if *that* is not graceful? *They* ought to know what is attractive, I reckon. No, sir; your proof is irrelevant, and I rule it out.'

"*Fenimore.*—(The sweat starting.) 'Well, your honor, I have evidence to prove the said plaintiff is slouching in dress; goes bent like a hoop, and so rocking in gait, that he goes down both sides of a street at once.'

"*Judge.*—'*That* to prove homeliness? I hope you don't expect a man of ideas to spend his precious time before a looking-glass? It would be robbing the public. "Bent," do you say? Is n't the curve the true line of beauty, I'd like to know? Where were you brought up? As to walking, you don't expect a "man of mark," as you called him at Ballston, to be quite as dapper and pert as a footman, whose walk is his hourly study and his nightly dream—its perfection, the sum of his ambition! Great ideas of beauty *you* must have! That evidence wont answer.'

"Now, Fenimore, brother in adversity! wouldn't you begin to have a realizing sense of your awful situation? Wouldn't you begin to wish yourself somewhere else, and a great deal further, before you came into court to justify, legally, an *opinion*? Wouldn't you begin to perceive that the application of the law of libel in its strictness to a mere expression of opinion is absurd, mistaken, and tyrannical?

"Of course, we shan't take advantage of your exposed and perilous condition, for we are meek and forgiving, with a hearty disrelish for the machinery of the law. But if we *had* a mind to take hold of you, with Richard to help us, and the supreme court's ruling in actions of libel at our back, wouldn't you catch it? We should get the whole fund back again, and give a din ner to the numerous editorial contributors. *That* dinner would be worth attending, Fenimore; and we'll warrant the jokes to average a good deal better than you cracked in your speech at Ballston."

The *Tribune*—never behind its competitors in news, always independent and out-spoken in its criticisms of public action whether individual or assembled, often exposing itself to the bitterest attacks of its political enemies, yet always able and strong in defense—continued to increase in prosperity through the early years of its existence. Though it had able contributors, its master-spirit, the life-giving heart of its system, was Horace Greeley. With new type and the paper increased one third in its original dimensions, he entered the labors of 1844, strong in purpose and full of vigor. It was now the leading whig paper of the country. This was to be, to its controller, a year of the most intense application, both mental and physical. Henry Clay, the favorite of Greeley's boyhood, the political idol of his riper years, and now almost his God, was the candidate for president. Of the amount of work which Mr. Greeley performed in that campaign, no one can have any conception who has not addressed public meetings five or six times a week, traveled by all the hours of sunlight, written twenty private letters a day, besides an average of twenty pages of foolscap daily for the press. It was well, perhaps, for the cause of American reform, that Clay was defeated; the overthrow of his darling candidate was the first blow toward Horace Greeley's emancipation from the bondage of party and political servitude. It was soon followed up by another, which was the annexation of Texas. Greeley now opened his eyes to the encroachments of the slave power. He discovered that he had made a slight mistake in supposing that by keeping still and letting the south have her own way, our rights would be best secured to us. He was feeling his way along to truth upon *this* question, when, in the early morning of February 5th, 1845, the office of the paper was destroyed by fire. Scarcely anything was saved but the mail books, which had been deposited in the safe. The city papers, however, kindly turned out to him their spare printing materials, and, the next morning, the best *Tribune* of the volume appeared at its usual hour, and soon everything was restored to its uniform order and regularity.

In the autumn previous to this casualty, Mr. Greeley became acquainted with Margaret Fuller, through the pages of the *Dial.* The richness of her style, the purity and originality of her sentiments, and her force of diction, induced him to ask her assistance in the literary department of the *Tribune*, and she replied favorably. Her first essay was published in December, 1844. Her average amount of writing was three articles weekly. She brought to the *Tribune* a mind crammed with the first literature of both hemispheres. Her talent for criticism was the most acute of any woman of her time. She appreciated the beauty of a literary performance and acknowledged it instantly, where others read and re-read, and withheld their opinion till some one spoke first. During the time of her connection with the *Tribune*, she resided in Mr. Greeley's family, upon the banks of the East river. After fourteen months she went to Europe, expecting to return after a temporary absence; but the vessel on which she embarked came almost within sight of her home, and there, with its cargo and passengers, sank forever!

We shall proceed to give specimens of Mr. Greeley's style, which are strongly flavored with the vituperative. They occurred during the years 1846 and 1847, when the *Tribune* was at war with almost all the educated professions of America. We give merely an occasional paragraph:

"The *Journal of Commerce* is the most self-complacent and dogmatic of all possible newspapers."

"We defy the father of lies himself to crowd more stupendous falsehoods into a paragraph than this contains."

"The villain who makes this charge against me well knows that it is the basest falsehood."

"Mr. Benton! each of the above observations is a deliberate falsehood, and you are an unqualified villain."

"The *Express* is surely the basest and paltriest of all possible journals."

"Having been absent from the city a few days, I perceive with a pleasurable surprise, on my return, that the *Express* has only perpetrated two new calumnies upon me of any consequence, since Friday evening."

To an article recommending the secession of the slave states from the Union, he replies thus:

"Dr. Franklin used to tell an anecdote illustrative of his idea of the folly of dueling, substantially thus: A man said to another in some public place, 'Sir, I wish you would move a little away from me, for a disagreeable odor proceeds from you.' 'Sir,' was the stern response, 'that is an insult, and you must fight me!' 'Certainly,' was the quiet reply, 'I will fight you if you wish it; but I don't see how that can mend the matter. If you kill me, I also shall smell badly; and if I kill you, you will smell worse than you do now.'

"We have not yet been able to understand what our disunionists, north or south, really expect to *gain* by dissolving the Union. * * * * 'These valuable slaves escaped,' do you say? Will slaves be any less likely to run away when they know that, once across Mason and Dixon's line, they are safe from pursuit, and can never be reclaimed? 'Every slaveholder is in continual apprehension,' say you? In the name of wonder, how is disunion to soothe their nervous excitement?

They 'wont stand it,' eh ? Have they never heard of getting 'out of the frying-pan into the fire ?' Do let us hear how slavery is to be perpetuated and fortified by disunion ?"

In reply to an article in the *Courier and Enquirer*, upon his eccentricity and style of dress, he has the following paragraph :

"As to our personal appearance, it does seem that we should say something, to stay the flood of nonsense with which the town must by this time be nauseated. Some donkey a while ago, apparently anxious to annoy the editor of this paper, and not well knowing with what, originated the story of the carelessness of his personal appearance ; and since then every blockhead of the same disposition, and distressed by a similar lack of ideas, has repeated and exaggerated the foolery ; until from its origin in the *Albany Microscope* it has sunk down at last to the columns of the *Courier and Enquirer*, growing more absurd at every landing. Yet all this time the object of this silly raillery has doubtless worn better clothes than two-thirds of those who thus assailed him—better than any of them could honestly wear if they paid their debts otherwise than by bankruptcy ; while, indeed, if they are more cleanly than he, they must bathe very thoroughly not less than twice a day. The editor of the *Tribune* is the son of a poor and humble farmer ; came to New York a minor, without a friend within two hundred miles, less than ten dollars in his pocket, and precious little besides ; he has never had a dollar from a relative, and has for years labored under a load of debt, (thrown on him by the misconduct of others and the revulsions of 1837,) which he can now just see to the end of. Thenceforth he may be able to make a better show, if deemed essential by his friends; for himself he has not much time or thought to bestow upon the matter. That he ever *affected* eccentricity is most untrue; and certainly no costume he ever appeared in would create such a sensation in Broadway as that James Watson Webb would have worn but for the clemency of Governor Seward. Heaven grant our assailant may never hang with such weight on another whig executive! We drop him."

To explain the last few sentences, it need only be remembered that Colonel Webb had been sentenced to prison for two years, for fighting a duel, but he was pardoned by Governor Seward, without a day's imprisonment.

Being accused by the *Evening Post* of knuckling to the slave interest, Greeley commenced his reply in these words: "You lie, villain: wilfully, wickedly, basely lie!"

In the Taylor and Fillmore campaign Mr. Greeley at first opposed, then wavered, and never heartily supported the nomination. He thought that General Taylor was not a man qualified to be president of the United States, but he was prevailed upon to support the nominations with a view to the triumph of free soil doctrines. The whigs were successful, and thereby Horace Greeley was elected to a seat in congress for three months, to supply the vacancy occasioned by the death of a New York representative. While there, he was too industrious to be esteemed by lazy aristocrats; too economical in "Uncle Sam's" interests to be popular among his nephews; and too much a hater of vice to be loved by her devotees. The measures which he labored upon mostly were the reform in mileage; the land reform bill, and the bill for the reduction of naval expenses. He also made some "plain and forcible" hits upon the tariff question, and the slave-trade in the District, and took part in the famous (or infamous) "battle of the books." During the intervals of session he wrote many articles for the *Tribune*, among which, the most prominent, and the one which procured him immense odium among the members was the "mileage expose." But we cannot stop to trace his course while here. He was completely disgusted with the management and duplicity of the "honorables," and especially with that crowning master-piece of shame, "the last night of the session." He wrote a long letter to his constituents, upon his return, of which we give the closing paragraph:

"My work as your servant is done—whether well or ill it remains for you to judge. Very likely I gave the wrong vote on some of the difficult and complicated questions to which I was called to respond AYE or NO, with hardly a moment's warning. If so, you can detect and condemn the error; for my name stands recorded in the divisions by Yeas and Nays, on every public and all but one private bill, (which was laid on the table the moment the sitting opened, and on which my name had just been passed as I entered the hall.) I wish it were the usage among us to publish less of speeches and more of propositions and votes thereupon; it would give the mass of the people a much clearer insight into the management of their public affairs. My successor being already chosen and commissioned, I shall hardly be suspected of seeking your further kindness, and I shall be heartily rejoiced if he shall be able to combine equal zeal in your service with greater efficiency—equal fearlessness with greater popularity. * * * I thank you heartily for the glimpse of public life which your favor has afforded me, and hope to render it useful henceforth, not to myself only, but to the public. In ceasing to be your agent, and returning with renewed zest to my private cares and duties, I have a single additional favor to ask, not of you espepecially, but of all; and I am sure my friends at least will grant it without hesitation. It is that you and they will henceforth oblige me by remembering that my name is simply

"HORACE GREELEY."

The year 1849 exhibits an amount of talent in the *Tribune* office which defies competition in America. Besides Mr. Greeley, principal editor, there was C. A. Dana, of brilliant talents, assistant; George Ripley, a profound scholar and classical critic; W. H. Fry, from the scorchings of whose *brain-pan* many an unlucky culprit has wished himself in the fire; Bayard Taylor, with imagination and memory stored with wealth from the plains of California and Europe, and G. G. Foster, a rapid workman in the city news department. Need it be wondered that the *Tribune* grew and thrived in spite of its independent fearlessness?

Mr. Greeley's cares were much lightened by such an able corps of men, and he found considerable time to travel. He took a tour to the west, lectured upon agriculture, and kept wide open his eye for observation. It has been affirmed by many, and believed by some, possibly, that he was an advocate of the doctrine of "spiritual manifestations." He was not. He examined the subject with care, as every honest man should, and did *not* find evidence of its truthfulness.

In regard to the woman's rights theory, he wrote as follows: "It is easy to be smart, to be droll, to be facetious, in opposition to the demands of these female reformers; and, in decrying assumptions so novel and opposed to established habits and usages, a little wit will go a great way. But when a sincere republican is asked to say in sober earnest what adequate reason he can give for refusing the demand of women to an equal participation with men in political rights, he must answer, none at all. * * * * However unwise or mistaken the demand, it must be conceded."

The *Tribune* had now become a lucrative concern.

It was the first enterprise in which Horace Greeley had so succeeded as to make it "pay." Instead of heaping up a princely fortune upon the receipts, as he might honorably have done after so much hard labor to establish it, he and Mr. McElrath determined to make an experiment of the doctrine of "associated labor," and to it they devoted the *Tribune*. The concern was divided into one hundred shares, of a thousand dollars each, and (excepting a reserved portion for the original partners) they were sold out to such of the men in the establishment as could pay for them. Each share entitled its owner to a vote in proceedings of the company, and it so continues to this day.

In 1851 Horace Greeley attended the General Exhibition for Industry, at London, and while there was appointed one of the jury on hardware. As the steamer glided down the harbor, the Napoleon of the New York press stood girt in the immortal "white overcoat," while crowds of friends upon the dock sent up enthusiastic cheers. His passage to England was a tempestuous one, and being sea-sick most of the way over, he enjoyed it but little. He visited the principal cities of England, commented upon everything he thought worthy of note, and in the columns of his paper criticised what he disliked, as freely as at home. He was invited by a parliamentary committee of the first men in England to give them the benefit of his experience in the matter of cheap periodicals. His information was well received, and seemed quite satisfactory to the committee. After nearly two months' stay in England, he went over to the continent, visited Calais, Paris, and Lyons; went across the Alps to Turin, and spent three weeks among the principal cities of Italy. Returning through Switzerland, Germany, and Belgium, the 21st of July found him again in London. He closed his European tour by a hasty trip through the north of England, Scotland, and Ireland, and on the 6th of August, in the Baltic, started for home. He wrote under date of that day the following paragraph:

"I rejoice to feel that every hour, henceforth, must lessen the distance which divides me from my country, whose advantages and blessings this four months' absence has taught me to appreciate more dearly, and to prize more deeply, than before. With a glow of unwonted rapture I see our stately vessel's prow turned toward the setting sun, and strive to realize that only some ten days separate me from those I know and love best on earth. Hark! the last gun announces that the mail-boat has left us, and that we are fairly afloat on our ocean journey; the shores of Europe recede from our vision; the watery waste is all around us; and now, with God above and death below, our gallant bark and her clustered company together brave the dangers of the mighty deep. May Infinite Mercy watch over our onward path and bring us safely to our several homes; for to die away from home and kindred seems one of the saddest calamities that could befall me. This mortal tenement would rest uneasily in an ocean shroud; this spirit reluctantly resign that tenement to the chill and pitiless brine; these eyes close regretfully on the stranger skies and bleak inhospitality of the sullen and stormy main. No! let me see once more the scenes so well remembered and beloved; let me grasp, if but once again, the hand of friendship, and hear the thrilling accents of proved affection, and when, sooner or later, the hour of mortal agony shall come, let my last gaze be fixed on eyes that will not forget me when I am gone, and let my ashes repose in that congenial soil which, however I may then be esteemed or hated is still 'My own green land forever!'"

He reached New York in safety, having stolen a march on the daily papers, by arranging the foreign news all ready for publication, before leaving the vessel. Rushing from the steamer, he carried the "copy" to the *Tribune* office, and while the compositors of the other papers were setting up their type, the *Tribune* boys were shouting the arrival of the Baltic.

In 1836, Mr. Greeley married Mary Y. Cheney, of Litchfield, Connecticut, by whom he has had six children, four of whom, alas! are now sleeping in the grave. His domestic afflictions and his constant and severe toil have given to his brow a weary, worn look, like that upon the countenance of a sorrowing, suffering man. And now he begins to talk of growing old. He says most beautifully:

"As for me, long tossed on the stormiest waves of doubtful conflict, and an arduous endeavor, I have begun to feel, since the shade of forty years fell upon me, the weary, tempest-driven voyager's longing for land, the wanderer's yearning for the hamlet where in childhood he nestled by his mother's knee, and was soothed to sleep on her breast.

"The sober down-hill of life dispels many illusions, while it develops or strengthens within us the attachment, perhaps long smothered or overlaid, for 'that dear hut,' our home. And so I, in the sober afternoon of life, when its sun, if not high, is still warm, have bought me a few acres of land in the broad, still country, and, bearing thither my household treasures, have resolved to steal from the city's labors and anxieties, at least one day in each week, wherein to revive, as a farmer, the memories of my childhood's humble home.

"And already I realize that the experience cannot cost so much as it is worth. Already I find in that day's quiet an antidote and a solace for the feverish, festering cares of the week which environ it. Already my brook murmurs a soothing even-song to my burning, throbbing brain, and my trees, gently stirred by the fresh breezes, whisper to my spirit something of their own quiet strength and patient trust in God.

"And thus do I faintly realize, but for a brief and flitting day, the serene joy which shall irradiate the farmer's vocation, when a fuller and a truer education shall have refined and chastened his animal cravings, and when science shall have endowed him with her treasures, redeeming labor from drudgery while quadrupling its efficiency, and crowning with beauty and plenty our bounteous, beneficent earth."

In another place he writes thus eloquently of growing old:

"Is it well to desire and pray for length of days? I would say, so long as our mental faculties remain essentially undecayed, it is well, it is desirable to live. The love of life is not a blind, irrational instinct, but has as its base a just perception that existence is a blessing, and that even in this "vale of tears," its joys outweigh its woes. And besides, our terrestrial course prepares and shapes us for the life that shall succeed it, which will be, to a great extent, a continuation, or second edition of this, with corrections and improvements. Doubtless, Infinite Mercy has means provided whereby the millions to whom this life was a blank shall nevertheless be prepared for bliss in the next; and I trust even those who have misused and culpably squandered this stage of being will yet be ultimately fitted for happiness in another. But opportunities wasted can never be regained; the memory of past unworthiness must ever be humiliating and regretful to the redeemed soul. In vain does Joseph, revealing himself in Egypt to his treacherous brethren, entreat them to 'Be not angry with yourselves that ye sold me hither, for God did send me before you to preserve life;' the view of God needed no vindication, while theirs do not receive any. I apprehend that flagrant transgressors (and who is or is not of this number, who shall here say?) will ever feel consciousness of inferiority and self-reproach in the presence of those who walked worthily on earth—that retrospect of their darker hours can never be joyful nor welcome to Judas or Magdalen. So long as we may grow therein in wisdom and worth it is as well, it is desirable to live, but no further. To my view, insanity is the darkest, the most appalling of earthly calamities; but how much better is an old age that drivels and wanders, that misunderstands and forgets? When the soul shall have become choked and smothered by the ruins of its wasting, falling habitation, I should prefer to inhabit that shattered tenement no longer. I should not choose to stand shuddering and trembling on the brink of the dark river, weakly drawing back from the chill of its sweeping flood, when faith assures me that a new Eden stretches green and fair beyond it, and that the baptism it invites will cleanse the soul of all that now clogs, clouds, and weighs it to the earth. No, when the windows of the mind shall be darkened, when the growth of the soul here shall have been arrested, I would not weakly cling to the earth which will have ceased to nourish and uphold me. Rather 'let the golden cup be loosed, and the pitcher broken at the fountain;' let the sun of my existence go down ere the murky vapors shroud its horizon; let me close my eyes calmly on the things of earth, and let my weary frame sleep beneath the clods of the valley; let the spirit, which it can no longer cherish as a guest, be spared the ignominy of detention as a prisoner; but, freed from the fetters of clay, let it wing its way through the boundless universe, to wheresoever the benign Father of spirits shall have assigned it an everlast- home."

The defeat of General Scott in 1852 emancipated Mr. Greely and the *Tribune* from the shackles of party and the tyranny of conservatism; it made him the most free of successful editors, and his paper the ablest and most fearless journal in America. We will close our sketch of his life by a glance at him in his office.

In visiting the *Tribune* establishment, one should by no means be content with an introduction into the editorial *sanctum*. He should first *descend* into subterranean regions where the press-work of the *Tribune* is executed. A view of the mammoth press, which, with its iron fingers, throws off fifteen thousand impressions an hour, will give him an idea of the business of the establishment. It is a press which has little rest, for the aggregate circulation of the *Tribune* is over one hundred and seventy thousand copies! Ascend to the first floor, and view the place where the business of the paper is conducted—where its immense advertising patronage is received and accounted for—where all bills against the firm of Greeley & McElrath are settled! Mount still higher, and see the printers at their work. If it is day, a busy scene will present itself, yet utter silence pervades the apartments. If it be night, it is still the same—each case is manned, and the work progresses under a new set of workmen, as rapidly as by day. Floor above floor, is occupied by the industrious printers, and the clerks who each day send off tens of thousands of papers, and one day in each week, more than one hundred thousand. But we have not visited the place where the burning thoughts which are the life of the *Tribune*, are put upon paper. It is in the highest story but one, fronting on the park. We first enter a long room fronting Spruce street, and extending to Nassau street. Here the sub-editors work. A row of them, each seated at his desk and plying the pen or scissors industriously, attracts our attention. George Ripley, a fine, manly person, with dark hair and darker eyes, sits at one. He is the literary editor of the *Tribune*, the book critic, and one would hardly suppose from his bland manners that his business, like that of a surgeon, consists in cutting people up! A book lies open before him—he is marking passages for extraction, and to-morrow morning we shall read them in the moist pages of the journal, as we sip our coffee, together with the critic's remarks. Bayard Taylor, perhaps, sits at another desk, just returned from a profitable lecturing tour, and we stop to gaze at the brilliant young traveler. Not far off sits white-haired "Solon"—Solon Robinson, the author of "Hot Corn"—the agricultural and city item editor of the *Tribune*. We skip the other editors in this room, and pass into a smaller apartment looking out upon the City Hall. The room is newly carpeted —in one corner, there is an old-fashioned sofa—easy chairs, three or four, are to be seen, and in one corner at a desk stands a slim, black-haired, brilliant-eyed man, in a pair of exceedingly old and easy shoes. His name is Charles A. Dana, and he is editor-in-chief when Greeley is out of town, and is usually termed the foreign editor of the *Tribune*. In another corner of the room a man sits writing at a desk which is just even with his chin, so that while he pushes his pen swiftly over the paper he sits perfectly straight in his chair. He is a short-sighted, and his eyes hug the desk. He is a strange looking mortal. His head is almost bald; what hair there is, is of a light, sandy color, and is exceedingly fine. He is dressed—well, we may as well speak it right out—abominably. It is Horace Greeley, the chief editor of the *Tribune*, upon his throne! It is the poor plow-boy controlling the grandest, the most powerful press in America. He turns to welcome us, and we notice that after all he has a fine face—a gentle look it ever wears. The eyes are not harsh or bold, but mild and honest. And though his manners are not of the Lord Chesterfield stripe, they are those of a man who values trifles *less* than realities. His thoughts are bold and striking; he has charity for an honest opponent; if we differ from him upon any point, we shall not necessarily lose his esteem, for though a man of fixed opinions, he is not an egotist. Spite of a thousand things which at first prepossessed us against the man, we like him better and better, the more we see of him and hear him talk. Our opinion of his intellectual powers and his moral qualities of course cannot be altered by any personal contact with the man. We have known him as the invisible soul behind the *Tribune* for years—and now we gaze upon—the *Tribune* made flesh and blood!

Engraved by J.C.Buttre from a Daguerreotype.

Yours for the War,
Thurlow W. Brown

THURLOW WEED BROWN.

One of the most powerful advocates of the temperance cause is the man whose name heads this brief sketch. He is powerful in a somewhat peculiar way, not like Choate or Phillips, with the very highest order of eloquence, nor like Sumner, with a chastened, classical eloquence. He is powerful with *the people.* Upon a vast gathering of sturdy yeomen in one of "God's own temples," he will make a most profound impression. He overflows with *natural eloquence.* He knows little of the schools of rhetoric, but he knows the human heart. His own is sensitive as a girl's. No wrong can be perpetrated upon one of his fellow-men without rousing his indignation. He knew in childhood what it was to suffer from intemperance of the nearest friends, and he grew up hating the traffickers in "liquid damnation" as he hated their father, the devil. He utters to the people before him words which burn—sentences which blaze with fire. They are not smooth, are not always elaborated, but they find their way to the hearts of his hearers.

The following extract from his "Temperance Tales and Hearthstone Reveries," presents at one view the causes of his temperance predilections, his direct and vigorous style, and his warm domestic attachments, as shown in the finest tribute to a mother which we have ever seen:

"Lastly, we are against it for a mother's sake. To her we ascribe the holiest of our temperance teachings, and to her history that deep and sleepless hatred of the rum traffic. A tear will come to your eye as we write of that hallowed name. She sits before us now, and we look with a holy love and a misty eye upon the locks fast silvering with gray. That idol has been shivered at your own hearth-side, but her temperance teachings and fervent prayers for her wayward boy will not, cannot be forgotten by him.

"A vision passes before us. There is a home, in New England, of happiness and comfort, and a lovely matron makes one of the links of the family circle. Again she stands at the altar, and weaves her destiny irrevocably with that of the man of her choice.

"Years pass happily and swiftly by, and the young bride is a happy mother. Fresh blessings are added to the first, but in the mean time a shadow has fallen upon that heart and its home. A tempter has glided into the Eden, and wreathed its coils around the husband and father.

"Other years go by, and ruin is in that home. The mother weeps and prays, and gathers more closely her children around her, as the storm bursts in its fury. Want, neglect, and abuse wring her aching heart. She fades out like the autumn leaf, and with a crushed heart sinks to the rest of death, and is borne to a pauper's grave; and ten brothers and sisters weep over the last home of one who can no longer shield them from hunger or the cruel blow.

"An officer steps within the abode of poverty and wretchedness, and drags away all to satisfy an execution in favor of the rumseller, who has swallowed the living of that family and placed the mother in her grave. The once high-minded, but now lost and imbruted father, sells the cow and riots the proceeds out at a drunkery, and leaves the children to the charities of friends.

"A girl of fifteen summers toils in a factory until her heart and brain ache, and she turns away to the lone group at the desolate hearth, and sinks *hungry* to her fitful rest. The cold-tongued bell breaks in upon short slumbers, and drives the slight and weary frame again to its bitter task. Saturday night finds her turning homeward with a feverish cheek and a heavy step. A father calls at the office of the superintendent, secures her earnings, and during the Sabbath squanders it all at the grog-shop with his boon companions!

"The factory girl once idolized that father. But hunger, and poverty, and abuse, have taught her to hate him; and as he goes to the groggery in the morning, an involuntary prayer goes up from the child's heart that he will no more return. So accursing are the effects of rum!

"Long and weary days pass away, and yet the factory girl toils, and at night gathers with her brothers and sisters gratefully around a loaf of brown bread. There is a jug of rum on the shelf, and an imbruted father slumbering on the hearth.

"—A dark and cheerless pathway opens to the factory girl.

"The worse than orphans are driven out from the wretched home and scattered here and there as paupers, kept by the town. One little girl, a fair-haired, blue-eyed, beautiful creature of three summers, is taken by a family. Away in an entry-away, without sufficient clothing, hungry, and no eye but God's to look kindly down upon her, she dies in the winter night—dies cold, hungry, and covered with vermin!—and the older sister could not even weep upon the child-pauper's grave, her of the fair hair and wild blue eye.

"With the brand which society once cruelly affixed upon the brow of the drunkard's child, the factory girl entered into the great battle of life. Without education or friends, she was compelled to perform the most menial drudgery. The shadows that then clouded the sky of her youth have mingled with and darkened the happiness of after years. Her brothers grew up, and some of them followed in the footsteps of their father, and became drunkards. One was drowned near Albany. Another rests beneath a southern soil. A younger one, a faultless model of manly beauty, and as noble in heart as in form, was taken by pirates at sea, and killed only when he towered the last of his crew upon the slippery decks, and his arms were hewn from his body. Two others wrestle now with an appetite which dogs their footsteps with remorseless craving, and but one lives the soul of manhood and honor.

"Thus were those linked to her by the strongest ties that can bind us to each other, wrenched away, and driven up and down the world. The father lived on a drunkard, and at a ripe old age died a drunkard by the roadside, and not a stone tells where he sleeps.

"Such are but the outlines of a childhood and youth of suffering, humiliation, and sorrow. The details are known only to the sufferer and to God. Memory rolls back upon its bitter tide the history of such scenes, the fountain of tears is opened afresh, and flows as bitterly as in the past. Childhood without sunshine! The thought is cold and dark indeed.

"This hasty sketching would apply to unnumbered thousands of such cases. As the sands upon the shore, the blades in the meadow, or the leaves in summertime, or the stars that glitter in the blue above, are the histories of such ravages upon the hopes and happiness of youth. They will never be known until the record of the angel shall be unrolled at the judgment.

"That factory girl—that drunkard's daughter—that child-pauper, who toiled while a drunken father drank down her wages—who went hungry for bread—who was deprived of society and education, and entered upon life's stern realities with no inheritance but poverty and a father's infamy—IS OUR MOTHER!

"God! how the veins knot and burn as the tide whose every drop is bitter with the memory of her wrongs sweeps to our fingers' ends. Our soul throbs firmly in our nib, until we clutch involuntarily for a good blade, and wish the rum traffic embodied in one demon form, that we could go forth with God's blessings and smite the hell-born monster. We look upon her head, now thickly flecked with threads of silver, and wish that the temperance reform could have dawned in her day. We look upon the tear that steals down her cheek as the dark days of yore are called up, and our manhood's cheek burns with indignation. She was robbed—cruelly, basely robbed. She hungered for bread to eat! She was threatened with the vengeance of a rumseller if she would not toil in his household for the merest pittance! She was shut out of society and its privileges because she had no home. She was pointed at as a drunkard's child! She toiled until her heart ached with pain, and the rumseller clutched from the hand of an imbruted father the last penny of her hard earnings! OUR MOTHER! God of justice and truth! give us but the power to-day, and we would strangle every hydra whose breath is blasting the hope of others as it blasted hers.

"To that mother we owe the most of our hatred to the rum traffic. We imbibed it from her breast, and learned of her in childhood. A father, too, his strong form untainted by the scourge, has taught us the same lesson. The memories of his own childhood are darkened by the thoughts of a drunken father. He grappled alone with life's difficulties, and commenced his career by working to pay rumsellers' executions against his deceased father.

"Thus from the cradle have we been educated to hate the scourge. That hatred is mingled with every pilgrim drop in our veins. It grows with our growth and strengthens with our strength. In the high noon of manhood we swear, by friends on earth and God in heaven, a lifelong warfare, if need be, against the traffic. There can be no compromise. It is a conflict of extermination, and the blows will only fail when the battle of life is ended, and our strong right arm is mingled with its mother dust. We will wear our harness to the grave, and make Hannibals of those who come after us, to fight on."

As a writer Mr. Brown has no mean reputation. His characteristics as such are similar to his peculiarities as a speaker. There is this difference: his intense love of nature, and of the beautiful everywhere, gushes forth with more ease and freedom in his writings than in his speeches. This is very natural, for the beautiful is born of quiet.

Mr. Brown was born in Preston, Chenango county, New York, in the year 1819. His father was a farmer and carriage maker. He came originally from Connecticut. Thurlow's mother's maiden name was Wood. He learned the carriage-maker's trade in his father's shop, working in it till May, 1839, when, with his parents, he moved into Sterling Cayuga county, New York, working on the farm and in the shop alternately until 1847. He had before this several times ventured to address meetings in the "rural districts" of the county, and had written articles for the local journals, though he had received but a spare common-school education. During the license law contest of 1845 he labored incessantly for the triumph of temperance at the ballot-box. He was often carried by his father from a sick-bed to attend temperance meetings, for the father was full of ardor which he infused into his son. In the latter part of this year Thurlow wrote a series of articles for the *Star of Temperance*, a weekly journal, published at Auburn, which attracted much attention. Their eloquence impressed its patrons as well as its publishers deeply. He was at length invited to occupy its chair editorial. And rough, rustic, and unused to any but country customs, he went to Auburn. In April, 1848, the *Star* was removed to Rochester, and he withdrew from it. When he took hold of it, its circulation was but four hundred; when he left, it had risen to three thousand—the best compliment any editor can receive. In January, 1849, he issued the first number of the *Cayuga Chief*, of which he is an editor now. He started with a capital of *seven dollars*, and a circulation of one hundred and seventy! Under his editorship and management it has risen to a circulation of three thousand copies. His mechanical genius is worth noting, and as he had no money to commence his enterprise with, he actually made, with his own hands, much of the furniture of his office. He worked on bravely, industriously, and eloquently. This year he married a woman worthy of himself, and to whom he is ardently attached. Home is his peculiar element; and his "Hearthstone Reveries" give unmistakable evidence that his chief attraction, the center of his happiness, is there. Long may he live to battle manfully in the cause to which he is so earnestly devoted.

The following, on the death of his beautiful boy, the lovely Willie, is one of the most sweetly pathetic things in our language:

"A BROKEN HOME."

A short time since, we left the cherished idol of our hearth circle in the full promise of health and life, and returned but to see him die! Our home is desolate, for its purest light has faded out. Willie is dead!

O God, how we loved the boy! He was a child of more than rare promise — a brave, beautiful, noble-hearted being and all manhood in every pulse. His mind was almost masculine, and he wrestled with death with the calm patience and judgment of maturer years.

Would that in the spring-time he had gone to his long night-rest of death, when the flower, and leaf, and tiny blade were bursting out from their earth-sleep to clothe the fields in beauty. But it matters not. He wandered not alone through the dark valley, "for of such is the kingdom of heaven." The warm sunbeam and raindrop of spring-time will deck the resting-place of the little sleeper with smiles. Little will he heed, however, either sunbeam or cloud on earth, for there is no winter shadow in the eternal summer-sky of bliss.

Blessed hope, that death is not an "eternal sleep!" The beautiful tenement of a soul of two summers will mingle with its pillow of earth; but in the silence of the night-time we shall listen to the tripping of little feet, and the low whispering of a silvery voice; to the sweet rustling of two little angel-wings, and feel the pure touch of a tiny palm upon the feverish cheek. One of the strongest links of earth has been broken but to bind us the closer to heaven. God's will be done!

The little playthings are all put away. A deep tide of

bright hopes has been rolled back in a bitter flood upon the heart. Crushed and broken, we bow to the storm that has swept our earth, and thank God that there is a better world than this for the child.

—WILLIE! our own loved, beautiful, gentle boy, good-night!

www.ingramcontent.com/pod-product-compliance
Lightning Source LLC
LaVergne TN
LVHW020105110826
845151LV00001B/67

* 9 7 8 1 4 2 5 5 4 3 7 0 9 *